A KINGDOM OF WATER

Indians of the Southeast

A KINGDOM
OF WATER

Adaptation and Survival in
the Houma Nation

J. Daniel d'Oney

UNIVERSITY OF NEBRASKA PRESS
LINCOLN

Library of Congress Cataloging-in-Publication Data
Names: D'Oney, J. Daniel, author.
Title: A kingdom of water: adaptation and survival in the Houma Nation / J. Daniel d'Oney.
Description: Lincoln: University of Nebraska Press, [2020] | Series: Indians of the Southeast | Includes bibliographical references and index.
Identifiers: LCCN 2019030113
ISBN 9781496218797 (hardback)
ISBN 9781496220066 (epub)
ISBN 9781496220073 (mobi)
ISBN 9781496220080 (pdf)
Subjects: LCSH: Houma Indians—Louisiana—Politics and government. | Houma Indians—Louisiana—History.
Classification: LCC E99.H72 D66 2020 | DDC 976.30049738—dc23
LC record available at https://lccn.loc.gov/2019030113

Set in Adobe Caslon by Mikala R. Kolander.

He did not say, "Thou shalt not be tempested, thou shalt not be travailed, thou shalt not be dis-eased." But He did say, "Thou shalt not be overcome."—JULIAN OF NORWICH

Contents

Illustrations

Acknowledgments

One of the great pleasures that researching and writing this book afforded me was the opportunity to meet some truly extraordinary people. In archives, private homes, libraries, and fishing boats, people invariably went out of their way to help in my research. Total strangers spent hours sifting through archival basements to help me find an obscure source or drove me to a distant relative's house so I could listen to elders recount an ancestor who was long dead but hardly forgotten. Looking back, I'm humbled by how generous so many people were, and it's a great pleasure to offer brief, albeit too brief, thanks for their kindness and support.

Initial thanks go to my maternal grandparents, JC and Myrtle Rae McGowen, who imparted their love of history to me. Cotton farmers in northeastern Louisiana, both were deeply interested in every aspect of their world and by far the smartest people I have ever known. They taught me a profound respect for both the written and spoken word, a deep awareness of the link between people and their natural environments, and a comfort with knowing that the world owes you nothing. The hours they spent recounting family histories to me are among the happiest in my life. Similarly, I owe a great debt to my parents, who pushed me to constantly question the world around me, made a lot of sacrifices for my benefit, encouraged me even as they sometimes wondered when I would ever finish school, and have been my most ferocious supporters.

Several teachers made all the difference in my life, particularly Mary Jayne White, my senior English teacher at Bastrop High School. Retired in 2016 after fifty years, Mrs. White exemplifies what a difference the right teacher can make in the life of a student, and her hours of instruction, guidance, and patient mentoring serve as a guide for how I hope I am with my own students. She would be followed by Emily Batinski of the Latin Department at Louisiana State University (LSU) and James Hardy of LSU's Honors College, who offered unconditional support to their students while also setting a very high bar. At Arizona State University, Peter Iverson and Robert Trennert encouraged me to look back to my home state when devising a course of research and gave me the freedom to choose my own path. Nancy Hawkins mentored me when I interned with the Louisiana Division of Archaeology, and her professionalism and class still give me a yardstick against which to measure my own behavior (I invariably fall short in comparison, I should add).

Institutions that generously helped me locate sources include the Louisiana State Archives, Louisiana State Museum, Louisiana State Library, Terrebonne Parish Public Library, Ellender Memorial Library at Nicholls State University, the National Archives, LSU Law Library, Louisiana State Division of Archaeology, Northwestern State University of Louisiana, University of Louisiana at Lafayette, the Earl K. Long Library at the University of New Orleans, the Historic New Orleans Collection, the Smithsonian Institute, the Bureau of Indian Affairs, the Terrebonne Parish School Board, and the Lafourche Parish School Board. The majority of my sources were in Hill Memorial Library at Louisiana State University, where I owe a special debt to Germain Bienvenu and Judy Bolton. Last, the librarians at Albany College of Pharmacy and Health Sciences (ACPHS) were tireless in getting sources for me, either by borrowing the documents or by acquiring scans. Many thanks to all the ACPHS librarians, but especially Lauren Grygiel and Kate Wantuch.

Several organizations were very generous in their funding. Albany College of Pharmacy and Health Sciences awarded me two Summer Scholarship of Discovery awards, and I am very grateful for working in such a supportive environment. The Louisiana Endowment for the Humanities (LEH) awarded me a Louisiana Publishing Initiative Grant at exactly the right time, and they will never know how grateful I am for the financial help and kind words. John Kemp of the LEH was particularly unflagging in his support and enthusiasm for the project and offered much helpful and timely advice. The T. Harry Williams Oral History Center at Louisiana State University was very generous with equipment, technical expertise, and occasional financial aid while I was conducting oral interviews.

I would like to extend my thanks to Matt Bokovoy and his associates at the University of Nebraska Press for their professionalism, courtesy, and patience, and to the four anonymous reviewers who read this book at different stages. These scholars offered thoughtful and meaningful advice about strengths and weaknesses in my work, taking time out of their schedules to help me make this a stronger book. For that I am very grateful.

I would also like to thank Theda Perdue, one of the pioneers of Southeastern Native history, who introduced herself at a conference years ago and asked me to submit my manuscript to the University of Nebraska Press. She remained unfailingly supportive and patient in following years and was gracious enough to include me in a 2011 National Endowment for the Humanities Summer Seminar at University of North Carolina Chapel Hill so that I could interact more freely with others in my field. Dr. Perdue has offered valuable criticism, advice, and encouragement over the years, and I can say with absolute certainty that this book is much stronger for her help.

This book would have been impossible without the generosity and help of many, many members of the United Houma Nation (UHN). Each one of the hundreds of people I met was kindness itself, and though it is impossible to thank all these people, there are four I would like to single out. I met (now Dr.) Bruce Duthu of Dartmouth when I was a student at LSU and he was a young lawyer giving a class presentation about the Houma; he was the first person to make me aware of the UHN. I met Kirby Verret during my archaeology internship when I drove to Dulac; he was working on his home's plumbing at the time and spoke with me while I helped him dig up his front yard. Kirby was very generous in making my first introductions to UHN members, and I am deeply grateful for that. Likewise, former Principal Chief Brenda Dardar Robichaux made time in her busy schedule to speak with me on a number of occasions, and her experiences gave me insight into many unrecorded but vital facets of Houma history. Lastly, Michael Dardar has been a great sounding board and friend over the years. Michael serves as the tribe's unofficial historian and has a lengthy publication record of his own. He provided valuable criticism and gave me one of the nicest compliments I've received when he said that this isn't the kind of book a Houma would have written, but that the Houma are okay with it.

Last, a word on reciprocity, an often-debated topic among indigenous peoples and those who work with them. I lived in the town of Houma for a year while conducting research in bayou communities and, both during my time living there and in the years since I left, absolutely everyone treated me with courtesy and respect (I must add that this kindness came not only from Houma Indians but also non-Natives and Indians of other tribes, even when those people maintained tense relations with the UHN). Though not a coffee drinker, I learned to appreciate the high-octane beverage served in households I visited, which could not be refused without offending the host; within several weeks I was close to addiction. While I can still thank some of the many Houma who shared their memories and experiences even when they had better things to do, passing years have made it impossible to thank others. Still, we do the best we can, and reciprocity is vital in our dealings, as scholars and as human beings, with people who extend their trust to us. I turned over copies of previous drafts and research materials to Brenda Dardar Robichaux with a request that they be used for good. Likewise, I lodged my oral interviews at the T. Harry Williams Oral History Center at Louisiana State University and made sure that the UHN would have access. In terms of reciprocity, can I ever repay the kindness extended to me? No, of course not. But I have done my absolute best to not abuse that kindness, to show gratitude, and to help others along the way. And that's the best I know how to do.

Introduction

To Cast a Wide Net

In August and September 2005 the world watched on television as hurricanes Katrina and Rita swept across the Louisiana coastline with the force of two invading armies. Either storm would have been catastrophic in its own right, but the combined force of these hurricanes hitting less than a month apart was like something out of a nightmare. One of the world's great cities flooded, and smaller but no less culturally rich communities were more than a dozen feet underwater. Homes that had stood for generations buckled, and millions of people fled as far from the invading waters as they could. Katrina shattered levees in New Orleans but also southward along the Mississippi, flooding bayou communities and creating a vast, unbroken sheet of the Mississippi Gulf. Roofs were ripped off, and when Rita hit several weeks later there was little to stop downpours from above and storm surges from below. And amid this devastation and mayhem, many heard for the first time of a tribe that had lived along the waterways of southeastern Louisiana for centuries: the Houma nation.

Any person with loved ones in the paths of Katrina and Rita surely felt the expected mix of emotions: anger, fear, frantic worry. For those of us who had friends among the Houma, though, there was a further concern: How could these people survive as a nation? Many Houma had fled from Katrina to relatives in bayou communities that now sat directly in the path of Rita. When Rita hit, nine feet of storm surge water went into districts that had offered refuge. Over four thousand Houma Indians had lost their homes to the first storm, and five thousand more lost theirs in the second. Other tribes had been moved from their traditional homelands, but at least these lands remained. How does a nation survive when its very soil is eroded from below and flooded from above?

From the vantage of a decade later, fears that the Houma would dissolve as a nation in the same way as their homeland have proven to be just that—fears. Far from an anomaly in its history, Katrina and Rita were simply further disasters with which the nation had to grapple, and the Houma regrouped, recovered, and rebuilt the same way they had for centuries. They appealed to outside communities, used the media to their advantage, and forged alliances with traditional rivals when it was to their advantage to do so. Far from defining them as a people, Katrina and Rita simply made the Houma exercise behaviors they had mastered over preceding centuries as they interacted with a variety of tribal, colonial, federal, and state officials.

A Kingdom of Water is not a tribal or cultural history, though it is couched in a narrative that examines the nation's history after 1699. Rather, it is a study of how one Native American group successfully navigated a constantly changing series of political and social landscapes between 1699 and 2005 while maintaining its identity as a nation. Even before the arrival of the French, the Houma had formed alliances either with or against other Indian peoples. After 1699 they included the French in their networks and played a vital role in the early history of *Louisiane*, ironic given that a French governor came dangerously close to exterminating them. After 1763 and the Gallic retreat, both the British and Spanish laid claim to tribal homelands, and the Houma cleverly played one empire against the other until the Americans took control of the region. Some alliances were advantageous and others disastrous, but all reflect Houma awareness of their changing political and social landscapes. Moreover, these alliances also reflect the Houma's understanding that they lived in constant danger and that perpetual movement and change was the only way to navigate dangerous waters.

When they first met the French in 1699 the Houma lived on the eastern bank of the Mississippi River, just above modern Baton Rouge. Several years after that an epidemic devastated the nation, and they attempted to rebuild their numbers by absorbing the Tunica tribe. Somewhere between 1705 and 1709 the Tunica rose up against their hosts, slaughtered many of them, and drove the remainder south. Survivors fled downriver to Bayou St. John but moved back upstream a few years later to escape the corrupting effects of New Orleans. Settling in modern Ascension Parish, the

Houma were forced to relocate once again in a few decades by pressure from surrounding farmers and hysteria over Native uprisings. Just before the Louisiana Purchase, they began their last migration, a journey down the waterways of southeastern Louisiana that would take them ever closer to the Gulf of Mexico. Houma tradition maintains they relocated down Bayou Lafourche to modern Houma, Louisiana, where they spread out along bayous radiating from that town like fingers from an open palm.

After 1763 settlers kept pushing the Houma farther into the marsh, and with the change in environment their world changed dramatically as they turned this refuge into a new homeland. Fishing and shrimping became mainstays of the Native communities, Indian women intermarried with nearby Euro-Americans and produced large families with French last names, and the nation adopted Catholicism as its dominant religion. After the Civil War and consequent restructuring of class systems, the Houma found themselves caught in a three-tiered system of segregation. Realizing that education was one way to retain lands constantly under assault from trappers and oil companies, the Houma fought to keep from being shunted off to black schools during the Jim Crow era. The first attempt to integrate Terrebonne Parish schools began in the early twentieth century and was not resolved until five decades later. Currently, the tribe is fighting for federal recognition.

Placing the Houma at the center of their own history is a great challenge given the gaps and biases throughout the archival record. René-Robert Cavelier, Sieur de La Salle sailed past the tribe in 1682 and missed them because a thick fog prevented him from seeing what stood only a short distance away, and this first mention of the Houma serves as a metaphor for the subsequent historical record. Almost every account from the colonial period to the modern era mentions the Houma solely in light of what the observer valued, and readers must examine these sources accordingly; in no way were these documents unbiased or complete in their perspective. French priests and explorers made only the briefest visits to the nation, and primary documents devote little attention to the culture of the Houma, concentrating instead on practical concerns such as food, the time it took to get to a village, diplomatic protocol, and the number of warriors the nation could provide. The French made incidental references to cultural aspects such as gender—a deceased female warrior who dressed as a man and led other warriors into battle, or that three matriarchs presented Iberville with foodstuffs during a ceremony— but with absolutely no interpretation of what this information might mean.[1] Likewise, the archaeological record reveals little. The Houma village of 1699 has never been definitively located and would have been influenced by later Tunica arrival, in any case. Likewise, many early village sites along southeastern Louisiana's lower bayous have been either eroded or inundated. Until now only the Grand Village in Ascension has garnered excavation, and even that was very brief.[2] While other sites might reveal a wealth of information in the future, they have not yet.

Even determining how many Houma there were based on primary documents is impossible. Colonial estimates varied wildly, not surprising given that Houma settlements were some distance from each other and visitors invariably recorded traveling to only one village. Moreover, the Houma were seasonally mobile, and this would have greatly influenced the number of people in a village at any one time. Adding to the confusion are multiple spellings of the same name, something that began in the colonial era and continued well into the twenty-first century; this includes the name of the tribe itself, names of individuals within the tribe, and names of non-Natives interacting with the Houma. Amid the welter of languages, colonial powers, and individual actors, it is not unusual to see the same person referred to by six or seven variations of their name.

As with the French, Spanish and English officials valued the Houma for what the nation offered, and when the tribe's influence waned so did colonial interest. Much of what we know about them from the late 1700s and early 1800s derives from a lawsuit and the writings of Louis Judice, a colonial official tasked with maintaining peace in one section of the Mississippi River. After the early 1800s the Houma lived at the very ends of bayous in extreme southeastern Louisiana, places they relocated to specifically so they would be ignored and left in peace. Newly arrived Americans were only too happy to oblige them. This stemmed partly from how the new federal government recorded Indians, the inaccessible location of Houma villages, and the fact that settlers had driven the nation down the bayous and were pleased to erase them from the American consciousness. As in the colonial era, population estimates and the spelling of names varied wildly.

So, is it impossible for the Houma to take their place at the table of history based on surviving materials? Whatever the archaeological record might reveal in the future, it does not reveal much now. Archival documents from the French, Spanish, and English are biased and contain gigantic gaps both in material and interpretation. Federal and state records were maintained by people who, at best, were completely uninterested in the nation and, at worst, had a vested interest in their being forgotten. There were no Houma Indian newspapers or essayists such as one finds among the Cherokee or other Southeastern tribes, and personal documents were invariably lost when hurricanes washed over bayou communities. Though John Swanton had conversations with tribal elders via translators, the first oral histories of the nation only began in the late 1970s.

Examining the Houma through surviving materials seems like a bleak task; yet, when one carefully studies the sources one begins to hear these people speak. I knew that I would never be able to base this book on traditional archival materials and therefore would have to cast a wide net in primary and secondary sources. My research path included as many areas as possible—archaeology, legal cases, records of the Catholic and Methodist faiths, references to the Houma in biographies of the region's notable people, school board records from Lafourche Parish and Terrebonne Parish, newspaper articles, courthouse records, oral interviews from the Houma Bicentennial Commission and Bruce Duthu, hurricane chronicles, personal letters, immigration records, lists of land purchases and sales, tax records, federal census figures, academic theses and dissertations, photographic archives, and a variety of other sources. My greatest primary documents were the people who spoke with me. Some of these were members of the United Houma Nation and other tribes who consented to recording, some were Indians and non-Indians who spoke with me but chose not to go on the record, and some were people who had never heard of the Houma. In this last group, the deckhands, pilots, and captains I interacted with during my time as a historian with Delta Queen Steamboat Company were invaluable in helping me understand the rivers, bayous, marshes, and swamps of southeastern Louisiana, a region as much "waterscape" as landscape and to which the Houma nation is inextricably tied.[3]

Neither my research nor my writing of this book took place in a vacuum, and I am indebted to many, many people whose scholarship suggested a theoretical framework for my own work. Ironically, H.L. Bourgeois and his virulent 1938 "Four Decades of Public Education in Terrebonne" gave me one of the best perspectives, because it revealed what challenges the Houma faced in the early twentieth century more eloquently than any other source. Ernest Downs's and Jenna Whitehead's 1976 "The Houma Indians: Two Decades in a History of Struggle" was invaluable, as were the publications of Janel Curry-Roper in the 1970s and 1980s. They were among the first scholars to look at the Houma from a variety of perspectives, and their work set a very high standard. Bruce Duthu's articles on the Houma remain a model of clarity and insight besides offering a valuable legal perspective. Bruce is also the first member of the Houma nation to write about their history, which gives his work a very scholarly yet very intimate perspective. Nicholas Ng-A-Fook's *An Indigenous Curriculum of Place: The United Houma Nation's Contentious Relationship with Louisiana's Educational Institutions* links many challenges facing the nation today with their historical struggles. Michael "T-Mayheart" Dardar has written widely on the Houma nation, but his *Women-Chiefs and Crawfish Warriors: A Brief History of the Houma People* stands out as a publication by a tribal elder and historian. Mark Miller's *Forgotten Tribes: Unrecognized Indians and the Federal Acknowledgment Process* is a wonderful examination of the federal-recognition bids of the Houma and several other tribes. All of these authors influenced my own work and, in the case of Bruce, Michael, and Mark, challenged me during spirited debates.

On a broader level, Daniel Usner's works on Natives in the Lower Mississippi Valley remain seminal, and his *Indians, Settlers, and Slaves in a Frontier Exchange Economy: The Lower Mississippi Valley before 1783* endures as the standard against which I measure writing in this field. I should add that reading his book while in graduate school at Arizona State University made me look back to Louisiana for my own research, so it is quite an understatement to say that he merely influenced my theoretical perspective. Now retired, Dr. Carl Brasseaux remains one of the major historians of Louisiana, and his numerous works on Cajuns, Creoles, and Native Americans offer a model of clarity and interpretation.

He was also extremely generous in making documents available to me and gently nudging me during our discussions, for which I will always be grateful. Jay Precht's work with the Coushatta and Brian Klopotek's examination of the Louisiana Choctaw are outstanding and offer comparative models against which to examine the Houma. Susan Sleeper-Smith's publications on Indian women and French men of the Great Lakes might seem geographically removed, but they offer a valuable framework for examining gender relations in the Lower Mississippi Valley. I would also be remiss if I did not mention Robbie Ethridge's pieces on the shatter zone and cultural adaptation, Malinda Maynor Lowery's writings on the Lumbee, and Theda Perdue's works on women and culture change as influences on this book.[4]

I received valuable feedback on my work from colleagues and several anonymous reviewers, and one rhetorical question I repeatedly heard was, "Why should we care about the Houma?" Other peoples, both Indian and non-Indian, have adapted to changing environments; indeed, this is a primary characteristic of human beings throughout history. Acadians, Yugoslavs, Canary Islanders, Germans, and various other ethnic groups have settled along the waterways of southern Louisiana and tied themselves to the landscape, so this certainly is not specific to the Houma. Other Native Americans of the Jim Crow era endured segregation and later fought for public education. Likewise, women of various ethnicities partnered with European men and created children from those unions, to which New Orleans's nearby free people of color attest. Certainly, indigenous peoples around the world have been relocated when a dominant power desired their homeland. One can isolate almost any facet of Houma history and find that same experience in another culture, particularly among Louisiana and Southeastern tribes. So what makes the Houma different?

When I was a teenager I read a definition of great literature that has stayed with me since: a great story is absolutely specific to its time and place while rising above its time and place. *The Great Gatsby* and *War and Peace* are forever tied to their eras and locations while at the same time revealing something greater about the human condition. I think this is true of any great story, and the Houma nation has a great story. Their experience is unique to them, and there is no way to mistake it for the history of any other Native American nation. In their colonial interactions, their lawsuits, their embracing of Catholicism and the French language, and their adaptations to the bayous of southeastern Louisiana, they stand alone. At the same time, their story illustrates themes shared by a number of other indigenous peoples—their struggle to survive and adapt in a hostile world, to create new homelands, to pull from the dominant society as a means of protecting their core identity.

One last point about what readers will find missing in this work. Southeastern Louisiana is both extremely rich and extremely complicated in its geographic and cultural fabrics. So too is the Houma nation. While writing this book I went into great detail on contexts and nuances that people might not understand unless they are from the area. Unfortunately, that resulted in *A Kingdom of Water* stretching over five hundred pages in its initial form, which made it somewhat unwieldy. I was ruthless in my edits and also placed many details in notes so as not to slow the narrative. Looking back from the other side of massive cuts, I found that streamlining my work made it stronger and more concise but eliminated many points that were, in the words of one of my reviewers, "very interesting but not vital to the story." Bearing these cuts in mind, I want to remind readers that the historical players in this work were far more than statistics or names in a census record. They were human beings—passionate in thought, energetic in action, chiefly concerned with their own goals, and every bit as vital as we are now.

Historians usually end the first section of their works by claiming any inaccuracies as theirs alone. I will follow tradition and say that any errors of fact or reconstruction fall on me and only on me. *A Kingdom of Water* is one person's interpretation of how the Houma nation adapted to the changing political and social climates of Louisiana between 1699 and 2005. But it is only one person's interpretation, and readers should view it in that light. This is the first full-length monograph on the Houma nation's history, and I hope it encourages others to continue this research. If anyone finds errors or draws a radically different interpretation from mine, I will be delighted, because this means they are further examining this important topic and either correcting things that should be corrected or simply drawing their own conclusions. Either will make me happy.

A KINGDOM OF WATER

I

"He and I Shall Be but One"

The Forging of Houma and French Alliances

At 10:30 in the morning of March 20, 1699, a group of three Houma ambassadors stood on the eastern bank of the Mississippi River and greeted a party of nine men paddling upstream toward them. Though neither group could know it at the time, this meeting would change their respective histories and usher in political and social change neither group could have imagined on this fresh spring day. But all that lay in the future. All the Houma ambassadors knew for certain at this moment, while the Mississippi's surging waters rose as they had for centuries and the sun rose above their heads, was that a group of eight Frenchmen led by a hated Bayougoula tribal leader was paddling toward them. These visitors could furnish military and economic advantages against rivals such as the very Bayougoula who was singing a greeting, and the next few hours would thus be critical in forging alliances. Raising calumets over their heads and singing loudly in welcome, the Houma men greeted the landing party.[1]

The Muskhogean-speaking nation that welcomed their guests had emerged from the Lower Mississippi Valley shatter zone of the 1500s and 1600s. They had once been part of the larger Chakchiuma group located in north-central Mississippi at the confluence of the Yazoo and Yalobusha Rivers and were distantly related to both the Choctaw and Chickasaw.[2] By 1682 the Houma had migrated southwest and established villages on the Mississippi's east bank. While they shared linguistic patterns and cultural ties with several surrounding tribes, the nation viewed itself as a separate people, sui generis. *Shâkti Humma*, or "red crawfish," indicated not only the giant crawfish that created the world by pulling up mud and kneading its claws but also its earthly cousin, a tiny creature that raised its pincers in aggression no matter how large the enemy.

"Houma" in all its pronunciations and later spellings meant "red," and the nation's warriors maintained the red crawfish as their war symbol.[3]

The nation's leaders had good reason to be cautious, flanked by adversaries and with possible foreign enemies now stepping on their shore. Their homeland stretched between the Koroa tribe to the north and the Bayougoula to the south, encompassing parts of modern East Baton Rouge Parish, West Feliciana Parish, and Wilkinson County, Mississippi. This territory was attractive to both their neighbors, and, indeed, competition for land was what turned the Houma and adjoining Bayougoula into rivals.[4] They regularly engaged in combat over natural resources and jealously guarded their boundaries.[5]

Surrounding tribes certainly would have coveted Houma territory. Geography, wind, and river currents joined forces to make the west bank of the Mississippi and the east bank to the south completely flat, but not the hills stretching behind the Houma party. On the contrary, the eastern shore's level floodplain of rich, dark, river-deposited soil rose quickly to high, steep bluffs. Eons of wind currents depositing Chinese glacial silt made these bluffs an ideal habitat for the Houma nation—free from flooding, lushly fertile, and difficult to take in warfare. The ground rose sharply in timbered slopes above the floodplain, and clear streams raced quickly through quiet, peach-colored valleys. The area assured a constant food supply, be it from rich stores of corn, beans, and squash or from abundant wildlife in the river and air as well as on land. With villages overlooking the greatest water route in North America and backed by footpaths winding through the region, the Houma sat at a transportation crossroads and had no intention of losing this treasured place to traditional enemies such as the Bayougoula. Thus, their welcome to the French was as much a pursuit of allies as it was hospitality.[6]

Houma distrust of the Bayougoula was amply justified. Indeed, the only reason the French arrived at the Houma village at all was because of tribal conflict. The exploration party was led by Sieur de Iberville, a scion of one of New France's most powerful families, and he was tracing the steps of René Robert Cavelier, Sieur de La Salle.[7] La Salle had sailed downriver past the Houma village during the foggy night of March 31, 1682, and continued to the river's mouth, where his proclamation on April 9 united French Canada and the French Caribbean.[8] It brought the mightiest river in North America, one of the mightiest in the world, under Gallic control and legally supported the French's claim, in their minds, to an empire stretching from the Appalachians to the Rockies. Thus, the party was exploring the Mississippi to ensure the continued growth of French power.

Rowing upstream from the Gulf of Mexico rather than downstream from Canada, Iberville sought proof that he indeed traveled the same river La Salle had in 1682 and was particularly interested in finding the major fork in the river described by Chevalier Henry de Tonty, one of La Salle's lieutenants. Called Le Bras Coup or La Main de Fer (The Iron Hand) because of the metal appendage he wore, Tonty explored on his own during and after La Salle's trek and claimed to have met the Houma in 1686.[9] Iberville checked landmarks and spent several days questioning the Bayougoula about the fork in the river, but his efforts were bedeviled by inconsistencies in the La Salle accounts and doubts of Native trustworthiness. Frustrated and convinced that the "intelligent and cunning" Bayougoula leader was feeding him false information to prevent his meeting the Bayougoula's traditional enemies, he had no alternative but to continue upstream and spend several days with the Houma.[10] Thus, if the Bayougoula chief's plan was indeed to derail a meeting and possible alliance, as Iberville believed, it backfired.

Before the Houma ambassadors and Iberville ever caught sight of each other, political alliances of the Lower Mississippi Valley had laid the foundation for their first encounter. On February 17, 1699, Iberville had sung the calumet with Bayougoula ambassadors who acted as proxies for other tribes and by doing so became a formal ally with four nations west of the river and seven nations east of the Mississippi, the Houma one of the latter.[11] Thus, in one of the ironies characterizing the intricate politics of Indian nations along the Gulf Coast, the Houma had already symbolically absorbed the French politically due to the efforts of their rivals the Bayougoula, the very nation attempting to derail an alliance between the two in March. The French thus technically stepped ashore not as strangers to the Houma but as political allies.

The Houma party and the Bayougoula leader sang to each other for several minutes and then reached upward to honor the sun, rubbing their hands over each other's faces and chests and then those of their visitors.

All fourteen men smoked and parleyed for thirty minutes, after which the Houma escorted the visitors to their village, singing effortlessly even though the party climbed steep hills the entire way. Around one o'clock a separate delegation of three Houma men relieved the previous group and repeated the calumet smoking ceremony. This new delegation led the French party to three huts about three hundred yards from the village, where they stayed until word came from the *Ouga*, or tribal leader, that they had permission to enter.[12]

Their Houma escorts ushered the party into the village and introduced them to the Ouga and two of his principal men, who greeted the party while carrying small white crosses. Even at seventy, the chieftain stood five feet, ten inches tall, strong and vital. Iberville's host and another leader grasped the thirty-eight-year-old under his arms and guided him to his seat for fear he would stumble or otherwise hurt himself while under village protection, a paternalistic gesture the older man repeated several times over the next few days. Ever the political animal, Iberville noted that the Ouga also had a son of around thirty whom he was grooming to succeed him.[13]

Just as the Houma leader made it clear to Iberville and his men that they were under his protection, so were all formal interactions and festivities over the next few days designed to project an image of strength tempered by hospitality. After the Ouga and his principal men embraced Iberville and his party, the Houma guided them to mats in the middle of a well-maintained village square about two hundred yards across. Surrounded by several hundred villagers, they again smoked the obligatory calumet and exchanged presents in front of the temple. For the Houma, this gift giving was much more than a mere exchange of material goods. On the contrary, as with so many tribes, the goods themselves were secondary at this point in Houma history and indicated a cementing of bonds between allies. "Proper" gift giving and trade were inextricably bound with ceremony, discussion, and the forging of social alliances.[14]

The next few hours were devoted to dancing, an entertainment particularly suited to displaying both strength and beauty. Around four o'clock Houma musicians and singers assembled with gourd drums and were in turn joined for three hours of energetic dancing by twenty young men and fifteen young women "splendidly adorned in their style, all of them naked, wearing nothing except their *braguets*, [loincloths for men and short aprons for women] over which they wore a kind of sash a foot wide, which was made of feathers or fur or hair, painted red, yellow, and white, their faces and bodies tattooed or painted various colors, and they carried in their hands feathers that they used as fans or to mark the beat, some tufts of feathers being neatly braided into the hair."[15] The gestures of hospitality had ranged from parleying and smoking to gift exchange and the beauty of a dance, but all were designed to pull the French into the Houma sphere of influence.

The French were drawing conclusions about their hosts based on several hours of interaction, and it would defy human nature to believe that the Houma were not doing the same. These arrivals brought very real danger of a colonial–Bayougoula alliance and thus a passing of military technology to the Houma's traditional enemy. The French had good boats, plentiful firearms, and skilled warriors, which warranted cautious diplomacy on its own merits, but the possibility of their traditional enemies acquiring those advantages would have struck terror into Houma military hearts. Any concerns about the Bayougoula poisoning diplomatic waters were amply justified, as the "cunning" leader had already cautioned Iberville that the Houma were treacherous and bloodthirsty and that the 1682 slaughter of Tangiboa mentioned by the La Salle party was a Houma atrocity.[16]

The Houma and Bayougoula definitely had reason to be wary of each other, and at the time of Iberville's visit the Houma maintained a slight advantage that would collapse if the French intervened. In 1699 they maintained 140 huts and 350 men at their main village, with a total village population of probably around 1,200.[17] By comparison, the main Bayougoula village contained 107 huts, between 200 to 250 men, and few women and children; the population had been reduced by 25 percent because of a smallpox epidemic, and in 1700 the Bayougoula would be reduced further due to intravillage warfare.[18]

Small conflicts between the two groups would erupt again in June and August 1699, and these illustrated why both tribes were so eager to form an alliance with the French against the other. Conflict escalated in October when the Houma staged a surprise attack and carried off twenty-five prisoners. On March 5, 1700, Iberville negotiated for the

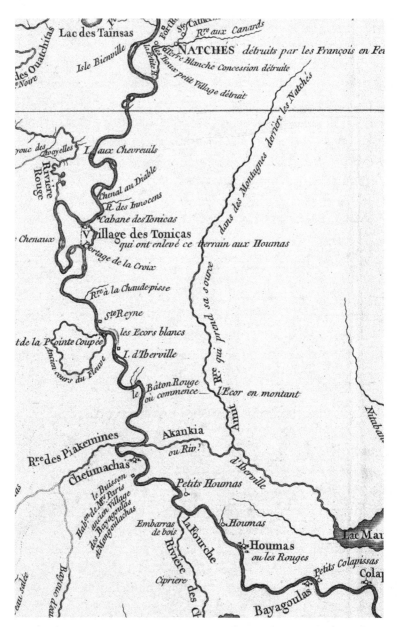

Map 1. Detail of Carte de la Louisiane, drawn in May 1732 but published in
1752. Jean Baptiste Bourguignon d'Anville. This image shows the Houma villages after the nation had relocated to Ascension. The "Village des Tonicas"
is approximately where the Houma lived in 1699. The Historic New Orleans
Collection, gift of Richard Koch, 1957.26 i, ii.

captives' release and asked why the Houma had broken the peace. Elders countered that the Bayougoula had first attacked. Rather than torture prisoners or incorporate them as either slaves or surrogate kin, the nation would gladly release them in exchange for apologies and presents. The Houma tribal elders were only mollified when Iberville apologized in proxy and offered trade goods with the caveat that Bayougoula elders would arrive shortly and sing the calumet.[19] Invariably, conflict stemmed from disputes over tribal hunting grounds, and the two nations habitually marshaled forces when the other crossed a recognized landmark.

Iberville had sought the river's fork rather than a tribal struggle but watched the political ballet with interest. More important, on the night of March 20, 1699, he watched several hundred Houma warriors dance for hours around a fifteen-foot pyre of river cane, the shafts exploding like gunfire as flames cast tortured shadows across the village square. Pierre Le Moyne, Sieur d'Iberville, sprang from one of Montreal's foremost political dynasties and had distinguished himself as a ruthless soldier many times over, most recently via the swath of destruction he cut through English Canada during King William's War. A few feet away from the battle-hardened veteran sat his younger brother Jean-Baptiste Le Moyne, Sieur de Bienville, barely nineteen but already displaying a toughness and political skill that would propel him to the governorship of French Louisiana two years later, and then for four terms between 1701 and 1743.

Though twenty years apart in age, both brothers instinctively sought the advantage in any situation. Moreover, both could resort to violence quickly and effectively if needed but realized that diplomacy invariably brought more rewards than war. In coming decades the French would become the region's dominant colonial power, but absolutely nothing was predestined in March 1699, and both brothers knew it very well. Fort Maurepas would not be founded on the Gulf Coast until the following month, Mobile not until 1702, and New Orleans not until 1718.[20] Looking around them in the Houma village, they silently agreed that diplomacy was the wiser option in this setting. The Ouga had shown through his actions that he was a strong personality, not afraid of outsiders and able to defend his territory. The nation produced large quantities of food and could be generous with it. Most important, the hundreds of warriors dancing before them "with their bows and arrows and head-breakers and war equipment" illustrated that the nation could quickly marshal soldiers for itself or, by extension, its allies.[21] Attempting to create a wedge between the French and Houma, the Bayougoula leader had succeeded only in creating a coalition.

By the end of the visit the French and Houma had forged a much stronger alliance than had existed two days before. Iberville and his party had sought only the route of the Mississippi when they arrived but were impressed by the Houma's warriors and horticultural wealth. In contrast, from the time Iberville entered the Bayougoula village he found them the poorest, "most beggarly" people he had ever met, with inadequate housing and a deficient work ethic. Any possible military union between the two was out of the question, as he thought the tribe's men nimble and well-made but "not much inured to war."[22] Moreover, soldiers and habitants could never draw upon the tribe for foodstuffs, as the surrounding fields were quite small. In short, the Bayougoula did not compare well to the Houma and through the rest of their history were never able to draw the French to their side despite regular entreaties.

The Houma Ouga and several hundred villagers escorted the French party back to their boat on March 21, with the Bayougoula singing the way and Iberville's men saluting the party with two musket firings. The Houma gave presents of corn and pounded meal, and in turn they received presents of "axes, knives, kettles, mirrors, scissors, awls, needles, shirts, blankets, and jackets made of red cloth."[23] In their parting ceremony the Houma mentioned how another Frenchman with a metal hand had stayed at their village a few years ago. This could only be Tonty, but to avoid any doubt in the matter Iberville continued upstream to the Koroa, then stopped at the Houma village again on March 23 as he made his way downstream. Iberville was a keen political animal and noted many things about the Houma that impressed him, but he had overlooked many things also. Though interested in the number and strength of his host's warriors, he completely missed that at least some women fought in battle as well. Shortly before his arrival a female warrior had died, a woman so honored for her bravery and logistical skill that an entourage of four young men preceded her through the village. Since she had died shortly before and only the Bayougoula leader could communicate directly with the Ouga, this is an understandable omission.[24] More surprising is that Iberville carefully observed how the Ouga's "son" was being groomed for leadership but made no mention of the leader's sister or that the heir might actually have been selected due to his matrilineal status. Most surprising of all is that Iberville either overlooked or minimized the important role that groups of three matriarchs played in ceremonial exchanges, astonishing given his careful scrutiny of foodstuffs and their future value.

Neither leader knew exactly what each was missing about the other, but both knew they were missing important nuances. The only way that they could communicate was through the Bayougoula chief, whom neither of them trusted. Obviously, this was not an acceptable option for either, especially since primary points of future communication would be food, trade, or warfare, the very points rival tribes strove to thwart. Fortunately, both men came from cultures long engaged in the adoption of children. For the Houma this meant ritual adoption with formal instruction in tribal mores, while the French practiced unofficial adoption via accepting a homeless child as a household member or standing as a godparent at a child's baptism.

Iberville departed Louisiana for France on May 4, 1699, and took with him a twelve-year-old Bayougoula boy that soldiers nicknamed *Mousquet* (Musket). The child had been previously captured in battle and then adopted by the Bayougoula leader before he was given to Bienville in late March. Bienville in turn entrusted the boy's training and acculturation to his brother. Sadly, Mousquet would not serve as a bridge between the two cultures, for his tale would be a brief one. He left France with his protector in December 1699, and on January 19 he fell ill with a throat ailment. He died on January 23, 1700, as the ship lay at harbor in Bay St. Louis.[25]

Adoption held a happier ending for the six cabin boys Iberville left behind when he sailed home, boys who would play a critical role in the area's history.[26] Over the next few years they fanned out in waves to Indian villages as emissaries of the French crown, and it is a sign of their immersion in Indian communities as adopted sons that they all but disappeared from the historical record. In 1700 the eleven-year-old Saint-Michel was sent to live with the Houma. His biological father had been the harbormaster at Rochefort, but the boy quickly gained new parents in the Indian community. He was instructed in tribal arts by Houma elders and blended so seamlessly into the cultural fabric that in May 1702, Bienville sent him to the Chickasaw after that nation asked for a child to adopt. Bienville reasoned that Saint-Michel's already-fluent Houma would allow him to pick up Chickasaw very quickly.[27]

The fourteen-year-old entered his second Indian nation not as a child picking up a new language but as a youth trained in tribal cultures, whose linguistic skills allowed him to communicate with both the French and almost a dozen tribes. His status was so prominent that in 1703 the Choctaw attempted to use him to start a war between the French and the Chickasaw. They told Monsieur Boisbrian, a French official who had journeyed to the Choctaw village, that the youth had been burned at the stake by his second adopted nation. The situation quickly escalated and was only put to rest when ten Chickasaws delivered Saint-Michel safely to Mobile.[28]

The life of Saint-Michel reflects a great irony. That this young man all but disappeared from the historical record and dictated or recorded nothing of Houma culture means that he was doing exactly what he was meant to do: blend into Indian communities. A continuation of this irony was that the priests who wrote the most about the Houma circa 1700 were the people least accepted by them and often those least comfortable with Native mores. In 1699 Iberville had brought the Recollet priest Anastase Douay with him, in part because Douay had sailed on La Salle's ill-fated last expedition to Texas. Douay proved more trouble than he was worth, however, after he lost both his journal and his breviary in late March while with another French party at the Bayou-goula village. Weeping, he accused several locals of taking his religious items. The accusations so angered his hosts that the chieftain told the French party to leave immediately, and the matriarchs took back bread they had prepared for their guests. These were signs of the highest displeasure, and when the party made it back to the Gulf and told Iberville what had happened, the latter barely contained his anger. The two men exchanged harsh words, and around April 20th, 1699, Douay requested release from expedition duties so he could return to his French monastery. Thus, Douay not only could not further alliances with local tribes but proved a liability. The Jesuit Paul du Ru was assigned to the expedition, and on February 3, 1700, du Ru entered the Mississippi's mouth with Iberville's second expedition.[29]

Douay had completely failed to grasp the nuances of local politics, but Father du Ru quickly ascertained something the Houma and their enemy had known all along, that a primary motivation was to pull European newcomers into traditional conflicts. On February 4 du Ru met his first Bayougoula, "more dried up even than the bear meat and venison."[30] By February 5 the old man had come to his tent to entreat the French to join forces against the Houma. He went on at great length about the aggression and violence of his enemy, but the Frenchman refused to sympathize. Deeply troubled by what he saw and heard, du Ru wrote in his journal that war was often an immoral act and always a risky one, "and it would be more so in this country, where the enemy lurks in the forest like beasts of prey and is harder to find than to fight."[31] Du Ru's refusal to engage in warfare did not prevent his asking the elderly Bayougoula to teach him that nation's language, as the priest had heard it was similar to those of surrounding tribes. The elder assured him that nine or ten surrounding nations spoke the same dialect, including their traditional enemy the Houma. By February 8 du Ru had already learned fifty of the most important words and a variety of basic linguistic rules, such as the complete lack of *r*'s and *d*'s in the language.[32]

Du Ru was not a stupid man, and when he entered the Houma village on March 5, 1700, he realized not only that he was welcomed due to Iberville's and Bienville's influence but also that the Houma wanted to draw him into their orbit as well.[33] Yet, he missed point after point of the culture in which he was a guest. Houma religion was characterized by a strong preoccupation with the sun; in the temple an elderly holy man tended a perpetual sacred fire (*loüak* or *loughé*) that represented the celestial fire.[34] The priest misunderstood this and saw no deeper meaning to why chickens and roosters were venerated or that they might be associated with the rising sun. Du Ru's description of shamans bridging spiritual and physical worlds in healing ceremonies as "less horrible but more ridiculous" than some other Houma customs is particularly ironic given that, with a few words changed, he would have described the Catholic rites he administered as a priest almost exactly. Perhaps, given his opinion of these medicine men as charlatans and tricksters, du Ru did not feel they represented anything close enough to religion to contradict his theory that the Houma simply honored the dead.[35]

Why would the Houma villagers have tolerated this man who clearly did not understand them and whose only goal seemed to be to destroy what he did not understand? Their actions make a great deal of sense when viewed from a tribal perspective. Their secondary goal was the acquisition of trade goods, which might make life easier but were by no means necessary. The Houma's primary goal was to keep these items from falling into the hands of the Bayougoula and other enemies. That was *very* necessary. The Houma were interested in reaching across boundaries insofar as it helped them achieve their own goals. They eagerly formed political and economic alliances and also willingly exchanged children with Europeans. Religion was another matter, and even though Bienville had introduced du Ru as "a great chief" and the Ouga suffered to be catechized by the priest, the majority of Houma were not particularly interested in Catholicism.[36] On the contrary, they watched politely as Jesuits celebrated mass, then went about their business.[37] If the Houma had railed against missionaries, this at least would have given a visible enemy against which to fight, but politeness and religious tolerance proved more stymieing than the most rabid apostate.

On March 9, 1700, du Ru recorded a type of religious success when a Houma man finally expressed interest in Christianity of his own accord. Adding to this victory was the man's prominent position in the village. The prospective Christian accepted du Ru as "a friend of the Great Spirit, Ouga, that is to say, the universal chief of all the nations of the world and he is very desirous of being also one of his friends. To him, says he, he and I shall be but one. *Jeheno, Yno, Nanhoulou toutchino atchota.*" The Houma man chatted with the priest often and sat near him at all counsels, observing the priest's actions from a close vantage. The Jesuit saw enough potential in him to give the Indian a high-quality shirt as a means of forging further bonds, but the man's attentions eventually grew so obtrusive that when the French party attempted to leave, du Ru was forced to hide in the bushes to avoid his first potential convert.[38]

Clearly, something more was at play than simple religious interest. Though their conversation was recorded from the Jesuit's perspective, its phrasing and word choice reflected Houma cosmology. What du Ru saw as childlike devotion even as the rest of the village listened to his religious teachings with coolness and detached politeness was much more likely an attempt to garner spiritual power. The man was already prominent and might have been attempting to further elevate his status, but one thing is absolutely certain: this "convert" reached across religious boundaries with such aggression that the priest eventually had to flee from him, even as the Indian couched his interest in traditional Houma terms. Interpreted from the modern perspective, this seems a classic maneuver to investigate what the French found important and use it for the benefit of either the nation or the individual garnering knowledge. The religious actions of this "convert" would thus be very much in keeping with political actions of other Houma the year before, of seeking an alliance with the French for personal gain.

On March 24 du Ru returned to the village, said mass, and persuaded the Ouga to begin a church in the village square, naming St. Francis Xavier as its patron. Du Ru constructed a model and left his French servant with the tribe to conduct the work, then sailed downriver.[39] No description or drawing of this chapel exists, but du Ru gives an excellent description of the church he and the Bayougoula villagers built over the next week at their settlement, and described the structures as looking much alike: about fifty feet long and twenty feet in width, framed by posts and rafters. Its general shape was a European nave, the walls stuffed with moss and plastered with clay, and the roof made with woven matting. A small cross was placed over the door and a large one, about thirty feet high, placed in the square. Made without nails, hammer, or chisel, the chapel was a mixture of traditional Indian building techniques and European planning.[40]

Du Ru's physical presence among the Houma ended on March 24, 1700, but he would be succeeded in late November first by Father de Limoges and then Father Gravier. Gravier had a very businesslike attitude toward conversion and made close inspection of both the Houma temple and Catholic chapel before speaking directly to the new Ouga, probably the man Iberville saw being groomed for power the year before. This gentleman conversed pleasantly and assured the priest that he only acknowledged one "Creator"; at the conversation's end the elder had utilized a time-honored political tactic of saying little without ever specifying the "Creator" to which he was referring. On the other hand, Father Limoges had arranged for Gravier to baptize a three-day-old boy, "the first fruits of his mission," named St. Francis Xavier in honor of his patron. The child died shortly after, but the Houma seem not to have associated the child's baptism with his death.[41]

Du Ru, Limoges, and Gravier walked every day through the Houma village. They passed shrieking children, strutting roosters, and hunters carrying white-tailed deer back to the village. In journals they recorded intricate details such as dress, sport, village location and population, and even the decorations of the Houma temple. In short, though they closely observed and lived surrounded by the people whose souls they had traveled far to save, they never understood the Houma. They never grasped the importance of women, the power structure that supported an Ouga, matrilineal kinship, or other underpinnings of tribal culture. Most of all, they never understood that they were guests rather than guides. The Houma had their own motivations and agendas, and the Jesuits changed nothing in the former's culture. Gravier performed the village's first high mass on December 3, 1700, but it takes more than one believer, one church, and one baptism to claim a faith, and it disappointed him that the Houma showed neither anger nor interest.[42]

What Father Gravier did not grasp during his two weeks in the village was that the Houma were carefully observing him and his fellow Frenchmen for possible political or economic advantage. From their first meeting, the Houma elders witnessed a constant fusion of religion, politics, and the military on the part of their visitors, and it was no small thing to have in their village holy men so respected by colonial leaders. That they were fluent in French and could also communicate in the Houma dialect was no small thing either, especially given that the Europeans and Houma were exchanging young men specifically to learn the other's language. From a strictly utilitarian point of view, if a series of French emissaries stayed in the village and offered access to the new culture without causing too much difficulty, then it was no hardship to erect a church and cross, to allow a little water to be placed on a child's head, and to tolerate some puzzling but harmless eccentricities. The Houma did not consider themselves sheep being led to God. On the contrary, their polite but disinterested tolerance of the new faith reflected not only their grasp of a broader political perspective but also a determination to place themselves at the forefront of negotiations.

When the Ouga escorted Iberville and Bienville back to their boats on March 21, 1699, both parties had made formal alliances and sized up the other's strengths and weaknesses. Both groups had decided that the other could prove useful, and in following months the Houma pursued this alliance enthusiastically. They welcomed a French cabin boy as a bridge between the two nations, helped construct a chapel, and housed priests passing through the village. Whether the first convert actually embraced Catholicism or was more attracted to the power du Ru obviously held among the French is debatable, but the Houma were savvy enough to realize the advantages of sheltering holy men given the latter's perceived status in colonial society.

By the time Gravier performed the Houma's first mass in December 1700 the nation had taken its initial steps onto a world political stage. What had started with three Houma ambassadors raising their hands toward a rising sun had quickly blossomed into a series of alliances with soldiers, holy men, and, by extension, a powerful king. Adapting quickly to a changing world had provided these advantages and, just as important, kept those military and economic benefits from flowing to the Bayougoula. The Houma acted to their own advantage, and in all appearances their strategy was extremely successful. What the nation could not foresee was how forging coalitions would bring down the wrath of other tribes and colonial powers. Within a few short years conflict would spread into their homeland, and the Houma would be pulled into global conflicts in a way they could not have imagined.

2

"We Should Be Obligated to Destroy Them"

Houma Remove to Bayou St. John and Ascension

By January 1701 the Houma were slightly less than two years into their alliance with the French, but international conflict was already appearing on the horizon. Far to the northeast, New France and New England had raged against each other for decades, and hostilities along the Southeastern borderlands were quickly escalating. Lower Louisiane had been spared this fate primarily because it lacked enough colonists to be a target, but in 1718 Bienville established the city of La Nouvelle Orleans just a few hundred miles south of Houma territory, and in 1722 his political machinations moved the capital there from Mobile. Close to the mouth of North America's mightiest river yet within easy travel of Houma territory, New Orleans would emerge over the next several decades as one of France's colonial capitals. That gave the nation access to goods and alliances they had not enjoyed before but also put them in danger, as the English and their allied tribes sensed a threat to their east.

After 1701 the European settler population increased, and escalations of colonial violence spread conflict from the Atlantic seaboard to the Lower Mississippi Valley. This would shortly engulf the Houma. Between 1701 and 1763 the nation was forced from its homeland by a closely related tribe and relocated twice, first suffering societal disruption and then emerging as one of the dominant political entities of the Lower Mississippi Valley. That they survived attacks from English-allied tribes and thrived in a new environment testifies to the Houma's ability to adapt. Ironically, the fact that they escaped slaughter at the hands of the French does as well.

Though the Lower Mississippi Valley conflict reached a fever pitch in the early 1700s, it had actually been building for several years along the Gulf Coast. In May 1699, less than two months after he had first met the Houma, Bienville and a group of Frenchmen happened upon some members of the Colapissa (or Acolapissa) tribe, a Muskhogean group living just above the mouth of the modern Pearl River.[1] The Colapissa were set to attack the colonials, but Bayougoula traveling with the explorers narrowly averted a slaughter by vouching for them. During a parley, Colapissas said that shortly before two English men and two hundred Chickasaw had attacked their village and carried off fifty of their tribe as slaves. They thought that the French party was returning for a second attack. The Bayougoula assured them that, though white, their companions were traditional enemies of the English, and what had started as certain death for the Gallics ended with the groups forging a common bond and a common enemy.[2]

Though this slaughter by the Colapissa was averted, other conflicts that arose as European powers jockeyed for supremacy in North America did not end so well. For decades Carolinians had fretted over the Spanish directly to their south, but now vague unease changed to outright alarm with growing numbers of Catholic French in the Lower Mississippi Valley and the attendant possibility that Catholic nations would jointly invade English colonies. Launching preemptive strikes in 1702 and 1704, respectively, the English attacked St. Augustine and then pillaged, with their Creek allies, Mission San Luis along the modern Florida panhandle.[3] Later that same year the British and their Indian allies harassed the new French settlement at Mobile. Whether it resulted from their own provocations or not, English fears were realized in 1706 when a combined French, Spanish, and Native American force laid siege to Charleston in a concerted effort to destroy the city. Worse even than a combined army of Papists was that, through small rivers winding back from the Gulf, the French now had political and economic access to tribes living inland. In short, what had been a disturbing situation for the English quickly morphed into one they found as terrifying as it was unacceptable.

Lower Mississippi Valley nations were particular targets not only because of their convenient location but also because they often stood as traditional enemies of Native slavers. Conflict only exacerbated with the rise of the highly profitable Carolina deerskin trade. The Creek and Chickasaw were major English allies and trading partners, and, with the demand for deerskins and subsequent wildlife depletion, huntsmen from these tribes moved west and removed occupants of the land, thus reaping the double benefit of capturing not only slaves but also new hunting grounds. In 1705 chiefs of the English-allied Coweta, Alabama, Kashita, and Okmulgee signed an agreement with the Carolinians to either exterminate or capture as slaves all French-allied tribes; later that year, three thousand hostiles staged a surprise attack on Choctaw villages. By September 1709 tribal warfare prompted Bienville to lament, "The English of Carolina are sparing nothing to induce their Indians to destroy those who are allies of the French." Even worse, information from spies indicated that attacks from the east would only escalate in the next several months.[4] The pressure placed upon tribes along the fringes of Creek and Chickasaw lands to move or be enslaved ensured that they, in turn, put pressure on other nations whose territories they invaded.[5]

Like many other tribes, the Tunica nation to the northeast of the Houma slowly began to crumble under attack from the larger and English-allied Chickasaw. The Tunica in 1700 centered along the Yazoo River in modern northwestern Mississippi, and from the time of French contact they had formed an early alliance, trading with the French and allowing Jesuit Father Davion to settle with them. Their political alliances and geographic position thus made them particular targets of the Chickasaw and other English-allied tribes.

The main reasons the Tunica emigrated southwest in 1706 were disease and warfare. Obviously, they could not move east or north, as those directions were controlled by enemies and they would have had to join a tribe that welcomed an influx of settlers. The southern-dwelling Houma lived far enough away from the Creek and Chickasaw to offer safety and were not nervous about refugees settling amid them. On the contrary, the Houma had recently suffered a 50 percent mortality rate from a 1700 epidemic that raged in the tribe for five months.[6] Incorporation of smaller bands to increase group strength was a time-honored tradition for the Houma, especially in the wake of a deadly epidemic.

French accounts differ on what happened in the months immediately after Tunica relocation. Both the modern Houma nation and the Tunica–Biloxi nation diplomatically avoid the topic today, but a contemporary French observer stated that the two nations engaged in formal negotiation and merger, after which the Tunica rose up and slaughtered half their hosts. After this massacre, Houma survivors fled to modern Bayou St. John. Whatever their motivations, by 1710 the nation had indeed relocated to the bayou, just inside modern-day New Orleans.[7]

Bayou St. John was a very attractive locale given that it was an important waterway and its banks provided high ground.[8] When looking at a topographic map of the Lower Mississippi Valley, one immediately sees the Mississippi, termed "Malbanchya" by the Houma, one of the world's most important waterways. Ironically, however, the numerous bayous and lakes around modern New Orleans were more important to the Houma and other settlers than the river itself. The nation could move quickly down the river, up Bayou Manchac, through Lake Pontchartrain, and up Bayou St. John, a major southward transportation route to their new home. Continuing south, various waterways connected Lake Pontchartrain to the Mississippi Sound. If the Houma canoed upstream from the Gulf, taking the Pontchartrain–St. John route rather than the Mississippi cut seventy-five miles off their trip besides saving the frustration of rowing upstream against a dangerous current.[9]

Unfortunately for the Houma, incoming French settlers found the area attractive as well. French competition for fertile land along Bayou St. John was not as sudden as the Houma rout at Tunica hands but, over time, just as inexorable. Bad living conditions and uncertain food supplies hindered immigration to Louisiana and caused severe unrest among colonists unable to leave, with the lack of wheat bread causing the largest number of complaints. Increasingly alarmed by what food shortages meant for the colony's future, the Count de Pontchartrain, French Minister of Marine, ordered Commissary General Martin d'Artaguette to rectify the situation. Looking about for likely candidates, d'Artaguette persuaded eight Mobile settlers to relocate away from the coast and grow wheat to supply the colony, in return for which he would arrange generous land grants. Moving west to settle high ground along transport routes, the Mobile party relocated to Bayou St. John. Though nearby Houma were fortunate with their cereal crops, similar good fortune evaded the colonists for several years. Wheat grew beautifully in the heat and rain but then withered and burned only a few weeks before harvest. Only a handful of habitants stayed more than a few years, but those who did switched to corn and then flourished as agriculturalists.[10]

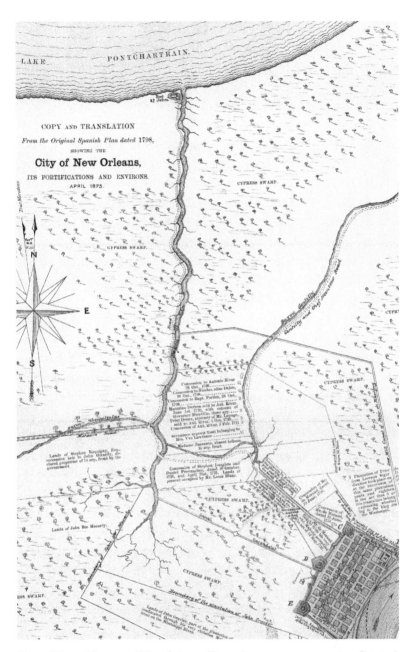

Map 2. Plan of the city of New Orleans, December 24, 1798, 1875 reprint. Original by Carlos Trudeau. Houma villages and the LaVigne land grants were just below the center of this image on the lines running back from Bayou St. John. The Historic New Orleans Collection, gift of Body Cruise and Harold Schilke, 1953.42.

French success came at the price of tribal dispossession, and the Houma quickly found themselves losing land through a series of French grants between 1708 and 1721. On October 28, 1708, the French government made a concession of 2 ½ arpents along Bayou St. John to Antoine Rivard de LaVigne, a concession of 2 ½ arpents to one "Nicolas," a concession of three arpents to Baptist Portier, and four arpents to Louis Juchereau de Saint-Denis; three other grants were made the same day to various colonists. As French arpents stretched roughly 180 feet across, and all the Bayou St. John concessions stretched backward forty arpents, the grants actually encompassed large amounts of Houma land. Ambitious and energetic, the LaVignes leveraged corn profits to buy three more arpents on June 1, 1720, and three more on October 4, 1720; they received yet another concession of three arpents on February 5, 1721. By November 24, the household had swelled to include six children, eleven African slaves, and two Indian slaves.[11]

Aside from settlers of comfortable means taking Houma land, other French colonists moved into the area and introduced disease and alcohol. Nations closest to the French were repeatedly struck with illnesses that reduced their numbers, and those epidemics only increased after the streets of New Orleans were laid out in 1721 and the city grew. That same year Bayou St. John had sixteen European family members, thirty-two African slaves, and eight Indian slaves; aside from permanent residents, its location along the trade route and the area's agricultural importance ensured heavy traffic from visitors.[12] The resulting epidemics were a very real concern, as was increased access to alcoholic spirits by young men of the tribe. Last, there was also the issue of erratic behavior on the part of French officials and colonists, some of whom created a toxic environment. Close proximity to the French thus made the Houma vulnerable.

Despite the area's attractions, the nation began moving back upriver and by 1718 had made at least semipermanent settlements about sixty miles upstream from St. John, along a large bend toward the Mississippi's east bank.[13] Modern Ascension Parish encompasses this bend and stretches across both sides of the river.[14] This second migration stemmed not only from the push factors in Bayou St. John but also the pull of the upriver location. Both French competition for land, especially cleared land at Indian villages, and the destructive influences of Gallic culture were decisive in pushing the Houma to their next location.

While the factors pushing them from the St. John area were complex, those pulling the nation to Ascension were fairly simple: transportation routes, natural bounty, and lack of competition for land and resources. Their new homeland sat in the Mississippi Alluvial Plain, formed by the river's floodwaters over centuries; the river rose gradually each spring and then receded to leave a rich layer of silt. Moreover, the area's position in the Mississippi Flyway and the region's abundant rivers, lakes, and bayous ensured excellent food supply from the air and water. In their new location the Houma created several communities of varying sizes. A "Grand Village" sat on a large bend of the river's eastern bank—modern day Houmas House Plantation—while another sat on the west bank's modern "Houmas Point," but other settlements ranged upstream and downstream, and hunters established seasonal camps along Bayou Manchac and other local waterways.[15]

In Ascension the Houma continued their tradition of living at a transportation crossroads. A bayou stretched directly back from the Grand Village and connected with a network of waterways on the river's east bank that wound through the swamps and to Lake Pontchartrain. On the west bank, the Rivière des Chetimachas, or Bayou Lafourche as it later came to be known, intersected with the Mississippi just upstream from the Houma settlements and offered entrance to a complex network of waterways stretching southwest and southeast through the interior and toward the Gulf. Thus, the tribe now lived along the major waterway of North America, at the termination of a complex series of waterways on the east bank and just across the river from the opening to a complex series of waterways on the west bank.

In their new locale the Houma grew more wedded to the French politically and economically. Just as they forged their first alliance by proxy in February 1699 and then in person in March, so too did they sing the calumet with the French governor and other tribes at Isle Dauphine in 1717.[16] Similarly, the two groups grew more wedded economically, especially in foodstuffs. In 1701 the colonial governor asked Father de Limoges to take fifteen livres worth of beads to barter with the Houma for corn and other produce.[17] The nation maintained a particularly robust trade position because of their strong agricultural history, familiarity with the geography of the Bayou St. John and New Orleans area, excellent relations with colonial leaders, and ideal position on transportation routes. By 1727 they were sufficiently entrenched in the city's economy to warrant one Pierre Ferand serving as their trade agent in New Orleans.[18]

The Houma shipped large amounts of cereal, fish, game, and medicinal herbs to the markets of New Orleans and in return reaped the benefits of trade. To a certain extent, growing tribal immersion in the new economy drew them away from the ceremonial giving that had characterized political relations in the past, but the end result was much the same in that imports could then be redistributed to the tribe. Grave goods dating to Houma occupation unearthed at two Ascension sites in the latter 1800s indicate a rich pattern of commerce: utilitarian objects such as iron pots, clay pipes, metal tomahawks, and several flintlock rifles from the mid-eighteenth century. Also found were items ranging from small metal trinkets to two separate pairs of earrings, one silver and the other high-quality gold. These sites and later archaeological digs produced a range of commercial goods, illustrating a rich level of trade between French colonials and the nation.[19]

Other tribes pondered and were very troubled by the strengthening bonds between the Houma and the French. If there were any doubt where the nation's loyalties sat, that question was laid to rest with the Natchez War of 1729. This was only the last in a series of skirmishes between the Natchez and the French, but it was undoubtedly the most traumatic for colonials. On November 28, 1729, the nation rose up and slaughtered several hundred colonials at Fort Rosalie, burning the fort itself and attacking outlying farms. A handful of French survivors escaped to New Orleans and informed shocked officials that the post had been exterminated. Over the next decade the French army and their allies waged a war of vengeance against the Natchez and later shifted their attacks to the Chickasaw, who had offered them refuge.[20]

Disgusted with the Houma, the Natchez had planned to exterminate them during the war along with European settlers. Ultimately unsuccessful in their plan, the Natchez were at least correct that political and economic bonds between the Houma and the French had grown so strong that the former would not desert the latter. Instead, the nation allied with colonials first in this war and later in expeditions against the Chickasaw. They served as scouts and guides for Europeans, guarding settlement routes and guiding militia patrols. French–Houma alliances were further illustrated in 1739 during the Chickasaw War, when the nation supplied colonial troops moving up the river with dozens of barrels of corn and other vegetables.[21]

The Houma's position as guides and scouts for the French aside, the Natchez War also reflected how the entire political landscape in which the Houma lived had changed. In 1730 Governor Périer allowed some Tunica to slowly burn to death a captured Natchez woman in New Orleans's central square. Rather than begging for mercy, the captive laughed at her tormentors and ridiculed their incompetence as torturers even as flesh cooked on her body. She also insulted the Tunica by calling them cowardly dogs hiding behind the French and warned that they and other tribes loyal to the habitants would be destroyed for siding with colonials. The Tunica did not have to wait long to see if her words were true, as a few days later a Natchez party scalped and killed their chief, killed several other members of the nation, and took prisoners; random attacks by the Natchez would escalate in the coming year.[22] By allying with colonials, the Tunica, the Houma, and other nations in this position had permanently severed bonds with many other tribes, both those allied with the English and many who had formerly allied with the French.

The irony of severing ties with Native groups and forging alliances with the French was that such a course of action did not automatically protect the Houma and other Native tribes even from their colonial "ally," as the Chouacha found out in December 1729 when Governor Périer launched an expedition against them. In the wake of an unsuccessful uprising of African slaves that Périer believed had been aided by local Indians—and of the Natchez Revolt in November that year, in which some slaves had joined forces with the Indians against their masters—he decided to drive a wedge between the groups once and for all. Arming black slaves in New Orleans, he ordered them to massacre a nearby Chouacha village to prove their loyalty to their French masters. The slaves did so admirably and forever sundered any hope of refuge or aid from Natives. Afterward Governor Périer mused that perhaps he should have ordered the slaves to destroy the Houma and all the other *petites nations* around New Orleans, given that they were of no use to the French and might potentially aid runaways.[23]

Though other officials and French colonists criticized this butchery of a tribe that had long maintained excellent relations with colonial habitants, the governor's tactic illustrated an important point: proximity to the French meant economic benefit but also danger and possible slaughter. What the Houma could not have realized was how close they themselves came to extermination. The newly arrived governor firmly believed they were complicit in the 1729 Natchez Revolt and noted, in an April 1730 letter, that the only reason he did not annihilate them was that in Ascension they were removed from his immediate sphere of influence. Had they been closer, he stated, the Houma's fate would have been dire: "We should be obligated to destroy them."[24]

Though Périer might have been delighted by the extermination of the Houma, French officials who were more effective realized the benefits of friendly tribes buffering against invasion and providing information and did everything they could to maximize political liaisons. Not only did the Houma serve as a physical barrier that hostile warriors would have to fight through on their way to New Orleans, but their location along the Mississippi, Bayou Manchac, and Lakes Maurepas and Pontchartrain also ensured they heard most rumors and could send word quickly enough for the French to arm themselves. French industrial goods always stood in short supply for gift exchange, but free gun repair and free—or very cheap—munitions for Native allies offset the lack of some other goods. Moreover, most governors were remarkably consistent in their dealings with the Houma and thus gained tribal respect, a respect that brought Houma warriors during times of conflict.[25]

While Houma residence patterns in widely dispersed villages made them valuable to the French, their far-flung remove made it difficult to determine tribal numbers. In 1699 Bienville estimated that the hilltop village contained 140 huts with perhaps 350 men and many children, while one year later Gravier recorded approximately 80 cabins.[26] In 1718 La Harpe wrote that the Grand Village alone contained 60 cabins and 200 men, whereas in 1726 the entire tribe contained only 50 warriors; in 1758 de Kerlérec estimated that the nation could still summon 60 soldiers.[27]

Obviously, officials ignored women and children and probably missed large numbers of men due to seasonal hunting patterns and the emphasis on recording warriors rather than tribal members overall, even when colonials actually made it to these dispersed villages. The first colonial official to live close to the Houma estimated the nation at 230 people in 1768, though he also noted that he based estimates on only the west bank and thus missed scores of people.[28]

The inaccurate listing of Houma demographics troubled neither the nation nor colonials in the early 1700s. French officials had no need to limit tribal lands and no desire to survey them, which meant they had no reason to define them. Colonials knew where to find the Houma, the Houma knew where to find colonials, and if either had to spend a day or so locating the other, such was life in the 1700s. To force a tribe that served as their eyes and ears to stay in a prescribed area would not have served French interests. On the contrary, it would have harmed both military and economic colonial interests, as the far-ranging Houma gathered plants and game during their seasonal migrations and then supplied these to New Orleans markets. Thus, the French did not draw up maps clearly defining Houma land and seem to not have been particularly worried about census figures, provided the nation could supply warriors in times of conflict.

Aside from their value to the French based on their location and military strength, the Houma were also valuable allies because their numbers were increasing rapidly. Bands of both Colapissa and Bayougoula settled in Houma villages. Both groups had valid reasons for seeking refuge with the larger nation. The 1699 raid on the Colapissa by Chickasaw and English slavers was not an isolated event, and the tribe endured subsequent attacks. The loss of tribal population to slavers was exacerbated by epidemics sweeping the area after 1699, further decimating the population. In the next several decades the Colapissa and Bayougoula were among the tribes hit hardest by English slavers, disease, and French brandy, resulting in further societal breakdown and severe cultural upheaval. The Bayougoula and Mougoulacha also suffered the impact of virulent epidemics and maintained tribal numbers only by desperately absorbing Quinipissa survivors of another plague, a futile effort in the face of further outbreaks and a rise in alcohol consumption.[29]

The Bayougoula and Colapissa thus faced the same choice that confronted many Lower Mississippi Valley nations: flee to a larger tribe for help or go extinct. Even though the Houma were also falling victim to some of the biological and societal issues affecting other nations in the area, they remained a strong people and had several traits in their favor. First, they had strong political ties to the French and good political relations with the nearby Alabamans and Choctaws.[30] Their location along the Mississippi was ideal as far as economics and transportation considerations went. Most important, the Houma put aside traditional animosities and extended the cloak of protection to former enemies. Indeed, a mutual thirst for survival united remnant bands of other tribes with the Houma and turned former enemies into tribal members, a trend that continued into the 1770s as some Houma women took Chickasaw husbands.[31]

Though the location and politics of the Houma changed dramatically after 1699, their religion proved an enduring cultural element. Its survival owed much to the tribe's position above New Orleans. Many priests were extremely reluctant to venture into the area, and the Capuchin Order that ministered to Houma territory was always desperate for men, in any case; there were only twelve Capuchins between the Yazoo River and the Gulf around 1728, with only two of them above New Orleans.[32] The corrupt Father Stanislaus's ecclesiastical parish theoretically encompassed Houma tribal lands, but his preference for business rather than religious affairs drew a strong reprimand from the governor in 1770, and local officials were cautioned to keep a tight rein as Stanislaus constantly strove to enrich his own pockets by forging bonds with wealthier colonists.[33]

While the Houma greeted the occasional visiting priest, traditional Catholic presence in Ascension truly dates only to 1772. On May 2 of that year a priest performed the first recorded baptism, and on August 15, 1772, Capuchin Father Angelus de Reuillagodos (Revillagodos) formally instituted worship when he established the church La Iglesia de la Ascensión de Nuestro Señor Jesús Christo de La Fourche de Los Tchitimacha. Despite a nominal Catholic presence, no recorded priest ministered to the Houma tribe and, in any event, only a few years separated the Church's arrival in the area from the nation's departure.[34] Thus, the Christian impact on the Houma while in Ascension was nil.

Between 1699 and 1762 Houma influence on French politics and culture increased dramatically. Quite simply, the fledgling colony could not have survived without the petites nations, whatever the misguided Governor Périer thought. As one of the most prominent small nations, the Houma provided soldiers for the French colonial army in a series of conflicts and supplied New Orleans with food both in peace and during war. In this sense, Bienville and Iberville had been very wise to forge an alliance with the nation. These ties were absolutely vital in the survival of the young colony. For their part, the Houma had become strongly wedded to the colonials—far too strongly wedded from the perspective of the Natchez and other tribes.

The Lower Mississippi Valley had changed dramatically for Native peoples since French arrival. The Chouacha had been extinguished as a group, the Chitimacha defeated and largely enslaved. The Natchez, formerly one of the most powerful nations in the Lower Mississippi Valley, had been defeated, hunted down, and their Great Sun sold into slavery in the Caribbean. Other tribes had suffered collapse via plague, alcohol, or enslavement by the English and their allies. The Houma had survived mainly because they could move quickly, first to Bayou St. John and then back upstream. Their capacity to adapt rapidly and well to a changing world provided a valuable geographic buffer from the French, while their familiarity with New Orleans and ability to supply the city's needs allowed them to pick the best of what the French economy offered.

In 1699 the Houma seized an opportunity to expand their power and influence. In the following years they cut ties with some tribes and made alliances with others, simultaneously maintaining and strengthening their political, military, and economic bonds with the French. In retrospect, the mid-1700s was the high point of Houma influence on the colony. Their role in the Lower Mississippi Valley had expanded in the first half of the century, but it would contract dramatically in the second as a new European power claimed their homeland and new neighbors arrived.

3

In the Shelter of a Duck's Nesting Place

Shifting Power and Politics along the Mississippi

From their villages on the banks of the Mississippi, the Houma watched a rapidly changing Lower Mississippi Valley. Over previous decades the region's balance of power had shifted dramatically with the destruction of several nations and the growth of French influence. The Houma again saw their world shift after the French and Indian War, which marked French departure and the division of their lands between Spain and England. The geopolitical realignment of the Lower Mississippi Valley after 1763 opened diplomatic and trade opportunities for the nation to play one power against the other. Conversely, it also opened the door to arriving settlers who usurped traditional Houma roles. Conflict between Acadian refugees and Houmas developed after the new arrivals were expelled from Canada and sought refuge to the south. Moreover, newly arrived Spanish officials decided the nation was no longer as valuable to European interests given the flood of settlers. Last, a combined force of plantation owners and colonial officials campaigned for Houma removal in the closing years of the 1700s.

Given their location along the Malbanchya and around New Orleans, the Houma invariably heard the latest political rumors earlier than many other nations and colonials. News of Gallic defeat in the French and Indian War and the consequent February 1763 treaty quickly made its way to their villages. In June 1763 a Houma delegation traveled to New Orleans to parley with Monsieur d'Abbadie, director general of the colony and acting governor. Disturbing reports indicated that French habitants would abandon lands along the Malbanchya and invite the English and Spanish into tribal homelands, which was especially unsettling given the English's history of murdering and enslaving Natives along the Gulf.[1]

D'Abbadie stood in a very unpleasant position: the French and Houma had enjoyed excellent relations for decades, but the director general could hardly answer their questions given the colony's state of flux. Governor Kerlérec had been recalled to France in the wake of a political scandal, and in February 1763 d'Abbadie had received explicit instructions from King Louis XV to keep all the tribes happy and make the transition between powers as smooth as possible. The French king's cousin sat on the Spanish throne, and in the recent treaty that kinsman and the English ruler had divided territory along the Gulf into East and West Florida. England had gained all territory east of the Mississippi with the exception of the "Isle of Orleans," claimed by Spain along with all territory west of the river.

As the Houma would have known from years of trading with the French, this "Isle" actually stretched quite a bit farther than New Orleans proper; the dividing line between West Florida to the north and the Spanish-held Isle of Orleans to the south would be Bayou Manchac, which flowed from near modern-day Baton Rouge on the river's east bank. Straddling the Mississippi as their villages did, Houma territory would thus fall into the westernmost section of English holdings and the easternmost section of Spanish territory, with New Orleans being the new Spanish center and several other trading posts falling under English control.[2]

In March 1764 another party met with the director and recounted how the English had sailed past their watchmen while traveling up the Mississippi. D'Abbadie thanked the Houma, explained that those were English on their way to take possession of their new lands, and stressed his pleasure that the Houma had honored new comrades acquired through parley. Gallic presence in the Lower Mississippi Valley was drawing to a close, and it was imperative for all parties to know what waited in coming days. Couching his words in political imagery the Houma regularly used, d'Abbadie reassured his visitors that the two emperors followed the white path. Above all, the Houma must remember that they were now joined to the English and pledge to be as good comrades to that nation as they had been to d'Abbadie.[3]

Though France left the Lower Mississippi Valley as an empire, its colonists remained, as did many of its former administrators. Spanish officials recognized these men for the skilled liaisons they were and requested that they retain their positions, albeit under a different king.[4] For their part, former French officials now in Spanish pay were terrified that heavy-handed Iberian policies would rend fragile alliances with the Houma and other surrounding tribes. Colonial circumstances had grown much more dangerous than in previous decades because of heightened English presence, and where Anglos and Latins had once glared at each other through a buffer zone, they now literally stood on either side of Bayou Manchac. If Luisiana Spaniards behaved in an authoritarian manner, they would drive former French allies such as the Houma into English arms, with a combined force exterminating the colony. The colonials keenly grasped that they teetered on a precipice's edge: "It is certain that if the Spaniards try to act the same way in Louisiana [as in other territories], all will be lost."[5]

Fortunately for all residents of the Gulf Coast, the arriving Spaniards proceeded with caution. In 1767 Governor Antonio de Ulloa instructed the first official Spanish expedition up the Mississippi to carefully note all tribes, take special care in recording the names and kin of primary and secondary leaders, and distribute medals to caciques in the name of the king.[6] A September 1768 census showed forty Houma men, forty women, sixty boys, and ninety girls, though the recorder noted that these were approximations and only included the Houma on the right bank of the Mississippi.[7] Though Governor Ulloa did not benefit from this knowledge since he was driven from power by revolting colonists shortly after, his successor, Don O'Reilly, studied these figures closely after retaking New Orleans the following year and estimated how many warriors he could muster if the English were to invade. Then he just as carefully planned how to make the strongest impression when first meeting potential warriors and decided to combine pageantry with strength.

Don Alejandro (Alexander) O'Reilly served the Spanish Crown as its military leader in New Orleans, and his background made him an ideal candidate for the position. One of the "wild geese" who fled Ireland and rose to high positions in other Catholic countries, he had served Spain in many capacities and successfully navigated several multicultural societies. Completely loyal to Spain and highly intelligent, O'Reilly was a polished, sophisticated leader with a pronounced ruthless streak. He adapted as quickly and well as the Houma and was a man one absolutely did not want to cross. In many ways he was remarkably similar to Iberville, the first European to forge close ties with the nation.

In October 1769 O'Reilly hosted the Houma cacique and chiefs of eight other tribes living within two hundred miles of New Orleans. Tribal delegations assembled at O'Reilly's home just before noon, and interpreters formally presented the Houma leader and his brethren to a collection of officers and important townspeople. As Europeans watched from under a canopy, the Natives placed their weapons at the Spaniard's feet as a sign of goodwill, then each chief saluted O'Reilly with a small feathered fan. Touching himself four times with his fan, the Houma leader gave it to O'Reilly and then steadied the calumet while the don smoked. Proper greetings observed, the Houma cacique extended his hand in friendship.[8]

The Bayougoula leader gave a formal speech on behalf of the delegation and, through his interpreter, reminded Spaniards of the strong bonds previously enjoyed with the French and that all the assembled nations wished for those bonds to continue with the Spanish. On cue, assembled Natives raised voices and pressed hands against their chests in assent. O'Reilly assured tribal heads that their continued loyalty was all he wanted but that he would accept nothing less. Strong bonds of blood and kin tied France's cacique with that of Spain, or else this transfer of a beloved land would never have taken place. The king of Spain stood in the tradition of the greatest warriors, whose strength and bravery were matched only by their wealth and loyalty to friends. He only asked that the Houma and other tribes not harm the English; though not related by kinship ties as the French and Spanish, the English were friends. O'Reilly then placed medals on scarlet silk ribbons around the necks of the Houmas, had them kiss the royal effigy on the medals, and used his sword to touch them on their shoulders and chests and make the sign of the cross over their heads.[9]

Following this bestowal of medals and a formal presentation of trade goods, a mass of Spanish soldiers assembled and paraded in full dress, entertaining delegates but also showing that the Spaniards made overtures from a position of strength rather than weakness. When delegates left the next day, the Houma cacique and his fellow chiefs departed with signs of great satisfaction, and even former French officials admitted that the tribes seemed extremely pleased with how the Spanish had treated them.[10]

This meeting formally instituted Spanish Indian policy in Louisiana and, in some respects, illustrated a reversal of the power dynamics of 1699. Upon meeting Iberville the Ouga showed via formal parleys and ceremonial giving that he understood diplomacy and was generous, just as the nighttime war dances proved that Bienville and Iberville were not to trifle with him. O'Reilly showed his generosity, pageantry, and military strength, but with the Spanish in a position of power. Landing with two thousand troops, he had easily retaken the city after Ulloa's expulsion and would put the rebellion's leaders to death two weeks after the tribal gathering. Courteous and polished as Don O'Reilly was, neither the nation nor the residents of New Orleans could ignore that his velvet glove covered an iron fist.

Unyielding as the Spaniard could be, he and other Iberian officials were no fools, and local fears that heavy-handed policies would drive tribes into English arms proved groundless. Defending against possible English invasion was paramount in the Lower Mississippi Valley, and warriors certainly counted for more than converts or slaves. The French had valued the Houma primarily as a buffer against invaders and starvation; Spanish administrators followed this same philosophy. In legal matters, the Spanish *Recopilación de las leyes de los reynos de las Indias* (often called the *Laws of the Indies*) was the official code, but O'Reilly had the *Recopilación* translated into French and, in time, conjoined it with former French edicts and customs into a hybrid legal system. In many instances, the new governors simply adopted French policies and couched them in Spanish terms.[11]

The *Laws of the Indies* recognized Native right to only one league of land, but colonial officials observed this matter solely in name. Houma settlements nestled along the Mississippi well below the Manchac boundary line, but their hunting grounds along Lakes Maurepas and Pontchartrain stood well within English territory. Like the French, neither the Spanish nor the English cared where the Houma roamed so long as they remained friendly and could quickly supply soldiers. As in the past, it was to their advantage to maintain a laissez-faire attitude that rewarded colonials with a constant supply of Houma game and crops as well as a ready supply of warriors.[12]

Advantages derived from maintaining good relations with the Houma would have evaporated if the Spanish had not been so fortunate in their list of provincial appointees. Now technically Iberians, these former Frenchmen maintained bonds with Natives and used those alliances in the service of their colony. Commandant Louis (Luis) Judice, a remarkably patient and efficient man completely at ease in different cultures, was a particular prize for the new Spanish rulers. Appointed administrator for the Lafourche des Chetimaches district, he was well acquainted with the Houma even before being made commandant.[13] Moreover, his familiarity with and respect for Native customs differentiated him from many officials and earned the respect of local petites nations.[14]

Judice served from 1770 to 1798 as Lafourche's first Spanish commandant, his area encompassing modern Ascension and several other parishes. His position required fluency in both Spanish and French, the former for official minutes and the latter for judicial and notarial documents. Judice combined a high degree of education and a remarkable sense of the region's place in history, to which the thousands of documents he created during his almost thirty years as Spanish commandant of Lafourche attest. Above all, his epistles show that the Houma were no fools and recognized their place on the chessboard of history.[15]

Both the Spanish and English wanted as strong an alliance with the Houma as that which the French had enjoyed, but the Houma would gain more if they stayed friendly with both sides. This was especially important since their settlements and hunting grounds were supposedly under the control of two different empires; British agent John Thomas noted that the "Spanish Indians Humas" ranged along both sides of the Mississippi but also eastward to the Amite and Iberville Rivers—a huge area.[16] Until they were driven out of the area during the Revolutionary War, English colonists enjoyed good relations with the Houma. Similarly, the Spanish and the Houma enjoyed good relations until the Louisiana Purchase. Forming alliances with one power and then the other was a consistent political tactic during the Houma's time in Ascension.

Nowhere was Houma skill in juggling European powers better illustrated than in 1765, when the English began wooing the nation to move to Bayou Manchac's northern bank. Illinois Natives had threatened the English and sent emissaries to the Houma and other local tribes, so English officials wanted not only to form long-term alliances but also to avoid immediate conflict. The British used diplomacy and high-quality manufactured goods to create bonds with the nation but, ignoring official policy as easily as the French and Spanish, they also used spirits. Natives knew that trappers and officials kept a ready supply of liquor for trade and personal use and generally drank when small groups parleyed. Social drinking occasionally smoothed political tensions but sometimes exacerbated them, as the British shortly found out.[17]

On August 27, 1765, Lieutenant Colonel James Robertson met with approximately fifty Indians at Fort Bute, on the intersection of the Mississippi and Bayou Manchac; the majority of the group was Alabama and Houma, but one Tunica, one Chickasaw, and one Okchina rounded out the party. Around noon they gathered in Robertson's quarters and smoked the calumet, but then things quickly took a turn for the worse. After talking the lieutenant colonel into sharing alcohol, the Indians became surly and aggressive. Within an hour they had cracked open the storeroom, growing increasingly drunker, and the situation escalated when they broke into the powder magazine. Fortunately for Robertson, he and the leader of the Houma party knew each other from previous hunting expeditions. Revealing that the Alabamas had suggested killing everyone in the fort, the latter counseled that the colonials must move to a secure location immediately. The Englishman quickly barricaded all soldiers, many of them ill, into his small room, with no path of retreat open and no canoe big enough to take them all.[18]

For two days soldiers listened to explosions outside their building and sweltered in the August heat and humidity, sweat turning their clothes dark and stinking. On the second night the Houma leader who had initially warned the Englishman knocked on the door and asked for admittance. The Native promised that the Houma men would not harm the colonists and pledged that they would not let the Alabamas harm them either. The next day the Indians left the fort in twelve canoes so heavily laden they barely stayed afloat, and the English stumbled out to a scene of total destruction. Indians had destroyed or stolen all the guns and every item in the storehouse as well as killed every animal in the fort. Three of the party had been killed by others in a drunken rage.[19]

The English hailed a passing French bateau and made it down to New Orleans, where Robertson put his dehydrated men in a hospital. On his way to the city, Robertson's Houma defender had hailed French officials, and the latter had sent an officer and eight soldiers to aid the English; Robertson and the French soldiers had sailed past each other in the night. The lieutenant colonel was grateful not only to the French for their aid and comfort in the days after the attack but also to the Houma, noting in a letter, "I really believe [they] were the Occasion of our not being killed."[20]

For their part, the British were neither upset with the Houma nor unduly angry with the Alabama. No one was harmed, and aggression was attributed to the mind-altering effects of alcohol rather than political liaisons, the latter being a far more serious matter. While the British were humiliated by their inability to defend Fort Bute and embarrassed by the French sending troops to protect them, the important thing was that the Houma had kept English soldiers alive and thus cemented political bonds. Certainly, both the Houma and the English thought so, as they happily parleyed on Manchac a few months later in December 1765.

The incident at Fort Bute occurred four years before the Houma forged an alliance with Don O'Reilly. In 1771 forty-six warriors presented British Indian Agent John Thomas with an eagle tail, symbolizing brotherhood with that nation.[21] These were only three in a series of meetings in which the Houma pledged an alliance with first one power and then another. That everyone felt comfortable with the constantly changing alliances stemmed in part from the area around Bayou Manchac being an illicit trade zone between the English, Spanish, and Indians; guns, liquor, and other items were frequently smuggled and exchanged despite the best efforts of some European administrators. Provided that everyone got along well, that no one raised a fuss that alerted superior administrators about illicit activities, and that colonists could draw upon advantages provided by the Houma in time of crisis, everyone politely ignored what others might view as political treachery.

The rapprochement that existed between the Houma nation and colonial officials would thin over coming years and snap completely toward century's end. With first the Bayougoula and then the Tunica, and then with settlers along Bayou St. John, competition for land and attendant control of transportation routes were issues for the Houma in the early 1700s. In Ascension that competition would take a different form, as increasing numbers of Acadians and Canary Islanders moved into the area.

War casts a long shadow, and Houma conflicts with Acadian settlers along the Mississippi stemmed from events thousands of miles to the northeast. After New France's transfer to England in the early 1700s, tensions ran high in the easternmost Acadian section. Simmering anger on the part of both former French colonists and British officials exploded after several generations. Maritime residents rose up and tried to expel the English but were instead defeated and deported from Canada between 1755 and 1763. The British scattered the survivors among American colonies, France, the French Caribbean, and numerous Spanish colonies. Many exiles eventually found their way to Luisiana.

Iberian officials welcomed Acadian exiles because they shared the Catholic faith, harbored no perceived interest in politics other than a common hatred of the British, and had farming skills. Moreover, just as the Houma served as a buffer against the English to the north of New Orleans, so would these new arrivals. In short, they were ideal colonists, and Canadian exiles arrived in waves after April 1764. They settled in Houma territory about sixty miles above New Orleans in a region termed "Cahabanooze," or "the ducks' resting place." Over the next three decades these arrivals in modern-day St. James Parish and Ascension Parish would give the riverfront yet another designation: the First and Second Acadian Coasts.[22]

Though the Acadians regrouped and rebuilt under Spanish protection, they still had much reason to worry about their future. In less than a decade they had been driven from maritime settlements, endured an appallingly high death rate with attendant physical and psychological trauma, and begun building new lives in a colony far from their old homes. Conflict with other settlers reminded them that their position in the region was uncertain, and the new arrivals especially dreaded war with nearby tribes.

These Acadian fears were certainly understandable given that there was an upswing in tribal conflict shortly after they arrived. In 1770 the Houma had relocated about two miles down Bayou Lafourche from its conjunction with the Mississippi to escape a raid by the Talapousa, a Creek subgroup migrating from Alabama. What the arriving Talapousa warriors did not know was that this settlement was so important precisely because it was *not* the main village. The Talapousa attacked only to find they had been decoyed into a faux hamlet and were in turn attacked by an alliance of Houma, Taensas, Chitimacha, Tunica, Hoctchianya, and Pacana. The Houma later kept some warriors at the Lafourche settlement but stationed the majority of their population at traditional river villages in case of further conflict. Increasingly concerned about incursions by migrating Alabama warriors, the nation erected a palisaded fort about sixty steps around in 1772, to which they could retreat in case of attack.[23]

Nearby Chitimacha Indians were also concerned about Alabama Indians migrating through the area in 1772 and fortified their village to prevent violence. Unfortunately, local settlers interpreted Chitimacha and Houma attempts to avoid assault as a step toward attacking nearby European settlements. A wave of hysteria concerning Indian raids swept locals of all ethnicities; nine Acadian families fled the area, and over two hundred threatened to charter a vessel and leave the colony altogether. The irony of interpreting Houma and Chitimacha fortifications as aggression is that these nations were themselves made extremely uncomfortable by other tribes migrating through the area and were ensuring peace through displays of strength.[24]

Tensions calmed somewhat over the next couple of years, but a series of small conflicts in 1775 convinced many local colonials that they would be in danger as long as Indians remained in the area. In early 1775 the Houma clashed with the Chitimacha and killed their chief. In February of that year a group of Chitimacha robbed several Houma while they were hunting, killing no one but taking their possessions. Even the normally cool Judice wrote nervously that he hoped this was not a prelude to escalating bloodshed. As it turned out, these incidents amounted to nothing, but later that same year the Houma attacked a group of Pascagoula as the latter ascended the river. This again raised fears that the area was about to see full-out war.[25]

The incident started simply enough. Both nations had been in New Orleans when several Pascagoula "wished to enjoy some Houma women," and the females quickly and ably defended themselves. Afterward the offenders threatened the Houma women and the rest of their group, only to be mocked. The women conferred with their men when paddling home and, as the Pascagoula moved upriver, the Houma leader Calabée hailed them from shore and called that perhaps they should stop and attend to unfinished business. The other group thought quickening their pace a wiser choice and rowed faster, only to have a volley of bullets from shore fall upon them. No one was seriously hurt, though the Pascagoula later complained of the incident to Commandant Acosta at Manchac and maintained their party had been maliciously attacked without provocation. Acosta wrote to Judice, who then asked the Houma leader what had happened. Upon hearing the full story, the Lafourche commandant told Calabée that he would have acted the same way and that both the Houma women and men had acquitted themselves well and maintained their honor. Given that they had taught the would-be attackers their lesson and that the whole incident made Acosta nervous, Judice would appreciate it if they let the matter drop. No more troubles resulted.[26]

The incident with the Pascagoula was only a minor altercation, but it fueled fears among local settlers that Houmas were prone to violence and that Europeans were in danger as long as Natives continued to live in the area; even if colonists were not directly attacked, they reasoned, they might very well serve as collateral damage. Ironically, the Houma were themselves the victims of many of these raids. Nevertheless, the threat of violence created such a tense atmosphere that when actual physical conflict exploded in the 1780s between the Houma and colonists, habitants viewed it as symptomatic of Indian character rather than aberrations from an otherwise peaceful nation.

The Acadians were, of course, only one of the groups that settled along the Mississippi River, but they were closest to the Houma and thus saw the most conflict. Even if the two groups had never clashed, however, the increasing number of refugees would have diminished Houma importance in the eyes of the Spanish simply because Acadian arrivals were excellent farmers and soldiers. For decades the Houma nation had benefitted from its geographic position above New Orleans and ability to satisfy the city's needs. Their position slipped slightly in the 1720s, as German farmers settled along the river and established themselves. Successful as the farmers were, there simply were too few of them to be a major threat to the Houma. That began to change in the 1750s with growing numbers of Acadian arrivals, and the scales of power tipped even further with Canary Islanders (Isleños) settling near the Houma in May 1779.

The Spanish placement of Isleños just down Bayou Lafourche from its junction with the Mississippi was no accident, and the move reveals much about the area's importance. On August 15, 1777, the Crown ordered the governor of the Canary Islands to recruit as many soldiers as possible for transport to the new colony. The first Islanders arrived in November 1778, and by the end of the following year had established four settlements that, together with the swamps and waterways that made invasion of the city so difficult, created a protective ring around New Orleans. Almost two thousand Canary Islanders relocated to these four settlements, a little over half of them wives and children of soldiers.[27]

The census record of two thousand settlers alone gives an inaccurate view of the situation. Canary Islanders moved into the Lafourche region slowly but steadily, and each passing month tipped the balance of power away from the Houma. Christmas Eve of 1779 saw six weddings and two infant baptisms; a few weeks later two more weddings occurred, and eighty additional Spaniards settled in the community. Even more important than the actual number of settler soldiers was that they quickly proved themselves reliable warriors, to the satisfaction of Iberian officials. With the nearby Acadians, who had also proved their mettle in combat, Spanish reliance on the Houma as a buffer against invaders shifted year by year toward the colonials.[28] This reliance grew even more pronounced after the fall of English forts after 1779.

The French and Indian War had influenced the colony in a profound but circuitous way. In contrast, the American Revolution affected colonials and Natives of the Lower Mississippi Valley directly. On June 21, 1779, Spain declared war on Britain, putting the Iberian section of the Lower Mississippi Valley at odds with the English territory next to it.[29] On August 27 a party led by Don Bernardo de Gálvez left New Orleans and ascended the river with 660 men.[30] During the journey they picked up 600 colonials and 160 Indians from along the river and from interior settlements, one location being the Acadian Coast.[31] The Houma and other Indians served as scouts moving ahead of the Spanish expedition, and they informed Gálvez when the party came close to Fort Bute. The post surrendered on September 7, and on September 21 Lieutenant Colonel Alexander Dickson surrendered both his fort at Baton Rouge and Fort Panmure at Natchez, giving the Spaniards complete control over the Mississippi River.[32] In March 1780 Gálvez took Mobile, and in March 1781 he took Pensacola, the English capital of West Florida. The Spanish thus wrested both the river and the Gulf Coast from English control.[33]

The Houma and other Native peoples had fought bravely in battles along the Mississippi, and in the short term their actions reinforced their standing with Spanish officials. In the long term, however, helping drive the British out of the Lower Mississippi Valley checkmated the Houma on the chessboard of empire. The English and Spanish courted them only as long as one could play the nation against the other or as long as illicit trade created profits. After the American Revolution and the subsequent loss of English power, Spain reigned triumphant in the Lower Mississippi Valley. Moreover, the population of colonials had increased to the point that of the 1,430 who moved toward Fort Bute and Baton Rouge, only 160 were Indians.[34] By the 1780s Acadians and Canary Islanders had come to serve as reliable soldiers and returned home to lush farms on some of the world's most fertile soil; the nation thus lost their status as not only warriors but also suppliers of foodstuffs for New Orleans. For almost a century the Houma had maintained their important position in the colony. Now, while still friendly to the nation, Iberia held the political upper hand. This was a new world for the Houma, and not a favorable one.

The political structure of the Lower Mississippi Valley had changed radically in just a few decades. From being a dominant player in the region's economy and politics, the Houma nation began to slowly move to the sidelines. Moreover, they were surrounded by new settlers who viewed them with distrust. In the 1770s and 1780s true conflict erupted between the nation and nearby Acadians, and behavior that might have been tolerated a few decades ago—alcohol-fueled violence and conflict over property—now served only as justification for Houma removal.

Around 1729 a group of French settlers moved into the area and began selling alcohol to the tribe. A few people immediately began to feel its ill effects but could not control their desire for more. By 1758 alcohol had infiltrated the Houma to the point that the colonial governor noted it in official reports.[35] The merchant Jean Baptiste Chauvin stood as a particularly incorrigible supplier of rum. One of his most profitable customers was the Houma man Pistolet, who drank almost beyond lucidity and then swaggered through both Indian and white settlements looking for trouble. Both the Acadians and Houma complained to tribal elders and Judice about Pistolet and other young men (both Indian and European) who followed his lead, but to no avail.[36]

Adding to tensions caused by increasing alcohol consumption were conflicts over ceremonial giving and property ownership. The nation did not particularly care that local Acadians were refugees. From their perspective the Acadians were settlers on tribal land and thus should engage in the elaborate gift-giving ceremonies characteristic of Houma social structure. Acadians initially had no problem with this, quick as they were to pick up on the intricacies of trade and free with goods in their own community. Their attitude hardened, however, as young Houma men grew increasingly belligerent. Native aggression stemmed only in part from the effects of alcohol, as even abstinent members of the nation saw how their landscape had changed with arriving settlers. Houma hunting areas were being decimated, and traps and trotlines were regularly harvested by settlers before their owners arrived. Each creature must eat according to its needs, and if settlers saw no problem with decimating the wildlife and plant species that had supported longer-established residents, then these residents saw no problem with harvesting pigs and cows that new colonists had introduced.[37]

Even as conflict escalated, many Houma and Acadians sought vainly to maintain calm. Elders struggled to rein in Pistolet and his cronies, who were drunk on brandy and bartering away tribal goods to English soldiers or to Chauvin, and even those who appropriated Acadian belongings as payment for lost property were urged to keep cool heads. For his part, Judice tried to calm angry farmers fuming about Indian youth stealing corn and hogs. When Joseph Landry lost sixty barrels of corn and aggressively demanded that Judice punish the tribe, the Spanish commandant parleyed with elders and warned them that if they could not curtail stealing, local militia would almost certainly attack and destroy the village. Some young Houma men viewed the following silence as weakness and started daylight raiding again with renewed vigor. When colonists tried to stop raiders, a band of warriors shot into homes and heightened already-smoldering social relations. Judice and angry Acadians tried to find the culprits, but three tribal factions blamed one another.[38]

Judice and the tribal elders exercised considerable diplomatic skill to defuse the situation, and relations improved in the fall of 1785 when twelve warriors joined forces with Acadians to put down a slave rebellion. This was no minor uprising but an attempted large-scale revolt that worsened each day. Raids on local farms yielded enough guns for thirty men, and an extensive slave network helped insurgents as they recruited supporters, ransacked homesteads, and fired upon white travelers. Unable to bring the matter to a conclusion despite continuous militia patrols, Judice appealed to the Houma in tracking rebels. The nation knew their landscape extremely well and quickly responded to the commandant's request. That they fought for the hundred-piastre reward offered for each rebel leader was irrelevant to the Acadians, who conceded that Houma warriors had fought better than the militia.[39]

This period of goodwill did not last long. First, hysteria over future slave uprisings swept the area when habitants realized how deeply the insurrection had run. Euro-Luisianans quickly fell into a garrison mindset and mentally divided their community into settlers versus everyone else, ironic given that the Houma had effectively ended the rebellion. Second, in 1788 a smallpox epidemic swept through the region and killed members of all ethnic groups. Acadians blamed plantation owners whose slaves introduced the disease, and the Houma blamed the Acadians. Amid the finger pointing, relations took a downward turn again.

Dealings between the Houma and Acadians started to fester again in 1789, when a small Choctaw band staying with the nation attacked a Lafourche farm belonging to Commandant Judice's son. They threatened to kill the younger man, and this time Judice's paternal motivations trumped his governmental position. Judice gathered a militia group and sped to the farm, where he stationed his men around the property. Calling upon the Choctaw to parley, the commandant approached only to find himself surrounded. Raising his hand as a signal, Judice ordered his band to move in and surround the raiders.[40]

The Choctaw realized their ambush had been trumped by a larger snare and fled, only to be fired upon by the militia; it gives some idea of Judice's presence of mind that he ordered his men not to shoot. They ignored him but hit no one because of poor nighttime visibility, though the party eventually captured the Choctaw and put them on trial in New Orleans. This conflict served as the final straw for local habitants. That the Houma had not actually attacked the farm was irrelevant to Spanish settlers. To their way of thinking, the Choctaw acted the same way the Houma had in the past, and the Choctaws had committed their attack while under tribal protection. In the minds of local habitants, the hosts were thus as responsible as their guests.[41]

Aside from physical conflict, pressure on the Houma to leave Ascension also stemmed from a supposed land sale to landowners Maurice Conway and Alexander Latil. According to what Conway and Latil claimed in court—some of their story solid fact, some of it fiction, some of it perhaps fact or fiction but unsupported by any original documents—on October 5, 1774, they paid a Houma chief named "Calabee" $150 in goods for all land east of the Mississippi, after which the tribe would relocate to the west bank. The men then petitioned Governor Unzaga—who owed his political position to Don O'Reilly, Conway's uncle—and on November 1, 1774, the governor formally granted a parcel stretching slightly over half a league along the Mississippi and forty arpents to the rear, or almost two miles across and one-and-a-half miles back. Latil then sold his interest to Conway on January 4, 1776, and on September 9 Conway petitioned Governor Gálvez for 180,000 extra acres to the original grant's rear, which the governor awarded on July 21, 1777.[42] The sections of land were termed "the Houmas Claim" in legal documents.

Judice noted several tribal leaders in official reports but never mentioned the "Calazare," "Colazare," or "Colazava" of the land transfer records. He did, however, record "Calab" as a tribal leader in 1768, and in the following years he and Calab/Calabee/Colabee enjoyed good political and personal relations.[43] This man appeared in an October 1776 gathering when the governor ordered Louis Andry, second adjutant in New

Orleans and a respected surveyor, to mark the boundaries of Conway's claim. Colonial witnesses to the survey were Maurice Conway, Louis Judice, and the owners of property just upstream and downstream from Conway's land. Also (and seemingly the only Indian) present was "the Chief of the Houmas and Bayougoulas, for whom Judice acted as interpreter," referred to in another source as "the said Indian chief named Calabee . . ." This tribesman witnessed the actual survey and signing of papers required after the survey.[44]

Whatever Calabee's qualifications as a leader, he had an unpleasant tendency to make decisions and then keep profits for himself. Indeed, on October 1, 1775, Judice frantically wrote Governor Unzaga that a Houma chieftain and several disgruntled followers were on their way to New Orleans to collect the governor's annual presents. Judice had tried unsuccessfully to stop them but said, "It was impossible for me to prevent them, their reason is that Calabee left before them, and that if he receives the gifts he keeps everything, without sharing with them."[45] Calabee obviously did not enjoy a high tribal reputation regarding the exchange of goods and, however legal the colonials might have thought their purchase of river property from one man to be, the nation as a whole seems to have had a markedly different opinion.

When Judice warned Unzaga that a discontented Houma party was on its way to New Orleans in pursuit of Calabee, he also included an update on possible Houma relocation. He had been on the verge on convincing the nation to reunite into one village and move down Bayou Lafourche on the river's west bank, "when an Indian named Pailmastabee, of the Choctaw nation, told them that they were fine as they were, and that they should stay there." They were now split into three groups. Natchiabe and about twenty men had moved two-and-a-half leagues upriver, where local settlers kept harassing them. Ironically, Calabee and about twenty men remained on Conway's land despite the latter's efforts to dislodge them. On the other hand, Tiefayo and eight families had removed to "the fork," as Bayou Lafourche was called, and were "doing very well."[46]

Judice found himself caught between many parties and desperately trying to keep the peace. Both Governor Unzaga and local habitants wanted all local Indians to move, whereas the Houma were determined to stay. Tensions over physical conflict escalated at the same time pressure over the land sale mounted. One group of Houma relocating down Lafourche was good, but that still left the other two villages. Judice tactfully requested that, since a Houma party was on its way to New Orleans, the governor "order them to withdraw to La Fourche, either at a distance of one league or half a league as [Unzaga] will judge appropriate."[47]

Based on Judice's letter, it is tempting to imagine a historical narrative in which the Houma split in discord over the land sale, after which Tiefayo relocated to unknown territory down Bayou Lafourche. However, the actual remove is likely much more complex. Obviously, there was disharmony with colonial settlers and officials before the land sale. Moreover, by 1774 at least some members of the nation had already acquired an excellent knowledge of the bayous and marshes to the south, as revealed in conversation that year between a Houma leader and geographer and surveyor Thomas Hutchins.

Hutchins served Great Britain for several years in West Florida and made extensive surveys on his own, particularly concerning the Mississippi and its outlets. The river's mouth remained unreliable until the latter 1800s, and he deemed the route through Lakes Pontchartrain and Maurepas too long.[48] Hutchins speculated on the existence of a bayou entrance to the Gulf south of the river's main course but was both puzzled and stymied by the fact that neither France nor Spain had produced reliable information on the coast west of the Mississippi. Turning to those with extensive knowledge of the area's waterways, he questioned local Houma, Alabama, and Chitimacha villagers and carefully noted their opinions, particularly those of "Natchiabe, an intelligent chief of the Humas tribe."[49]

The Houma man explained that the bayou indeed split about eight leagues down its departure from the Mississippi, with one distributary running southeast and the other southwest but both flowing approximately seven leagues before emptying into the Gulf. If Hutchins had been surprised at the Indian's depth of knowledge, he should not have been. Natchiabe and his nation had hunted and fished the large and small bayous running through the area for decades and knew them extremely well.[50] Modern maps correspond precisely to Natchiabe's description and show that in 1774, at least some Houma were intimately familiar with details most Euro-American waterway charts would not show for decades.

Natchiabe's knowledge of the region's bayous served him well two years later, when he fled questioning in his brother-in-law's murder and took flight for the coast. Judice wrote that "Nathiabée" was fleeing ever southward and hope of apprehending him among the maze of waterways was small. A man running for his life usually travels to areas he knows well, and Natchiabe must indeed have known the bayou lands intimately, since he was never apprehended until cleared of all charges. Other Houma Indians believed the man justified in the incident and thus refused to track him despite their knowledge of the region. To them, the bayous and coastal areas were not terra incognita but very much the opposite. They knew the area intimately and lived in part from its bounty. Bayou country was thus an extremely attractive locale when slipping from a Euro-American vise.[51]

In the modern era, multiple and independent oral narratives of Houma history as recited by tribal elders state that the nation split into three bands in the latter 1700s. The only divergence in these narratives is in how many bands traveled down Lafourche; some say that two went back upstream and disappeared from the historical record, while others maintain that only one sailed upstream as the other two went down Bayou Lafourche.[52]

Why some Houma began a migration down the waterway is easy to determine given the conflict in Ascension and that the entire river was falling rapidly to the plantation system. However convenient it might be to date their remove to 1774 or 1775 based on Judice's letter, it is impossible to determine a single year of departure given that there almost certainly was not one. Louis Sauvage, characterized by the Houma today as an ancestor, moved south "with the permission of the proper Spanish officer" sometime prior to 1803 and occupied 145 acres on both sides of Bayou Terrebonne at the time of the Louisiana Purchase.[53] Likewise, Marie Nerisse's claim to 321 acres was confirmed given that she had "obtained for this land a regular warrant of survey from Governor Miro, in the year 1788, and that the same was inhabited and cultivated by her on the 1st day of October, 1800."[54]

On the other hand, ten or twelve Houma families lived on the Cantrelle plantation in St. James Parish until around 1800; by 1803 only four families were left on the river, though there is no record of whether the others had traveled down Bayou Lafourche or relocated elsewhere.[55] On April 4, 1806, two Houma chiefs visited Territorial Governor W.C.C. Claiborne, and he presented them with two military jackets valued at forty-eight dollars. In his letter to the U.S. government asking for reimbursement, he noted that the "friendly tribe of Indians called the Hamos" still lived "on the waters of the Mississippi in the County of Acadia within this territory."[56]

Thus, the historical record reveals some very important things. First, by 1774 at least some Houma had been making inroads into the bayous and marshes of southeastern Louisiana for years. They knew the region well enough to describe it in detail to a surveyor and to flee there in times of crisis. Second, at least one group under the leadership of Tiefayo had relocated down Bayou Lafourche by 1775. All this can be determined from the colonial record without referencing oral tradition.[57] Tiefayo's group might have been later joined by other tribal members en masse or, more likely, there was continued and gradual migration down the bayou as the nation was pushed out of lands along the river.[58]

A more important question for some people is exactly where the Houma went as they traveled down La Fourche des Chetimaches, or Bayou Lafourche. A distributary rather than a tributary, the bayou "forked" from the Mississippi and flowed southeast through a region once associated with the Chitimacha Indian tribe, hence the name. In her research with the Houma, Dana Bowker Lee argued that the "fork" to which Judice referred was not the initial split between Bayou Lafourche and the Mississippi or even the bayou itself. Rather, she argued that the fork was actually a secondary division, that of Bayou Terrebonne from Bayou Lafourche. According to Judice, Calabee was clinging to the former village on the east bank, but Natchiabe had moved two leagues upriver, which means that these Houma were pretty much where they had lived since their arrival in Ascension. A removal to the initial fork by Tiefayo would only have relocated his village to the river's west bank across from the two other villages, precisely the area Judice was desperate for them to leave. Thus, the secondary split between Bayou Lafourche and Bayou Terrebonne could only be the fork to which Judice referred. Michael Dardar, a Houma elder serving as the nation's unofficial historian today, argues the same.[59]

Bowker Lee and Dardar made an important point, one that gives a different flavor to Houma migration. The nation fanned out along the bayous of modern Lafourche Parish and Terrebonne Parish over the next century. They settled either on Bayou Lafourche and Bayou Terrebonne or on smaller branching waterways. If the secondary fork farther down Bayou Lafourche was actually the one to which Tiefayo moved (at modern-day Thibodaux, Louisiana), that would place his village farther into bayou country and closer to the lands and waterways with which the nation would eventually identify.

The eighteenth century had proved a momentous one for the Houma. In its first half, the nation engaged in two massive relocations and rose to prominence based on their alliances with France, but the second half saw a steady shrinking in their power and prestige. Indeed, as the year 1800 grew closer, the Houma suffered one setback after another. Having formed coalitions with the French against other tribes in the Lower Mississippi Valley, the Houma saw their allies forced from the region after 1763 and their tribal homelands divided between the Spanish and English. Acadians colonized territory along the river and supplanted the nation as soldiers and horticulturalists. Arriving Canary Islanders only exacerbated this trend, and the English departure from the region took with it the nation's ability to play European powers against one another.

Thus, as the eighteenth century drew to a close the Houma were primed for a mass relocation from Ascension. Even if they had wanted to remain along the river, however, it would have been suicidal to stay. Governor Gayoso removed Commandant Louis Judice from office in September 1797 as a result of politics. Though ostensibly the man tasked with deporting the Houma from the region, Judice also was one of the few forces of calm amid ever-increasing violence. The American Evan Jones replaced Judice but lasted only until September 3, 1798, due to his abrasive personality and conflicts with local Canary Islanders. He was followed by Lieutenant Rafael Croquer, who was relieved of duty in November 1799.[60] Clearly, the world along the river had changed and would change even further with arrival of the steamboat era in 1812. By 1825 a highly profitable sugarcane economy dominated Ascension and most other areas along the lower Mississippi. This system forced out many early settlers and small planters who had themselves forced out the

Houma, some of whom would follow the nation down the waterways of southeastern Louisiana and compete for their new lands.[61]

Difficult as the century had been, the Houma were still standing at its end. This was more than many tribes and European powers could say for themselves. The nation had survived because of their ability to move quickly and to take the best of the world around them and make it their own. Their adaptations until 1800 had been primarily political, forming alliances with colonial powers or tribes as need arose. On a secondary level their changes had been economic, as the nation supplied the food markets of New Orleans. Over the next century their adaptations would be primarily demographic and social. In the coming decades they would fan out along the waterways of southeastern Louisiana. The Houma would relocate, embracing Catholicism and the French language, and Indian women would take French husbands. Likewise, their assigned racial status would change as the entire cultural fabric of the Lower Mississippi Valley underwent a massive shift after American arrival. The one thing that would not change would be the nation's talent for adapting quickly and well to a changing world.

4

A Kingdom of Water

Adaptation and Erasure in Bayou Country

Since 1699 the Houma had learned many lessons about colonials, but one of the most important was that these outsiders would not stop. Bayou St. John and Ascension had been lost to arriving settlers, and the nation could survive only by fleeing to an area the ever-increasing arrivals did not want. The bayous, marshes, and swamps of extreme southeastern Louisiana offered that hope. Radically different from the Houma's previous homes, it was a place as much waterscape as landscape, where the difference between the two was often determined only by a few inches in elevation. This new move would force environmental and social adaptations in a way none of their former homes had and link the nation inextricably with the bayou country. They changed their settlement patterns by fanning out along a series of small waterways while maintaining connections between communities. Women of the nation began taking husbands from outside societies, adopting French names and some aspects of French culture but pulling these men into tribal society; the resulting children would be viewed as Houma by both the nation and non-Natives. Moreover, the Houma embraced Catholicism as their official religion and began a shift to French monolingualism.

While the move to modern Lafourche Parish and Terrebonne Parish offered hope, it also meant that Houma political and economic worlds would narrow even further. More important for future generations of the nation, it meant that they would be ignored and eventually erased from the historical record. If the Spanish government had wanted to end an embarrassing situation in Ascension by moving the Houma out of sight, their desires were as nothing compared to those of Americans after the Louisiana Purchase. In 1816 American records mentioned the Houma of Terrebonne Parish and Lafourche Parish as a nation but only to deny them land rights. Census records added to the confusion by varying wildly in recording the supposed numbers of Indians in the area. Finally, many documents confused both the tribal affiliation and ethnic status of tribal members. In effect, these erasures were the first step in a process of ethnic cleansing, of creating a history in which the nation had ceased to exist.

Modern Bayou Lafourche bears little resemblance to what the Houma would have known as they traveled downstream. Visitors would never guess that until about 750 years ago this small waterway was the Mississippi's bed and that its silt-laden waters had formed the subdelta now called Lafourche Parish and Terrebonne Parish before the river changed course to the east. The erection of a dam separating the bayou from the Mississippi around 1903 was successful in that it protected the area against flooding, but it also brought about a stagnation of the distributary.[1] The Houma would have traveled a much wider outlet prior to the dam, with numerous waterways branching from it. From its separation point at modern Thibodaux, Bayou Terrebonne split from the larger waterway and flowed slightly southeast through modern Houma, entering the Gulf just below Montegut. Though Terrebonne is one of the most noticeable waterways, through much of the area's early history Bayou Black (also noted on maps as Bayou Bœuf) was the most important. Other major arteries in the area are Grand Caillou, Little Caillou, Dularge, and Blue; smaller waterways are L'eau Bleue, Pointe au Chien, La Cache, La Cire, and Sale. All these start in the north and run to the south and/or southeast.[2]

The Houma moved—or more accurately, were forced—down first these large bayous and then the smaller waterways at a much faster pace than they could have imagined. Widespread sugar cultivation along the Mississippi intensified around 1805 with the arrival of American capital, the decimation of cotton crops by an armyworm invasion, and the 1812 introduction of steamboats that sailed against the Mississippi current. By 1814 Ascension properties had skyrocketed in price, and they rose even higher after the 1822 introduction of steam processing in sugar mills and the particularly profitable 1828 crop. In the wake of these changes, many small farmers in Ascension relocated.[3]

Some yeomen farmers left Ascension in poverty, but others departed with tidy profits from land sales. Many of the latter chose to move farther

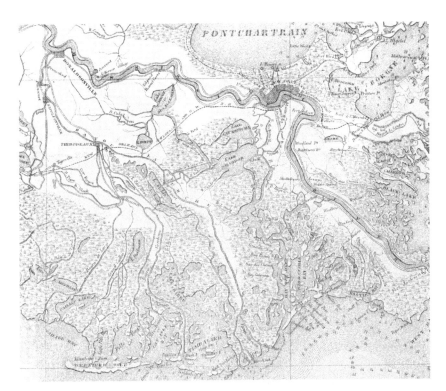

Map 3. Detail of hydrographical and topographical map of Louisiana, Mississippi, and Alabama. Published by Messrs. Holle & Co. The Historic New Orleans Collection, L. Kemper and Leila Moore Williams Founders Collection, 1953.128.

south, along Bayou Lafourche and eventually along Bayou Terrebonne.[4] These areas in turn saw a rise in population density and wealth much like that of the river parishes. In November 1806 Thomas Ashe visited the area, noting that the banks of Bayou Lafourche were already densely settled and that plantations stretched from the bayou's departure from the Mississippi for fifteen leagues. Tribal movement down ever-smaller bayous escalated in response to arriving waves of Euro-American settlers who fought with the Houma for high ground. A flood of habitants lured by lush soil and economic opportunity replicated the sugar economy of river parishes, which in turn replicated the conflict between the Houma and arriving settlers.[5]

In the approximately one hundred years after migration from Ascension, Houma families spread through the deltaic plain and divided into

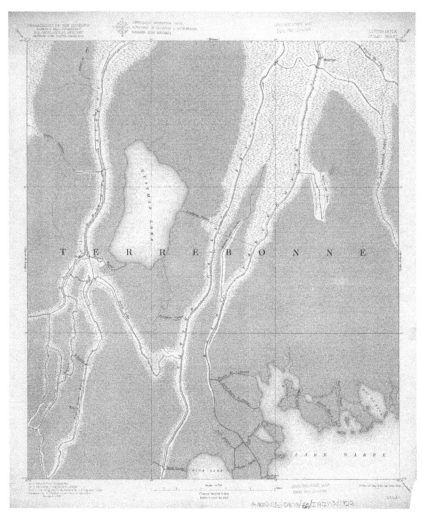

Map 4. Map of Dulac, 1894. Note the interconnected waterways linking lakes and bayous. One could quickly and easily travel across the landscape, especially given that there were even smaller waterways not listed on this detailed map. Louisiana State University Cartographic Information Center.

various bayou-linear communities linked by crossing waterways: Golden Meadow, Galliano, Grand Bois, Isle de Jean Charles, Grand Caillou, Dularge, Dulac, Larose, Montegut, and Pointe-aux-Chenes. Houma communities seemed far removed from each other as they grew in Terrebonne Parish and Lafourche Parish, but they certainly were not; one reason Bayou Black was so important was that it ran east to west across bayous flowing north to south. Even after decades of erosion and Indian-used waterways dissolving into the Gulf, there remain hundreds of bayous, canals, and traînasses one would never find on even the most detailed map. Houma Indians propelled shallow-draft cypress dugouts quickly and gracefully across the landscape to reach other tribal communities, easily maneuvering waterways stretching three feet across and a foot deep. Looking at an aerial map today, one sees very little distance *by water* between Houma communities. Continuing east, one also sees very little distance by water between Lafourche Parish and Jefferson Parish, where many Houma went to trap and hunt.[6]

In 1850 English travel writer Matilda Charlotte Houstoun visited Houma territory. Despite her experience as a world traveler, she was still disoriented by the "infinite number of crossed *water* roads, a species of natural canals, which grow more and more intricate in their turnings and windings as [her party] slowly wended [their] way through them." She continued at length about how fellow passengers were totally disoriented, but her guide and steersmen did not even hesitate at turnings.[7]

An Indian guide seventy years later showed that his people had lost none of this knowledge, when in 1919 a Methodist missionary named Anatole Martin traveled from Pointe-aux-Chenes to Dulac at the behest of a Houma family interested in his faith. His ferryman, Jacque Richard, used a flat-bottomed pirogue that skimmed the surface of water and grass, moving swiftly between settlements. Though a lifelong resident of the area, Martin was unaware of the intricate waterways linking Houma Indian villages until actually in them. Richard pushed away from his home at six o'clock in the morning and had Martin in Dulac before noon, a quick trip indeed for 1919.[8]

The Houma nation had been linked with water in all their previous locales, but in their new home along the myriad bayous of southern Louisiana they developed an even more intimate relationship with it. Simply put, it is impossible to understand the Houma without understanding their relationship to water. Water was their highway, their economic base, the producer of their food, their means of escape from enemies, and the route via which the nation maintained political and social ties with friends and family. In many ways it was more their home than land. Until one understands this, nothing about the nation truly makes sense, yet once one does grasp their relationship to a kingdom of water, everything else about the Houma falls into place.[9]

Just as the Houma adapted to a water-based environment, so too did they tweak other aspects of their culture during this time. The most important shift was intermarriage with non-Indians, if only because it affected so many other cultural features. From the colony's founding, both religious and secular powers had expressed concern about sexual relations between French men and Indian women, albeit for different reasons. Catholic leaders were concerned about soldiers and traders in Native villages debauching Indian women and defying Church power, while secular officials fretted that such unions damaged colonial growth through their instability.[10] Even worse from the perspective of government agents were stable unions in which the men did not leave their partners and eventually became enmeshed in Native cultures and kinship patterns. One militantly unenthusiastic official went on at great length in 1715 about French men marrying Indian women and decried how "those who have married them have become themselves almost Indian, residing among them and living in their manner, so that those Indian women have changed nothing or at least very little in their manner of living."[11]

Over the next several decades male arrivals to southern Louisiana joined Indian women as life partners either in Church-sanctioned unions or in "the fashion of the country," where bonds were recognized by a colonial or tribal official but not blessed by the Church until later, if ever. An order of December 16, 1792, from the Royal and Supreme Council of the Indies to the Bishop of Havana and the governors of East Florida and New Orleans decreed that marriage ceremonies be conducted only in the presence of priests and two or three witnesses, as dictated by the Council of Trent. The niceties of Tridentine marriage were often lost to the colonies, where priests were scarce and marriage was often an informal affair. The Bishop of New Orleans wrote Pope Leo XII that older priests believed the Council of Trent had never applied to the colony and asked that the pope correct the confusing situation. Realizing that this was a losing battle, Pope Leo finally issued a *sanatio in radice* on September 24, 1824, that validated previous marriages not conducted in proper form. Formal blessing of Houma marriages previously without benefit of clergy began around 1842 when missionary priests traveled to isolated communities.[12]

Though the Church might debate Tridentine marriages, the intricacies of Catholic edicts were of little interest to French men and Houma women coming together in bayou country. As in other parts of North America, marriage in the fashion of the country was duly recognized and couples clearly viewed their bonds as valid with or without clergy. By the 1820s unions had sprung up in Indian communities, with the highest concentration centering on Isle de Jean Charles and Montegut. Oral tradition maintains that men of European ancestry from Isle de Jean Charles traveled to nearby Montegut and brought Indian wives back to the island.[13] Almost all modern Houma trace their ancestry in some form to these unions, particularly the coupling of Jacques Constant Billaux (Billiot) and Rosalie Courteau. The seven sons of this couple are held as the progenitors of the modern Houma nation.

These European fathers gave children their surnames, but, in an ironic case of absorption, within a few generations those particular French names came to signify Native identity. In 1907 John Swanton noted that three major Indian families were "Couteaux," "Billiout," and "Verdine."[14] These were three of the most common family names, especially in the particular communities he visited, but other familiar Houma surnames were Chaisson (or Cbiasson), Billiot (Billeau), Sauvage (Sauvagin), Solet (Saulet), Verret, Jeanne (or Dianne, or Dion, or Ghianne), Courteau (or Houma, or Abbé), Verdin (or Verdun, or Verdine), Parfait, Naquin, Fitch, and Dardar. Adding to the confusion was that these surnames were strongly associated with both the Houma and with non-Indian communities. The name holder's ethnic group would be determined in conversation by factors such as spelling variations, different syllabic emphases, variations in vowel sounds, and the primary habitation of the name holder. The last point would hinge on if one were, for instance, a Naquin from Isle de Jean Charles—in which case one was almost certainly Indian—or a Naquin from Thibodaux or southwestern Louisiana, in which case one would be Acadian.

Unions between Houma women and non-Houma men were remarkably stable. Oral tradition absolutely maintains that these pairings were consensual and that each member brought something to the table, be it material gains or shared lifestyle.[15] Several modern Houma women who married non-Houma men interpreted their ancestors' outmarriage in the same way they viewed their own: a woman picks a man she is attracted to, whom she can get along with, who can help her family and protect her. All other cultural elements could be negotiated, especially since colonial men outnumbered white women in Louisiana at the time. For their part, Indian women served as guides and kept their mates alive through their knowledge of southern Louisiana landscapes and plant life—vital knowledge for newly arrived males not used to the area—and also played an active role in hunting and trapping. Families often ranged to a dozen children or more, as each child was a welcome addition not only to large kinship networks but also the family economy. An Indian priest maintains that the modern Houma's aversion to birth control and horror of abortion were not products of introduced Catholicism; rather, Catholicism reinforced preexisting codes of morality and family structures.[16]

Through subsequent decades, Houma women and their children chose what appealed to them in French culture but maintained their tribal identity. As had happened with the Houma each time they absorbed individuals or bands of outsiders, these women pulled their partners *into* the nation rather than being pulled out of it themselves. This stands in marked contrast to other ethnic groups in southern Louisiana that were consistently subsumed by Acadian culture after outsiders married Acadian women.[17] That it was Indian women mating with French men (some of whom had come directly from France and who thus did not have cultural ties spanning generations) is the main reason the Houma maintained their cultural strength.

Just as the nation asserted that children born to exogamous unions were Houma, so did members of the non-Indian community, albeit for different reasons. Many non-Houma maintained that the tribe was Indian, but others maintained it was composed of mixed whites, blacks, and Indians trying to pass as something they were not. To intermarry with them was to pollute the white gene pool, be that pollution via Indian or African ancestry. Thus, local non-Indians did not separate the nation's members according to degree of Indian versus African versus European ancestry. When looking at a mixed-race child they might use the term

"Indian," "Houma," or "Sabine" interchangeably, the last an extremely offensive moniker. These terms in no way indicated a recognized métis status, however, as they were used on both "full bloods" and tribal members suspected of mixed ancestry. Thus, many non-Houma adamantly agreed with Indians that children born of exogamous unions were not white, but based upon a different interpretation.[18]

Louisiana law reinforced social opinion. Article 10 of the colony's 1724 *Code noir* decreed that if a slave and free woman had a child, the child was freeborn based on the mother's status. Conversely, if a free man and slave had a child, then the offspring was born enslaved based on the mother's status. While the *Code noir* supposedly offered protection to slaves, it was often ignored based on what was convenient for those in power, and basing a child's status on the mother's rank was as much a matter of social norms as legal regulation. In much the same way, and especially given that throughout the colony's history it had a shortage of white women and thus a surplus of children born to European men and non-European women, a child's ethnic status invariably followed the mother's in much the same way its legal status did. This legal interpretation would only be reinforced after American arrival.

In sum, children produced by Houma women and non-Houma men took the status of their mothers. This was the ruling of the nation, of the outside community, and of the Louisiana legal system. European fathers introduced French names, blue and green eyes, auburn hair, and freckles to the nation, but they did not introduce white children, and the nation stood in direct contrast to Canadian tribes in that they never developed a métis community.

The shift to Catholicism and French as a primary language was not the direct result of exogamous marriage, but such unions sped transitions already underway. Du Ru's dreams of a Catholic nation had stalled for a century, but they began to flower in bayou country. At least some priestly inroads had been made in the early 1800s, for in May 1832 word came to Father Tomas Ponz in Donaldsonville that "L. Joseph Sauvage de la nation Houma" was dying and required last rites immediately. Father Ponz had served as assistant at the Church of the Assumption at Plattenville and briefly as priest at Ascension, two major churches along Bayou Lafourche. He knew both the Houma people and landscape very well, but even moving quickly down the bayou he was unable to reach the deathbed in time to perform the last rites. Ponz brought the body back to Ascension Catholic Church for burial, recorded a death time of 10 a.m., May 17, and made sure the records showed that the Indian man died in good standing with the true faith.[19]

The first priest who consistently ministered to the Houma was Father Charles Menard, born in Lyon, France, in 1817. During the early to mid-1800s Church officials heavily recruited young, enthusiastic priests to Louisiana from Spain, France, and Italy. The area then controlled by the Thibodeaux Diocese stretched from just above Thibodaux to the Gulf and from the Atchafalaya River in the west to Jefferson Parish in the east; at one time it also included southern Jefferson. Such a vast area required priests who combined dedication with stamina, and in both these respects the driven Menard stood out. An unusually energetic man who required little sleep and seemed happy only when moving physically and mentally, the twenty-five-year-old's high energy level and constant need for work led the Bishop to appoint Menard pastor of the entire parish in 1842.[20]

Disappointed that many of his Thibodeaux parishioners only attended mass on Palm Sunday, Easter Sunday, and Corpus Christi, the restless priest took special interest in communities down the bayous. In particular, he was upset that area people had been married for years without having unions blessed by priests and immediately sought to correct that. In 1842 Menard led the first recorded mass at Montegut, in the tribal heartland.[21] Menard's first recorded baptism among the Houma was on January 6, 1843, for Jacques Billaux, seven-year-old son of Jacques Constant Billaux (Billiot) and Rosalie Courteau, for which the family made the lengthy journey to St. Joseph's Church in Thibodaux.[22]

Jacques and Rosalie's was the most prominent exogamous marriage, and they were the first couple to choose baptism for their child. This sacrament thus stands as the true beginning of Catholicism among the Houma. Du Ru's and Gravier's efforts fell on hard ground, and Joseph Sauvage's last rites reflected the end of a life rather than a beginning. Even Menard's 1842 mass was his decision rather than the community's. On the other hand, young Jacques Billiot's baptism reflected a decision by the Houma themselves and began a religious shift that would come to full fruition in coming years. Jacques would be among the first generation raised in the faith, and by 1862 a small but strong core of Indian parishioners had developed in Montegut.[23]

Father Jean-Marie Dénecé made an even stronger impression because he actually lived in the Houma community and frequently traveled to different Indian settlements. In 1864 Archbishop Odin voyaged to France on a recruiting expedition and brought the young priest back to bayou country. A portrait from the time reveals a solid-looking youth with dark hair and brows, pale eyes and skin, and a full mouth that looks ready to laugh—the face of a country boy used to hard work and hard living. He was named founding pastor of Montegut and constructed the first church in the new parish, Holy Family, the Mother Church for the Houma. Teams of local workers labored on the new structure, and Indians noted with pride that a particularly skilled Houma named Joseph Duthu had created all the doors, windows, and pews.[24]

Father Dénecé remained as priest until his death in 1890, served his parish for twenty-six years, and until his death in 1890 enjoyed extremely good relations with the Houma. During his tenure he improved roads, built the first bridge over Bayou La Cache so he could move from settlement to settlement more easily, and learned to navigate small canals and bayous linking coastal villages. He traveled constantly, conducted marriages and baptisms, and celebrated mass every fifteen days in Montegut after 1866. After his death a succession of priests worked this vineyard and established churches in nearby tribal settlements. Whatever elements of the old religion remained in folk knowledge or in songs, by the end of the 1800s Catholicism was the official Houma religion.[25]

In large part because of the efforts of Menard and Dénecé, the Houma completed their shift to the French language that had begun in 1699. By the time ethnologist John Swanton visited the Houma in 1907, they spoke French exclusively and only a handful of elders remembered any Muskhogean.[26] The Houma ancestors initially learned French from youths left in their village and then refined their language skills with colonial officials and Jesuits such as du Ru and Gravier. Moreover, in the river parishes they interacted freely with local Creole and Acadian families, just as they had done with Commandant Judice. A colonial official recorded shortly after 1800 that Houma families living on the

Cantrelle plantation along the Mississippi were completely bilingual in "Choctaw and French."[27]

The Houma's absorbing the French language and refining their skills in it only continued with passing decades. Speaking freely in French to a journalist visiting Isle de Jean Charles in the 1940s, Chief Victor Naquin explained that many of the island's first males had arrived from Europe in the early 1800s and lived with Indian women. His own ancestor Jean Charles Naquin had come from France and was joined by other countrymen in following decades. French spoken in Houma dwellings was reinforced by missionaries who traveled down the bayous.[28] In particular, the missionary Fathers Menard and Dénecé taught French language classes from 1842 to around 1890, and both these highly educated men were excellent instructors. Language skills absorbed over decades through intermarriage and instruction by priests were strengthened by the arrival of Frenchman François Bordeaux on Isle de Jean Charles in the late 1880s. Trained as a teacher and visiting as a tourist, he decided that he liked the island and stayed through the 1880s and 1890s, educating young Houma in reading and writing French as well as refining their accents.[29]

By the beginning of the twentieth century, French was so deeply ingrained in the Houma nation that it was appropriate to label it their native language. A combination of parents, priests, and teachers took their duties so seriously that in 1948 a newly arrived priest was shocked at the high quality of French he heard on Isle de Jean Charles among the Indian community; while conversing with several men in their eighties, he learned that many elders could read and write fluent French as well. Given that many Houma Indians in the 1800s had access to informal but high-quality education, in 1948 many members of the older generation were, in fact, better educated in many respects than the younger generation.[30]

Cultural change did not come about simply due to non-Houma men being pulled into the Indian community through marriage. The loss of a village square would have happened in bayou-linear communities in any case, as would have tribal adaptation to new plants and animals. Nevertheless, new patterns of marriage were significant not only because they reflected Houma willingness to take the best of a new environment and make it their own but also because they reinforced change in areas such as religion and language. The key point is that, just as some parents came

Fig. 1. (*top left*) Houma woman weaving palmetto, Terrebonne Parish, ca. 1930s. Note the palmetto hat and raised home, both adaptations to the locale. Northwestern State University of Louisiana, Watson Memorial Library, Cammie G. Henry Research Center.

Fig. 2. *(top right)* Houma women and man, Terrebonne Parish, ca. 1920s. Northwestern State University of Louisiana, Watson Memorial Library, Cammie G. Henry Research Center.

from different cultural traditions to produce "mixed-race" children who were still very much members of the nation, so too these examples of cultural adjustment produced a stronger, better-adapted nation that was still very much Houma.

By 1900 the Houma had engaged in major geographic and cultural shifts to preserve itself as a nation. One of the horrible ironies of their history, however, is that even as they regrouped in a new home and adapted successfully to a new environment, they were being erased from the historical record. Whether deliberate or not, paperwork created by arriving Americans produced a welter of state and federal documents

Fig. 3. (*top*) Indian family on lower Bayou Caillou, Terrebonne Parish, ca. 1920s. State Library of Louisiana Historic Photograph Collection.

Fig. 4. (*bottom*) Houma man on quaking prairie with coffin, Point au Barré, Terrebonne Parish, ca. 1920s. Though likely only one or two feet in depth and not shown on maps, this waterway allowed people to move quickly. In this case, it allowed for transportation of a coffin. Thaddeus I. St. Martin Collection, Allen J. Ellender Archives, Nicholls State University, Thibodaux LA.

Fig. 5. (*top*) Houma man with pirogue and coffin, Point au Barré, Terrebonne Parish, ca. 1920s. The coffin was on its way to a cemetery, where a large family met for the ceremony. In ways such as this the Houma moved easily across the landscape of southeastern Louisiana, maintaining family ties and kinship networks. Thaddeus I. St. Martin Collection, Allen J. Ellender Archives, Nicholls State University, Thibodaux LA.

Fig. 6. (*bottom*) Cemetery at Point au Barré, Terrebonne Parish, ca. 1920s. Note the water in the background. Though relatively high ground in the 1920s, this area has since eroded. With coastal erosion have gone many signs of Houma presence. Thaddeus I. St. Martin Collection, Allen J. Ellender Archives, Nicholls State University, Thibodaux LA.

that erased the Houma from the landscape. Federal land records referenced the nation mainly to explain that their traditional rights did not have to be respected, then quickly moved to ignoring the group. Inaccurate census figures gave a stilted and inaccurate view of the region. Last, local ethnic and racial terms used to designate individuals varied wildly, even when describing the same person.

In the wake of the Louisiana Purchase, American officials codified land claims made under the French and Spanish governments. Landowners had to prove they had settled and/or occupied land prior to 1803 or lose their property rights. Thickly settled as the Lafourche region was, hundreds of claimants rushed to prove they had been granted land, had purchased it outright, or had settled and lived on it for years. Houma oral histories maintain that to reward the nation for past loyalty and moving south, the Spanish issued the Houma a grant encompassing land between Barataria Bay and the Atchafalaya River, a large area encompassing the present-day parishes of Lafourche, Terrebonne, and St. Mary.[31] While many individuals hurried to prove their singular claims, the Houma made a group petition on what would have been the heart of this area: twelve sections of land on Bayou Black (also called Bayou Bœuf).

The nation's claim to 7,680 acres was rejected in 1816. Significantly, the Americans did not deny Houma presence along the bayous or their history on the land, only their legal right to make such a claim. Under a subheading titled "Including Claims Not Embraced by Existing Laws," the rejection reads, "The Homas tribe of Indians claims a tract of land lying on bayou Bœuf, or Black bayou, containing twelve sections. We know of no law of the United States by which a tribe of Indians have a right to claim lands as a donation."[32] This went against a century of colonial protocol, particularly the January 1, 1798, proclamation by Intendant Don Juan Bonaventure Morales on land rights and distributions, with Article 31 stating, "Indians shall be protected in their holdings."[33]

This denial of the Houma land claim stood in stark contrast to their relations with the French and Spanish. Both colonial powers had understood that tribes would move as they chose. Indeed, the very mobility of Indian peoples made them valuable to first the French and then the Spanish. The United States made a complete reversal of this and leveraged an ambiguity in Article 6 of the Louisiana Purchase Treaty, the passage addressing the United States' agreement to recognize previous treaties and articles between Spain and Native tribes. U.S. officials determined that Spaniards had granted Indian peoples mere rights of occupancy at the will of the Crown rather than through treaty and that "the force and effect of prescription, in abolishing the Indian title to lands in Louisiana, is further established by the Indians permitting themselves to be removed from place to place by governmental authority."[34]

The 1816 decision that the Houma had no land rights as a nation would only be reinforced in coming years by federal census records that gave a highly inaccurate view of the region in general and the Houma in particular. Granted, French and Spanish officials had also compiled inaccurate Houma demographic records, but usually with the caveat that such records were approximations only and that many villages were ignored due to distance or terrain. Much more weight was given to census records after American arrival, however, despite their shortcomings. Beginning in the mid-1800s these records indicated wildly varying numbers of Indians in Houma territory, placing almost the total Indian population of Louisiana there in some years and stating the total absence of any Natives in others. The end result of this was to erase the Houma from the landscape of southeastern Louisiana.

Throughout the early 1800s the U.S. Census did not reference Natives. In Terrebonne Parish the 1840 census recorded 1,140 white men, 935 white women, 35 free people of color, and 2,294 slaves but made no reference to Indians.[35] In 1850 Terrebonne Parish, the census recorded 3,305 whites, 91 free people of color, and 4,328 slaves, again making no reference to Indians. The more densely populated Lafourche had 5,142 whites, 22 free people of color, and 4,368 slaves. Again, there was no mention of any group of Native Americans living either in those parishes or in St. Mary Parish, where some Houma had moved and where the Chitimacha nation already lived. That changed with the census of 1860.[36]

The 1860 census made separate designations for white males and females, free colored male and female blacks, free colored male and female mulattoes, male and female black slaves, male and female mulatto slaves, and male and female Indians. In contrast to those of later years, the 1860 census not only separated Indians from other free people of color but lumped all 173 Indians with whites in the final tally of population groups. Regarding Native Americans, the sex but not the tribal affiliation was noted. Though no Natives were recorded for Lafourche Parish, "St. Mary's" had 33 and "Terre Bonne" had 103, or 136 out of a recorded 173 Indians in the state of Louisiana.[37] The 1870 census recorded 569 Indians in the state in total; again, there were still no recorded Indians in Lafourche Parish but 50 in St. Mary and 199 in Terrebonne, the highest Native population in Louisiana. Calcasieu Parish was second at 105 and St. Landry Parish third at 83.[38] The 1880 federal census did not sort Indians into parishes but recorded 840 "civilized Indians" in Louisiana: 437 males and 403 females.[39]

In 1890 the federal census again distinguished between Indians living on the reservation and "civilized Indians" living in states and territories as an element of the general U.S. population. There were 627 civilized Indians in Louisiana, up from 848 [sic] in 1880, 569 in 1870, and 173 in 1860.[40] In 1900 a total of 593 Indians (338 males and 255 females) were listed in the state, with the Terrebonne population at "-", Lafourche population at 65, and the St. Mary population at 83.[41] In 1910 statewide numbers increased to 780 (385 males and 395 females), with Terrebonne at 125, Lafourche at "—" and St. Mary at 50.[42] In 1920 the census listed 1,066 Indians statewide, with a total of 550 males and 516 females constituting one percent of Louisiana's total population. The parish tally listed 639 Indians in Terrebonne, 5 in Lafourche, 83 in St. Mary, and 28 in Jefferson Parish, the first in which Jefferson showed an Indian population; according to Houma oral tradition, a few families had moved there to engage in the fur industry. The next closest was Allen Parish at 118. Allen was where the Coushatta nation was centered, which means that these five parishes comprised the overwhelming majority of Indians recorded for the state: 873 out of 1,066.[43]

Wildly varying figures continued in following decades. In 1930 there were 1,536 Indians listed in the state; Terrebonne had 936, St. Mary had 59, and Lafourche had 11.[44] In 1940 there were 1,801 Indians in the entire state, but no parishes were given.[45] In 1950 "Indian" was not included as a general category the way it had been previously; in Terrebonne, statistics were given for native whites, foreign-born whites, negroes, and "other races," with the last comprising 994 people. Census figures contradict each other because "Indians, Japanese, and Chinese, By Sex, for Selected Parishes and Cities: 1950" were recorded, but only those "parishes and cities with 10,000 or more citizens, or with 10 or more Indians, Japanese, or Chinese in 1950" were. "Indians" were not those of East Asian ancestry but rather American aborigines of either "full-blood" or mixed white-and-Indian ancestry if they were enrolled in a reservation or on a roll, or had a proportion of Indian blood at ¼ or greater, or were "recorded as Indians within the community." Parishes consistently recording the most Indians in previous decades now recorded none. Only St. Mary was still included, with 89 Indians. The next two highest parishes numbered 79 in Orleans—that is to say, 79 in New Orleans—and 49 in La Salle, with absolutely no mention of Terrebonne or Lafourche. Terrebonne had a total population of 43,238, Lafourche had 42,209, and St. Mary had 35,848, but it seemed as if the Natives of these parishes had simply vanished.[46]

Though these census figures might be tedious to review in detail, they reveal something very important. That is, whether by carelessness or by deliberate action, the Houma nation was being systematically erased from the historical landscape. Statistics varied wildly from one decade to the next even in the same parish, often bouncing from several dozen or several hundred Indians to none at all. It seems implausible that census figures, often considered the most reliable of public documents, could overlook so many people. Sadly, this was not uncommon in southern Louisiana. There were very pronounced reasons why the Houma were left off census rolls.[47]

First, census takers were prone to encounter both resistance in their position as government employees and outright hostility after the appointment of Republicans to compile the 1870 census. Combine this resistance and hostility with language barriers—many census takers either never could speak French or had lost their French-language skills—and inaccurate figures invariably result. Eminent Acadian historian Carl Brasseaux noted that southern Louisiana census figures must be taken with a grain of salt for all groups, as recorders, "often political hacks, were notoriously careless. Individuals residing at some distance from the main roads were routinely ignored."[48]

The Houma were much more than some distance from main roads. While Indians moved quickly across waterways and high ground from settlement to settlement, outsiders had the option of either traveling back up and down each bayou or cutting across marshes and swamps. The latter choice was often disastrous. In the late 1800s a local priest tried to walk the five miles from Theriot to Dulac, reasoning that he would be safe as long as he stayed on high ground. Veering into the swamp, he quickly found himself adrift in an unmarked green inferno. Routinely sinking to his knees in an unstable mix of mud and water, and sometimes sinking to his shoulders, the priest wandered for several days before he gave up in desperation, wrote his will on a slip of paper, and consigned himself to God. Meanwhile, several Indian families wondered when the father would arrive and sent word to Theriot, only to hear that the priest had left a couple of days before. Fanning quickly through the swamp, a group of Indians and Acadians found the priest, weak and dazed but alive. Their shock at his condition was equaled by his shock at how quickly they found him in the swamp that had nearly claimed his life.[49] This and similar stories were not lost on census takers. Estimating Houma Indians or any other group living in isolation was a matter of not only convenience but safety.

Moreover, some census takers were also hobbled by fears and stereotypes. Throughout south Louisiana history, "down the bayou" has denoted both a direction and a perceived way of life. Residents of more densely populated locales such as Houma and Thibodeaux admitted that the nation and other "way down the bayou" people were independent and feisty but also thought them dirty, violent, and hostile to outsiders. Many uneasy census takers reasoned that trappers did not care what one called them so long as one left them alone. Officials certainly were not about to ask a glowering patriarch if he or his wife were not white.[50]

Last, many members of the nation could not be located either because they lived in very isolated areas unreachable by roads or because they simply did not want to be found. The extreme edges of Lafourche Parish and Terrebonne Parish were exactly where one went when one wanted to disappear, and people living in inaccessible areas were unlikely to be counted unless visitors knew the area intimately. Being noticed had not worked well for the nation in any of their previous locations, and staying far down the bayous and away from prying eyes was the surest way to avoid conflict, violence, and possible removal.

Thus, there were some very pronounced reasons why census takers would have ignored the Houma. On the other hand, people who were a bit more adventurous in their travels reported very different demographics. In 1851 a reporter from *De Bow's Review* visited Terrebonne and wrote about "a tribe called the Houmas [who] once inhabited this section" and still lived in the area. Another writer traveling through the parish in 1892 included the Houma in an estimated aggregate of 336 New Orleans–area Natives.[51] Also in 1892 the New Orleans *Daily Picayune* reporter Catharine Cole traveled through Terrebonne and spent several days exploring the parish. She noted that the Houma Indians had settled in the area bearing their name "but now survive in a few palmetto huts—on the bayous near the sea marshes." While at the parish seat she befriended Mr. E. W. Condon, clerk of court for sixteen years. He informed her that if all eligible voters went to the polls, there would be 2,072 white and 1,992 colored voters. He then noted that 72 Indians of Terrebonne were eligible to vote, if they could make it to the polls, out of the 336 Indians in the parish.[52]

As the twentieth century dawned and more people traveled into Houma settlements, visitors came to a surprising conclusion: the Indian population was much larger than expected. In the early 1930s noted Terrebonne historian Randolph Bazet estimated the Houma Indian population at around 500, but in the late 1930s Frank Speck raised that number to a possible high of 2,000.[53] His estimate was not as high as Reverend Anatole Martin's, however. One of the most prominent Protestant missionaries to the Houma, Martin won friends among the Houma with his personality; they took him hunting and trapping and introduced him to people who lived miles from even the smallest Indian settlement.[54] After several years of ministerial work Martin started to count the people he met, and in 1937 he estimated there were between 4,000 and 5,000 mixed and pure-blood Indians in Terrebonne Parish alone, even as federal records recorded the evaporation of the Houma nation.[55]

Another thing that effectively removed the Houma from the historical record was the common use of multiple names and spellings. The practice had started under the French and continued with the Spanish, English, and Americans. Multiple naming was not a deliberate and calculated method of erasure so much as it was a product of various cultures and languages coming together. Moreover, many people in the region often went by nicknames that were listed in official documents as given names.[56] Nevertheless, the result of this practice in coming years would be to obscure personal identity and ethnic status. Such disorder would muddle the historical record so thoroughly that by the twentieth century it would be extremely difficult to trace ancestry for many Indians. To give one example among many, three documents concerning an Indian named Tacalobé illustrate how confusing this practice could be.

Tacalobé was among the first Houma Indians to settle permanently in bayou country. Oral tradition places him squarely within Houma kinship networks, but land transfers and wills display a variety of names and affiliations. On August 29, 1822, "Touh-La-Bay Alias Courteau of the Beloxy Nation" bought four arpents of land for $100 from Jean Billiot, a "free man of color." The purchased land along lower Bayou Terrebonne was bounded above and below by the property of "Alexandre Verdin." At the page's bottom, "Tough-la-bay" made his mark.[57] On June 1, 1829, "Toup-La-Bay, said Indian Courteau of the Biloxi Nation" sold that same section of land to "Alexandre Verdun" for $350. Verdun already owned the property directly above and below the section he purchased, so he was definitely the same man listed as "Verdin" in 1822.[58]

At the time of Tacalobé's death in 1844, his estate was divided and sold. His probate only gave one name when referring to him, but a deceased son was referred to as "Abé" in one section and "Abbé" in another; both names were used to describe the father as well in other documents. Marks at the bottom of the probate identified his children as Philorom Tacalobé, Antoine Tacalobé, and Rosalie Tacalobé. Rosalie Tacalobé was sometimes designated in legal records as Madame Jacques Billiot but was (and still is) consistently known as Rosalie Courteau, to whom most members of the modern Houma nation trace their ancestry.[59] One finds several other variations of Tacalobé's name in documents from Terrebonne Parish.

These three documents give only a taste of how confusing the historical record would become for the Houma. The two land sales and probate records give multiple spellings for multiple people and two different spellings in the same document for the same man. Moreover, they place a man strongly identified with the Houma nation into another tribe and then give that tribe's name two different spellings. If this pattern were confined to a handful of documents it would be a small matter to unravel them, but when it is multiplied over many members of the nation and across decades, its cumulative effect is to thoroughly muddle the historical record and, in effect, remove the nation from southeastern Louisiana.

But the confusion went even further. Just as in 1816 the United States had reversed French and Spanish attitudes on land rights to deny the Houma their claim, so too did it take preexisting racial codes and tweak them into a form neither colonial power would have recognized. Both French and Spanish records referred to Indians of the Lower Mississippi Valley as "Indiens," "sauvages" or "gens de couleur libres," but the region's intricate racial mores set boundaries between Natives and people of African descent. Post-Purchase officials maintained earlier terminology but began lumping different groups into the same category, as one of the most significant court cases from the era shows. In 1810 a young woman of mixed West Indian ancestry sued her master, arguing that she was free unless he could prove otherwise. The Superior Court of the Territory of Orleans, First District debated the matter and ruled in *Adelle v. Beauregard* that "Persons of color may have descended from Indians on both sides, from a white parent, or mulatto parents in possession of their freedom."[60] Negroes were understood to be slaves unless they could prove their freedom but, conversely, people of color should be regarded as free unless proven otherwise.

Adelle v. Beauregard was a complicated case that would have far-reaching effects for the Houma. On the one hand, it affirmed the Houma's status as free people.[61] On the other hand, it began the process of legally conflating Indians with people of mixed white and African ancestry. The process that began in 1810 would only speed up in coming decades before accelerating dramatically after the end of Reconstruction.

One Houma woman's example will be enough to illustrate how easily people could be moved from one racial category to another. Marie Nerisse had several alternate spellings of both her first and last names, but there was far more variation in her race. The federal land confirmation based on her declared 1788 Spanish grant does not list her race at all, but different local records refer to her as a "free women of color," a negress, and a griffe (triracial ancestry comprised of black and mulatto).

Her daughter Rosalie Francoise was referred to as a free quadroon, and other descendants were recorded as mulattoes, free people of color, Indians, and whites.[62] In coming decades, Houma identity would be determined by whoever recorded the legal document, and it was extremely common for various children of the same Indian parents to be classified as Indian, white, colored, and black.

Change was the one constant in the Houma nation's history, and through the decades of the nineteenth century they adapted quickly and well to their new environment. They migrated through the deltaic plain, pushed ever southward by newly arriving American settlers, some of whom followed them from their former home in Ascension. The nation traveled down Bayous Lafourche and Terrebonne and eventually pushed down even smaller waterways stretching to the Gulf. They made this place their own and established a series of small communities stretching down bayous and linked by tiny traînasses cutting across the landscape, waterways little bigger than ditches but through which people could skim like otters and maintain relationships between settlements. Indian women and non-Houma men formed lifelong partnerships that produced big families. After several generations, the children of these unions had French names, spoke French, and thought of themselves as good Catholics, yet they were recognized as tribal members by both the Houma and non-Houma.

Tragically, the adaptation that kept the nation alive as a people had a darker side to it, as it also made them invisible in many ways. Only a few decades after the United States denied the Houma's group claim to a large plot of land, census figures began completely overlooking the nation. Estimates varied wildly from year to year, but the end result was that there was no recorded Houma presence for a century —indeed, there was often no Indian presence at all—in the very area where the nation had established thriving communities. At the same time the welter of names and terms that were part of life in southeastern Louisiana would place the Houma in the wrong tribe or even in the wrong racial group. The United States used terms established under French and Spanish rule but then applied these terms in ways colonial powers would not have recognized.

That census takers overlooked the Houma and that civil servants placed them in a variety of racial categories cannot be explained away as simple treachery or a nefarious plot. There were many reasons why census takers might have overlooked the Houma, and carelessness rather than malice was likely the predominant factor. Likewise, people in southeastern Louisiana were making their way through a mélange of languages, legal codes, and ethnicities. That many Houma and their descendants were placed in the wrong category by civil servants is not shocking given the racial and ethnic gumbo that was southern Louisiana. Yet, deliberate or not, the erasure of the Houma from the historical landscape would later devastate them as a people.

During the same era that the Houma were expunged from the historical record, Louisiana was moving toward a division of its society into white versus nonwhite. After the Civil War Louisiana's delicately balanced racial categories collapsed, and all those who had been people of color—Indian, free black, or slave—were lumped into the same category. Houma removal from the historical landscape meant that whatever tribal references were actually in the public record would be interpreted against them. Erasing the nation from history picked up steam at the same time Louisiana was reshaping itself into two perceived races. One movement fed the other, and both grew in strength. It would not be an overstatement to call this an ethnic cleansing, a removal of Indian peoples from the public mind the same way their bodies had been removed from tribal homelands. This was a storm that swept the Houma before it, and in a few short years a man named H.L. Billiot would find himself in the center of that storm.

5

"So-Called Indians"

The Houma Quest for Education

At the dawn of the twentieth century a Houma elder could look back and ponder the very serious challenges the nation had faced in its history. Looking forward, they would face even more. Sloppy record keeping by officials had effectively erased the nation from public records, even as visitors to bayou settlements saw that the nation was thriving. Moreover, the exquisitely complicated multicultural and multiracial designations characterizing Louisiana for generations had already disappeared on a legal level, with ethnic groups now falling into binary categories of "white" versus "non-white."[1] Though the state ostensibly maintained a tripartite education system in coming decades, Indians were regularly lumped in with African Americans and denied quality education. Their lack of formal schooling would prove disastrous in the early twentieth century, when outsiders moved into Houma territory seeking fur, oil, and gas leases. Charlatans took advantage of the nation's inability to read English documents, just as they took advantage of previous marriages in the fashion of the country to dispossess "bastard" children.[2]

Since 1699 the Houma had adapted to a changing Lower Mississippi Valley by forming alliances with colonials, playing one power against another, moving to different areas and tweaking their own culture when necessary. None of these would help them now. Realizing that education in Louisiana schools was a new route to survival, the Houma launched a decades-long campaign to integrate schools in Terrebonne Parish and Lafourche Parish. Both to acquire quality education for their children and to protect themselves from trapping and oil companies, the nation repeated what they had done for centuries by continuing to fight while also forging alliances both within and beyond Louisiana.

Though cultural differences between the area's colonial population and Americans who arrived after the Louisiana Purchase have often been overblown, in numerous ways the two groups truly had definite and serious dissimilarities, particularly in how new arrivals viewed both race and the language used to quantify race. The Louisiana Superior Court's 1810 *Adele v. Beauregard* ruling had conflated the Houma's status as free people of color with those of mixed white-and-African descent, and in coming decades Americans passed legislation lowering the status of *gens de couleur libres* of African ancestry.

During Reconstruction a brief window of progressive racial reform opened in Louisiana, but this was slammed shut by Bourbon ascendancy after 1877 and the attendant drive to restore the status quo ante bellum. In 1890 the Louisiana legislature required railroads to segregate "Negro" or mixed-race passengers, leading to *Plessy v. Ferguson* in 1896. Miscegenation laws overturned during Reconstruction were reinstated in 1894 and reaffirmed in Act 87 of the 1908 legislative session.[3] The Louisiana Supreme Court debated these laws in the 1910 *State v. Treadaway* ruling on a white man cohabiting with an octoroon woman. The Court ruled in favor of the man and his partner, stating that "There are no negroes who are not persons of color; but there are persons of color who are not negroes."[4] The legislature pondered the court's ruling and, not admitting defeat, passed Act 206 in its 1910 session, amending the antimiscegenation bill to outlaw racial mixing between any white person and any colored or black person.

Though Americans implemented these codes to curtail the freedoms of African Americans, any such law also affected the Houma nation, subsumed as they now were under the general rubric of "non-white." The taint of post-Reconstruction nonwhiteness was particularly dangerous in education, which by its very nature raised fears of race mixing. Since schooling was the route to economic advancement, controlling what people learned and how they learned would likely determine whether the ruling class actually remained the ruling class. Moreover, since education was the domain of youth, and youth was perceived to be particularly susceptible to "free thinking" and the contaminating effects of racial mixing, this area particularly engendered conflict between the Houma and non-Indians.[5]

Terrebonne Parish had emphasized education from the time it was carved from Lafourche Interior. In 1819 the state placed public schools under the direction of parish police juries, administrative bodies that basically served as governing boards.[6] Officials immediately began creating a school system, and by 1851 Terrebonne contained thirteen public schools and a flagship high school in the parish seat of Houma.[7] Even with the establishment of free public schools, however, education was not necessarily open to everyone; not until the late 1920s did Governor Huey Long guarantee both free public schools *and* free textbooks that ensured poor children gained access to affordable high-quality education. Moreover, transportation along bayous and on bad roads was minimal at best. Most schools ranged directly around the parish seat, which meant that Indian communities far down the bayous but without public transport stood at a serious disadvantage.

The first demand for mainstream public education came in September 1916. *Plessy v. Ferguson* had legalized separate but equal schools, which was clearly not the case for Indians along southeastern Louisiana's bayous. Isolated pockets of private schooling were available for some Houma students and public teachers occasionally looked the other way when enrolling Indian students in white schools, but the Supreme Court ruling made no specific provisions for indigenous students. Menard, Dénecé, and Bordeaux had carefully educated tribal children, but their generation was dying out. Just as important, education had been in French previously, and a handful of ambitious Houma men and women knew that a second language was much more than a luxury in a changing world. Rather, English was the language of people steadily gaining control over every aspect of Louisiana society in the hundred years since the Purchase. Many members of the nation felt that public parish systems held the key to their educational future. H.L. Billiot was one such man.

H.L. (sometimes referred to as "N.L." or "Henry") Billiot had attended public school below Montegut with both whites and Indians in the 1890s. A man of property with strong and confident penmanship, Billiot at age thirty-two was comfortable in both Native and Euro-American worlds and attributed much of his success to education. He had moved to lower Bayou Dularge in Terrebonne Parish's tenth ward at age nineteen, and his home's position close to the Gulf offered no educational opportunities. Local schools admitted only white students, and his three sons were getting beyond the age at which he could tutor them. In 1913 he requested that, since his family was of mixed Indian-and-white ancestry, the Terrebonne Parish School Board allow his sons to attend the all-white Falgout Public School that stood about fifteen acres from their home; the board took no action. Just before the start of the 1916 school year Billiot spoke to Terrebonne Parish School Superintendent H.L. Bourgeois, who grudgingly agreed that the children could attend Falgout.[8]

On the morning of September 13, 1916, Madame Celesie Billiot sent Harry (age twelve), Walter (ten) and Paul (eight) to their first day of school. However, just as they were about to enter Falgout, all three boys were stopped by teacher Marie Lejunie, told they could not register at the white school, and sent home. Billiot returned with his sons only to hear the teacher reply that Mr. Bourgeois had changed his mind after several parents had protested about the Indian students, and Bourgeois had given specific orders not to allow nonwhite students to register. Rather than making a scene in front of children, Billiot spoke with Bourgeois and the situation quickly escalated.[9]

As the conversation progressed, Billiot realized that Bourgeois was even more opposed to Indian children attending the Falgout school than the teacher herself. The superintendent curtly informed his visitor that the children would *not* attend the whites-only school because they were not white and a petition had been passed demanding that Indian students be excluded from white schools. The boys could attend the school for African American children or they could go truant. Billiot replied that the school system was required to offer proper facilities for the educable, and he would not send the children to a black school because they weren't black; even if they were, the black school was substandard. Bourgeois countered that if Billiot felt his solution was not good enough, then the court system could decide. Enraged and realizing that the school year would expire before a lawsuit would conclude, Billiot appealed to the 20th Judicial District Court in Houma for a writ of mandamus on September 18, which was granted on September 30. He not only demanded admittance of his children to the white school but also noted that the superintendent's actions had inflicted slander upon his children and extended family to the extent of $1,000.[10]

H.L. Billiot stood as a good choice for a test case on desegregation. A man of property and a respected leader in the Indian community, he enjoyed the esteem of both Indians and whites and interacted freely with the latter. Most important, he was educated enough to understand the rudiments of the legal system and unyielding as a hurricane when he felt he was in the right. He had federal law, Louisiana law, and H.L. Bourgeois against him, and it is a testament that he stood up to those three forces for any length of time. *H.L. Billiot v. Terrebonne Parish School Board et al.* dragged on in starts and stops for months; it was scheduled to begin on October 6, 1916, but finally came in front of the 20th Judicial District Court in Houma on February 3, 1917, a delay that ensured the boys were excluded from school that year. The court record stands as a case study in how a respected leader is publicly humiliated when he refuses to bow to the mores of the dominant society.[11]

In his original statement Billiot testified that he and his family did not qualify as colored "as said word colored is used and understood in the state of Louisiana." He went on to say that he and his children were of mixed ancestry, "descended from the white race and the race of American Indians." Emphasizing his white heritage as much as possible, Billiot claimed the unspecified nation from which he descended "had long since lost their tribal relations." He continued that he himself had attended a school for children of mixed Indian–white backgrounds at Point au Barré, just below Montegut. Billiot stated categorically that he had always eaten with whites, sat on the white side of the courtroom, traveled in the white car on trains, and did not associate with people of African ancestry. His statements were supported by his father, seventy-seven-year-old Severin Billiot. Severin was born on Bayou Little Caillou, fought for the Confederacy at Vicksburg as part of a Terrebonne regiment, and had always enjoyed the privileges of white status.[12]

Severin Billiot's testimony raised many questions for the court. He maintained there was no Indian *or* African ancestry in his or his wife's lineage, though he admitted, "I am what we call in good French 'a bastard,'" and had no knowledge of his reputed father's ancestry other than his coming from Champagne, France. His mother's ancestry didn't match the genealogy he gave, though his knowledge of the southernmost bayou areas where his mother's family lived after supposedly moving from Brittany and Bordeaux was very detailed. Severin Billiot's gaps in knowledge concerning his own family and complete lack of knowledge concerning his wife's parents are almost impossible to believe in an area where people defined themselves through kinship networks. On the other hand, details of Severin's ancestry dovetailed nicely with an Indian mother who had produced a child by a European father and was herself the product of a white-and-Indian union.[13]

The lawyer questioning Severin definitely realized something was suspect, as both the types of questions and their rapidity reflect. The witness testified that his mother could not care for him because of her poverty, and so Etienne Billiot Sr. had adopted him as a foster son and raised him until age twelve. When asked why his son H.L. was so much darker than he if there were no racial mixing in his wife's family, Severin replied that variations in color were not uncommon in families and that two of his grandchildren looked so different one could not tell they came from the same mother.[14]

When the school board presented marriage records stating that at least one of the ancestors of Celesie Frederick, H.L. Billiot's wife, was a person of color, an ancestor named Etienne (King) Billiot Jr. became the focus of the case. King Billiot was both the foster brother of Severin Billiot and the maternal grandfather of Celesie Billiot. Etienne Billiot Sr. had raised Severin Billiot, and the resulting family remembrances were labyrinthine. Terrebonne Parish School Board lawyers maintained that Marianne Erice (very likely Marie Nerisse), the mother of Etienne Billiot Sr., was a negress from San Domingo, though witnesses maintained she was Spanish. Unable to derive specific answers from legal documents and family members but determined to prove there was negro ancestry in Billiot's family, the court called witnesses from communities where Billiot and his ancestors had lived. Men in their seventies and eighties who had known King Billiot testified, and all confirmed his status as a person of color, though they emphasized that he lived his life as a white man and was widely accepted as such before the Civil War. When asked whether they had ever associated with other negroes, witnesses pointed out that they did not view King Billiot as a negro, only as a man of color.[15]

Changing tactics, the school board's attorney attempted to clarify King Billiot's being a person of color, but witnesses hedged in how they defined the term, usually saying that they had interpreted his status as a person of mixed Indian-and-white ancestry. They evaded every question concerning his physical appearance, despite the lawyer's increasing frustration. When asked whether Billiot had kinky hair, a wide nose, or thick lips, they all stated they had never looked that closely despite being friends with him for decades. They admitted that he had a dark complexion but then pointed out that this could have come from any ethnic background and would not be that uncommon for whites. Without exception, they spoke highly of him and his extended kin.[16]

Not receiving a definitive answer from people who had known the family for decades, the court called seventy-five-year-old Felix Theriot, who had taught a young H.L. Billiot in 1897 at Point au Barré. Even calling a former teacher did not answer the question of ethnic status, however:

Q: Were you used to teach colored schools, Mr. Theriot?
A: You mean a negro school? I taught it as a mixed school.
Q: Mixed in what sence [sic], Mr. Theriot?
A: There were different nationalities of blood. That's what I mean by mixed.
Q: What were the nationalities of the ancestors of the children that you taught?
A: They must have been a mixture of white blood or Indian blood.
Q: Mr? [sic] Theriot, in order to fix in the record what you mean by a colored person, I ask you what you would class a child born by a full blooded white man and a full blooded Indian woman?
A: Class him as a colored child.[17]

Theriot avoided further defining a "colored person" and dodged questions at every turn when asked to give information on the Billiot family. Pressed by lawyers to describe the physical appearance of King Billiot and whether he looked African, a defiant Theriot said that he had never really noticed. Further pressed by the lawyers, he curtly replied "I never took his picture." The prevarication and refusal to give a conclusive response continued with witness after witness, and the only definite answer came with the last informant, Mr. Taylor Beattie: "He was not black, but he was a dark colored man ... King Billiot had in those days the reputation of claiming to be and being recognized as being the King or Chief of the Houmas Tribe of Indians that settled in this portion of the State. The Houmas Tribe of Indians are a portion or sub-tribe of the Choctaws and lived on the River and in Lafourche before the Americans settled in the Country. As to whether he was the Chief of them, I know nothing. That was his reputation." This is one of the few precise statements in the entire trial and seems to have answered many of the questions the court had. Unfortunately, Beattie had only met King Billiot once, and that was forty or forty-five years before the trial.[18]

Though many witnesses gave vague statements or outright refused to answer questions, only one definitely perjured himself. Marcel Falgout, seventy-four at the time of the trial, had built the Falgout Public School as a white facility and spearheaded the drive to bar Indian children from attending. Falgout testified that he had not broken bread with Celesie Frederick's family members or visited in their home—two of the most prominent signs of racial equality—though he had once eaten with King Billiot when they went hunting with two other white men. However, Celesie's brother Alcee Frederick later testified that Falgout had both visited his home and eaten there, thus privately betraying the racial code Falgout publicly claimed to uphold.[19]

As for other witnesses, self-preservation could not have been their motivation. Their own racial ancestry was beyond question. They owed H.L. Billiot and his wife nothing and could easily have classified her ancestor as black rather than consistently referring to him as "a man of color." But they did not. Rather, it seems these men closed ranks to protect a man who could no longer defend himself and, by continuation, his great-grandchildren. Even Marcel Falgout declined to say point-blank that King Billiot had been part black. A feisty Felix Theriot refused to betray his former student or be cowed by the lawyer in any way.

Not having determined the Billiot children's ancestry but satisfied they were mixed race on both sides of their family and that their mother's side might have African admixtures, the 20th Judicial District Court ruled for the Terrebonne Parish School Board on March 26, 1917. Admitting a child suspected of African ancestry would have shattered the framework of segregation. Desegregation in turn meant exploding the mechanism on which Louisiana's legal and social systems were in large part predicated, something the court could not permit. The ruling derailed not only the Billiot children's futures but those of hundreds of relatives, as public knowledge that one was related to a negro—or even might be related—was enough to ruin them all during the Jim Crow era.

Stricken, Billiot filed an appeal the same day of the decision. The case made its way to the Louisiana Supreme Court, which in April 1918 ruled that it had no jurisdiction if damages did not exceed $2,000 in value, the amount necessary to take the case to the next level. Determining the children's ages and corresponding lost education until graduation, the court ruled that each child's instruction would not have cost $10 a month, the amount needed to push it to the $2,000 level. Thus, it would not hear the case. At first the Supreme Court recommended the case go to the First Circuit Court of Appeal, then dismissed it entirely on May 27 with a notation that hearing was refused and the case would not go to appeal. *H.L. Billiot v. Terrebonne Parish School Board* was decided, completely decided, and both H.L. Billiot and the Houma nation had lost.[20]

No mention of *H.L. Billiot v. Terrebonne Parish School Board* ever made it to the Terrebonne Parish School Board's minutes, which is not surprising since H.L. Bourgeois kept them. What he did record was the October 1917 reference to Terrebonne Parish paying $120 for an unspecified number of students to attend school in Lafourche Parish for the 1917–18 school year. Lafourche and Terrebonne had reciprocal agreements for students living close to a school on the parish line's other side, but Terrebonne additionally sent Indians to school in Lafourche and paid their tuition, thus maintaining the illusion of no Indian students in the parish. Whether the 1917 transfer was an example of this or not, the transfer of students for political purposes was common.[21]

In the following years several new school petitions went before the Terrebonne Parish School Board. One 1922 request was for twenty-six white children on Bayou Dularge, the same area where H.L. Billiot lived. Bourgeois immediately provided facilities, and Billiot thus watched the erection of a new school his sons could never enter because of the 1917 court ruling. Two years later a group of Indians on Bayou Dularge requested a school for local children. In October of that same year a non-Houma named J.C. Munson appeared before the board and requested the superintendent's reasons for excluding Indian children from the public school system. The board ignored both actions, as it well could given the Louisiana Supreme Court's ruling. Legally speaking, after 1918 there were no Indians in Terrebonne parish. As Superintendent Bourgeois triumphantly noted in his master's thesis, the "so-called Indians" now occupied the legal status of blacks.[22]

H.L. Billiot v. Terrebonne Parish School Board would reverberate through the following decades. Under absolutely no circumstances could the ruling's monetary significance be reduced to a matter of tuition for three boys, as its economic cost would include not only lost tuition, or tuition for scores of Houma youths denied access to quality education, but also lost earnings for several generations. Even more important, potential for oil and gas revenue in coming decades vanished when tribal lands were appropriated. Ambitious people such as H.L. Billiot and his wife were effectively shut out of the educational system. Harry, Walter, and Paul Billiot would have been in the prime of their lives when Houma land was taken and presumably could have protected tribal members if armed with educations. Instead, their lack of English and formal education handicapped them in a shifting economy and devastated the nation when it fought for land, first with trappers and later with oil and gas companies.

In examining why Louisiana's fur industry expanded so rapidly in the early 1900s, context is important. In the latter 1800s and early 1900s the fashion for fur coats exploded and led to attendant overhunting in the Northeast. Seeking new supply areas, furriers shifted their attention to south Louisiana otter and muskrat. Though both animals produce excellent pelts, the latter was particularly valuable given that it could be trimmed and colored to imitate more expensive seal or mink fur. At the same time furriers turned their attention to southern Louisiana, there was an upswing in the region's muskrat population because so many of their predators had been overhunted. Thus, a combination of factors produced a greater need for muskrat skins, a supply shift to the Gulf Coast, and an attendant rapid escalation in prices.[23]

Prices for muskrat pelts rose from eight cents a skin to $3 for the best-quality merchandise, and this potential profit attracted buyers and leaseholders. In 1922–23 prices stood at $2 for a good pelt, and approximately ten million pelts were harvested. Trapping was intense work and required constant maintenance between November 20 and February 1, but a good trapper could bring in 150 pelts of "soft gold" a day and, depending on their quality, reap high profits. In comparison, the Governor of Louisiana made $7,500 a year in the 1920s, about the same amount family units could reap during trapping season with good pelts and a stable price.[24]

The epicenter of the southeastern Louisiana fur trade encompassed long-held Houma territory; though the nation saw an upswing in its economy, they benefited no more than other trappers. Moreover, they lost tribal lands under the onslaught of new arrivals. Many Indians lived on public lands that fur companies bought or leased, such as the extensive parcel purchased from the Atchafalaya Levee District in 1895. Companies then subleased rights to trap muskrat. The Houma thus had to negotiate to trap on land they already occupied but might not own. More important, even in cases where they had squatter's rights after thirty years of occupation, companies required that all tenants sign or make their mark on a contract. By signing the form showing that they subleased lands owned by the company, Houma trappers thus signed away all legal rights to the land. These leases could be easily produced in court at a later time. Moreover, fur companies maintained stores at which tenants sold pelts and bought necessities, and high credit rates ensured that Indians went into debt and were thus forced to sell land to which their legal rights had been stronger than mere occupation.[25] The Houma inability to read English and increasing inability to read French were major factors in these land swindles.[26]

Fraudulent land deals increased with the arrival of the oil and gas industries in the 1930s. Natural gas was discovered in Shreveport in 1870, and in September 1901 wildcatters brought in the Heywood oil well in the state's southwestern quadrant. In 1910 overwater wells began drilling on Caddo Lake. In 1916 drilling began in the Monroe Gas Field and ushered in an era of unprecedented wealth through the state's northeastern section. Newly wealthy oilmen looked around for even richer fields, and their gaze turned to southeastern Louisiana. Preliminary tests revealed the area held the same mineral wealth as other parts of the state, and frenzied competition for land erupted. On December 19, 1925, Terrebonne Chamber of Commerce manager Eugene Dumez took the nom de plume "Telesse Bodouin" and wrote a mock-Cajun-dialect letter to the *Houma Courier* decrying "Yankees" for illegally taking lands from trappers and small farmers that had been in the public domain for over 150 years.[27] Ironically, the most valuable land was that formerly deemed the most useless, where the Indians of Terrebonne Parish and Lafourche Parish were most thickly settled.

Many people saw what was happening as clearly as Dumez but could not stop the relentless flow of speculators.[28] In January 1933 an alarmed New Orleans lawyer named Frederic Querens, who represented several Houma Indian men, sent a letter to the Bureau of Indian Affairs (BIA) informing them of the land loss. The previous year these trappers' lands had been taken from them, after which the new owners placed an injunction to prevent "trespassing." The Indian trappers tried to work out a deal with the new proprietors, who delayed giving a definite answer until the beginning of trapping season, after which they denied entry. In December 1932 the Indian trappers had begun working their old lands despite the injunction but were immediately arrested and sentenced to federal prison. Querens wrote that the Houma's lack of education made them vulnerable and that traditional lands were being stolen at ever-increasing rates: "Can you, and will you please do something through your department for these unfortunate people before it is too late?"[29]

Querens's plea went unheeded. Commissioner Charles J. Rhoads replied that the Houma were only one tribe of many living away from reservations who had never compacted treaties with the United States. "In other words, the Houma Indians have never been regarded as government wards, which, under decisions of the Comptroller General, precludes the expenditure of any funds at our disposal for their benefit." The commissioner forwarded Qurens's letter to the Red Cross, with instruction that any further communications were to take place between the two. The Bureau of Indian Affairs was not to be involved any further.[30]

Land grabs only sped up in the coming years. Given the high profits to be made in the oil industry, hordes of people swept across areas in search of land leases, and some of these people were highly unsavory. Speculators used a variety of methods to take land from individual tribal members, such as researching who had not paid taxes, who had failed to file a deed, and who was susceptible to ongoing harassment by civil authorities. Other people realized there was profit to be made from southeastern Louisiana's Byzantine kinship networks and easygoing attitudes on paperwork, making great use of many Houma's inability to produce a birth certificate. A favorite tactic was to research if there had been a civil marriage ceremony (as opposed to socially or ecclesiastically recognized unions), which the Houma rarely had given their distance from population centers and lifestyle.[31]

This last tactic was especially devastating to the nation. In the early twentieth century Louisiana law was very explicit on rights and privileges afforded married couples and equally explicit on penalties for children of unmarried people. Even during the French and Spanish periods the difference between legitimate children, illegitimate children, and bastards was understood, but these distinctions were reinforced during the American period. As early as 1808, the Code mandated that the state would recognize marriage "in no view other than a civil contract" and that "such marriages are recognized by *law* as are contracted and solemnised according to the rules which *it* prescribes."[32]

These distinctions between types of unions applied directly to many people in southeastern Louisiana. The Houma had long had blessings said by a respected community member when they made public pledges. After 1842, priests such as Menard or Dénecé usually blessed these unions at a later date and made notations in Church archives, and few Houma couples went through the process of filing a formal declaration of marriage at the distant courthouse. It might take days to get there and back, and besides, their union had been recognized by the community after a proper ceremony. Moreover, it had been blessed by a priest as a sacrament and then recorded by him. This common and accepted practice of ecclesiastical and social unions over civil unions extinguished the rights of many Houma to their land.

In addition, Louisiana's Civil Code had many draconian sections referencing other marriage-related issues, particularly forced-heirship laws. These meant that parents could not disinherit children and had to divide all property among their progeny. Though forced heirship protected children against parental whims, it also ensured heirs had to run a gauntlet of substantiating lineal descent, for one was entitled to a share of property only if one were white and successfully proved relationship. Added to this was the desire by some whites to keep their race "pure" by ensuring mixed-race progeny could neither pass for white nor inherit their father's wealth. Stringent laws concerning marriage were avenues to accomplish both goals.[33]

Just as the 1808 Civil Code dictated what types of union were legally acceptable, so too did it prohibit marriages between slaves and free people and further state that "it is the same with respect to the marriages contracted by free white persons to free people of color."[34] Given that *Adelle v. Beauregard* had legally classified Indians as free people of color in 1810, the Civil Code and its later iterations would seem to preclude all unions between Indians and whites and also all unions between Indians and free blacks. However, Louisiana law waffled for the next hundred years on whether Indians could contract legal marriages with Euro-Americans and/or African Americans. The state's legal structure thus harmed the Houma on two levels. Clearly defined designations of Louisiana law made the Houma vulnerable to trappers and oil speculators swarming their lands, but, and just as important, the grey areas between the laws—what could be interpreted based on paperwork (or the lack thereof)—also worked against the nation. These matters would haunt the tribe in the twentieth century when inherited land was taken from them, land that had been passed to children recognized by both the Houma and non-Native communities as Indian.

Robinet v. Verdun's Vendees in 1840, sparked by an exogamous Houma union, illustrates how Louisiana law allowed the taking of property. On April 29, 1829, Euro-American Alexandre Verdun appeared before a Terrebonne Parish judge to make provisions for the children of Marie Gregoire, a "femme sauvage." Verdun and Marie had amassed sizable wealth and wanted to make sure their children were protected economically, especially given Louisiana's law that children of a racially mixed union and of unmarried parents would not inherit their biological father's property. At age forty-three Verdun began dividing and selling land to his children, making provisions without legal acknowledgment of paternity. Since Indian women could not manage estates, he appointed Jean Baptiste Gregoire his executor with the understanding that Gregoire would work closely with Marie. When he and Marie died a few years after he made his will, both had the satisfaction of knowing their children would rightfully inherit their property.[35]

Unfortunately for them, a white heir disagreed. In 1840 Melanie Verdun filed *Robinet v. Verdun's Vendees*, and her lawyer argued that land sales made to Marie Gregoire's children were a transparent attempt to circumvent Louisiana law by "selling" land to bastards who could not inherit their biological father's property. Their argument drew upon the Louisiana Civil Code's sharp distinction between illegitimate or "natural" children acknowledged by their father, who were thus entitled to a fraction of their progenitor's estate, and "bastards" not acknowledged by their father and who were entitled to nothing. Ironically, the law that white heirs used would guarantee Verdun's Houma children land if there were no blood link and exclude them if there were a biological bond. Against the wishes of Indian heirs and in violation of French and Spanish custom, the American court admitted evidence proving these children were the bastard progeny of Alexandre Verdun and "a squaw." They were therefore entitled to absolutely nothing. In this matter the Louisiana Civil Code was both explicit and unforgiving. Interestingly, the Gregoire/Verdun heirs are never referred to in the suit as Indian in ancestry but as colored.[36]

Almost a hundred years separate *Robinet* from the oil-and-gas era, but the same principles applied. Between not legally owning the land they occupied and not being able to inherit land their ancestors did legally own, the Houma were in a vulnerable position when someone wanted their property. As long as the nation stayed in communities far down the bayou and away from desirable lands, they were generally safe. When mineral resources were discovered, however, traditional land became very valuable indeed, and legal proceedings would begin.

When legal precedent did not apply, there were other methods. Unmarried couples could not be dispossessed under the Civil Code, but there was always the possibility of physical coercion, of permanently blocked roads, of marshes and freshwater lakes ruined by canals and wells, and of whole herds of cattle shot. Impersonation was another ploy for speculators. White men saying they were from the government came to homes and requested permission to pursue legal action against land speculators intent on taking Houma land. After serving several cups of strong black coffee and giving a signature, the Indians waved farewell. Several weeks or months later, they received notice that they had signed their land over and must vacate immediately or face eviction by the sheriff.[37]

The Houma looked around them in 1930 and saw the elements by which they defined themselves culturally being taken and new routes of opportunity being closed: loss of land, loss of natural habitat, exclusion from education, and exclusion from a growing economy. This was the single darkest period in the nation's history. The *Shâkti Humma* stood in very real danger of their culture shattering and becoming a nation of beggars, dispossessed and with no way to survive. But it says much about the Houma that their symbol has always been the red crawfish, a tiny creature that raises its pincers in aggression no matter how large the opponent and that will spar indefinitely with an adversary without shifting its gaze. It will conquer or it will die, but it will not admit defeat.

The Houma were no more willing to accept defeat than their symbol. Knowing the school board would ignore further petitions from them, Terrebonne Indians chose another point of attack. Just as they had long ago forged alliances with powerful French and Spanish colonials, they now began enlisting whites to help them, particularly those with influence. Because of Houma appeals and because of the time he spent in Indian communities, Dr. H.P. St. Martin introduced a motion with the Terrebonne Parish School Board in 1930 for Superintendent Bourgeois to assess the needs of Indians below Dulac and provide for them.[38] Though Bourgeois took no action, St. Martin and the Houma had taken their first step in forging a coalition that eventually would mount a combined attack on segregation.

In 1931 Louisiana congressman Numa F. Montet wrote the Bureau of Indian Affairs asking what measures could be taken to bring the Houma under the federal government's jurisdiction given their Native status. Commissioner Rhoads replied that if the agency assumed responsibility for the Houma then it would be required to assume responsibility for all Louisiana Indians. Natives were no worse off than blacks and poor whites in the same area, and to help Indians of Louisiana would handicap them and "turn the clock backward."[39] Correcting the poverty and poor education of Louisiana Natives was the responsibility of Louisiana, and the Houma were definitely not the problem of the BIA, an attitude very much in keeping with the era's assimilation policy.

Under constant assault by a handful of Louisiana state officials and members of the Houma nation, the federal government finally agreed to send a representative to the area. A special commissioner from the Bureau of Indian Affairs named Roy Nash visited the Houma in June 1932. His report made little change. After a visit of five days Nash concluded that the people were mixed French and Indian, but five percent reflected African ancestry. According to the racial codes of the time, that five percent was enough to damn the whole tribe.[40] When Nash's report was filed it included a memo from Assistant Commissioner Daiker that no further action was to be taken.

In March 1933 Dr. Carson Ryan, director of the Office of Education in the BIA, visited Terrebonne Parish but met only with the school board. He wrote in a 1934 letter to David Billiot—who was sending letters to Louisiana Governor O.K. Allen, President Roosevelt, and anyone else he thought could help—that he had visited the town of Houma the previous year and inquired about local Indians, but that Indian education was "entirely a State matter" and, while his office was corresponding with state officials, he would make no promises of assistance.[41]

The dark times of the Houma in the 1930s brightened a bit when anthropologist Frank Speck from the University of Pennsylvania accepted their invitation to visit. Robert Neitzel was supervising excavation work at Marksville, home of the Tunica–Biloxi, and he and Speck regularly exchanged information and sources. Speck asked Neitzel to collect songs, dances, and observations on the Tunica–Biloxi, then came south in 1938 to check the data himself. Once in Louisiana, he decided to accept the Houma's invitation to call upon them.

Intrigued by the landscape and accents of bayou country, Speck visited several communities and recorded aspects of Houma society, not only what remained from earlier generations but also what was changing. In particular, crop cultivation was growing less important with each passing decade. With movement toward the Gulf and corresponding increases in soil salinity, ever-increasing competition for higher levee ground, and trappers and mineral interests acquiring Houma land through any means possible, the nation was sliding inexorably toward a hunter-and-gatherer lifestyle. True, they still supplied oysters and clams to the New Orleans markets—called "harvesting" and viewed as a type of agriculture—but this was a far cry from when they had maintained French settlements during famines. Many Houma he met lived at least part of the year on houseboats and could erect a temporary palmetto dwelling within a day. The nation still ate well but their diet was shifting inexorably toward a seafood base, and they grew fruits and vegetables for personal consumption rather than for sale. Speck theorized that increased mobility was engendering an emphasis on location and that band rather than heritage and clan had begun to determine identity. Speck's conclusion was that tribal culture was indeed changing, but the Houma still survived as an Indian group.[42]

In September 1938, Speck met with Dr. Willard Beatty of the BIA's Education Division, Commissioner of Indian Affairs John Collier, and Louis Nelson of the Department of Education. John Swanton had visited the Houma in April 1907, and in either 1907 or 1908 M. Raymond Harrington had spent time with the nation, but no anthropologist of note had worked with them since then.[43] At Speck's request, Dr. Ruth Underhill was sent to investigate the Houma and found definite traditions of tribal descent. Underhill also had several meetings with Superintendent Bourgeois, and the two strong-willed individuals butted heads immediately. Each thought the other highly unpleasant, and Dr. Underhill noted in a report to the BIA that most of the Houma educational problem came from Bourgeois's obsession with race and that in the future they should deal directly with the state superintendent.[44]

While Speck was advocating for the Houma in the late 1930s, educational opportunities were opening, not through the actions of the BIA or the school boards of Terrebonne Parish or Lafourche Parish but through those of the Methodist Church, South. In 1910 a young woman named Ella K. Hooper had finished her degree in rural education at the Louisiana State Normal School and taken a position at Terrebonne's Cedar Grove School.[45] By 1917 Hooper felt that she was marking time. She and fellow Methodist Laura White traveled into the lower bayou communities to win converts to the Methodist faith but quickly realized that establishing schools was the greatest need of Cajuns and Indians. She asked her younger sister Wilhelmina to teach as a volunteer for two months at Dulac until muskrat season began in November and the school emptied. Wilhelmina stayed almost the rest of her life.[46]

The Hooper sisters and Laura White began working with Houma Indians at precisely the right time for them to make inroads, as some people were growing disenchanted with a Church that was not helping end segregation but seemingly furthering it. The Indians were troubled that they had to sit in a different section of the church and take communion after white neighbors despite being Catholic for several generations. They strongly respected the Church per se, but were troubled by how some priests differentiated based on skin color at the same time they said the Heavenly Father did not.[47] Moreover, they were extremely concerned that when they did listen to Protestants, the priests grew angry and threatened excommunication; in one case a priest refused last rites to an Indian who had expressed interest in the new faith. Several tribal members had already invited a Methodist to visit Dulac in 1917, and they invited him back in 1919 for extended ministrations.[48] The Hooper sisters thus began working with the Houma at exactly the right time, when Methodist schools offered opportunities denied via *H.L. Billiot v. Terrebonne Parish School.*

In October 1919 missionaries purchased the large Gagne home in the parish seat of Houma along with its eighteen acres along the Intracoastal Waterway and created what would become a center of Indian educational activity in Houma: MacDonell Wesley House, a boarding school ministering to all people regardless of race or religion. Houma converts saw the new faith as a route to better education and greater social equality. Moreover, they were still worshipping the same *Bon Dieu*, just in a different tongue.[49] The hurricane of August 26, 1926, only strengthened their opinion as it slammed into southeast Louisiana and killed at least twenty-five people. Communities were devastated, but the Methodists and Baptists quickly gathered resources and helped friends down the bayou. Indians who had never pondered conversion saw white men and women slogging through water as the dreaded Congo snake slid by and thought to themselves that any faith producing such people could not be all bad. Conversion increased markedly after this hurricane.[50]

In 1932 the Methodist Church, South purchased the large overseer's house of a former Dulac plantation fourteen miles below Houma, thereafter managed by Wilhelmina Hooper and two volunteer teachers. The curriculum at Dulac Indian Mission's school was the same as in any state school, and admission was open to all Indians regardless of religious belief. The fledgling school quickly found itself a victim of its own success, as the people H.L. Bourgeois had described as shiftless and uninterested in education flocked to its doors. Teachers scrambled to find seats for all pupils and sort them into manageable groups. This continued for several years, until in 1936 the Methodist Council developed an alternate plan of holding morning classes at Dulac and afternoon extension classes in smaller communities.[51] By 1939 the Dulac school was holding both, teaching sixty children from 7:30 a.m. to 12:30 p.m. and thirty adults from 6:30 p.m. to 8:30 p.m.[52] Even in these small communities, however, schools soon overloaded, and teachers again faced the problem of providing adequate education. Baptist and Catholic churches coordinated with the Methodists and also opened centers, but they soon faced the same dilemma and had to turn pupils away.

Thus, by 1938 a combined force of Houma Indians, anthropologists, religious organizations, and sympathetic citizens had converged. They came together for different reasons but with the same goal: to fight segregation and broadcast the conditions of the Houma nation to a broader public. Dr. Speck and others sympathetic to the Houma encouraged a series of highly romantic news articles. An *Associated Press* dispatch of February 5, 1938, examined at length "A virtually crimeless and extremely clean tribe of Indians living in the Louisiana bayou country . . . The people near Houma, Louisiana, [live] in comfort and simplicity in the vast marshes and cypress swamps in which the white man does not survive, said Dr. Speck. They are contented, peaceable, well-ordered, virtually crimeless, and extremely clean." A defiant Superintendent Bourgeois titled a chapter of his 1938 master's thesis "So-Called Indians" and in it replied, "One wonders upon what source of information this statement was founded. There is no Indian tribe in the parish, nor do the so-called Indians of Terrebonne Parish possess any aura of virtue as F. G. Speck ascribes them."[53]

Due to articles appearing in the national press, the steady stream of tribal members lodging complaints, and the force of its own members lobbying for change, the Terrebonne Parish School Board reluctantly agreed to rectify the situation. On August 20, 1940, Mr. William G. Price made a motion authorizing Bourgeois to provide a school for

Fig. 7. (*top*) Wilhelmina Hooper and students, Dulac Indian Mission School, Terrebonne Parish, ca. 1935. This school had originally been the home of a plantation overseer in Dulac. State Library of Louisiana Historic Photograph Collection.

Fig. 8. (*bottom*) Students, Dulac Indian Mission School, Terrebonne Parish, ca. 1935. State Library of Louisiana Historic Photograph Collection.

"the so-called Indian children living on Lower Point-au-Chien." On September 25, 1941, Reverend Abel Caillouet appeared before the board to request transportation for Indian children in his private school, and three members were appointed to ascertain transportation needs for the parish. Although there is no mention in the minutes of the Terrebonne Parish School Board of a school built or rented, in the roster of teachers confirmed for the 1941–42 school year there is a listing for "Montegut Indian School" included in the roll of white schools; the teacher assigned was Mrs. Valerie Babin.[54]

On November 5 the transportation committee submitted its report, referring to the Indian children exclusively as "so-called Indians." It found that there were 526 children in the group, 345 of whom were enrolled in the six church schools and 26 of whom were attending the parish school.[55]

The question before us is whether or not our board should provide transportation for these so-called Indian children who fall within the purview of the law in this regard. Act 254 of the Legislature of the year 1940 states that a parish school board has authority to provide transportation for children attending any school approved by the State Board of Education and living more than one mile from such a school.

Of the 345 children now registered in these private schools, 97 live at distances in excess of one mile from the school they attend. Where transportation will be provided under the auspices of each private school, our board can consider the advisability of appropriating for this service the sum of $11.36 per child per year, which amount was the average per pupil cost of transportation in our parish during the 1940–41 school year. A total probable cost of $1,101.92 is involved here if all private schools should accept this aid from the board.[56]

The transportation committee finished its letter with a comment revealing a keen understanding of broader racial issues and that making provisions for Houma children would open the gates to African American children as well: "A good number of Negro children, living more than a mile from the school they attend, fall in the category of the so-called Indian children under discussion. If these, as a matter of fairness, are included in an enlarged transportation program, the board will find it necessary to increase its revenues for this addition to its budget of expenditures."[57]

School board members voted to transport Indian children more than a mile from their school but, if they thought these measures would mollify the Houma or end educational tensions, they were very much mistaken. The nation continued to pursue educational facilities, and the director of Indian education for the Bureau of Indian Affairs also noted irregularities. In 1942 Willard W. Beatty found amenities provided for Indian children extremely deficient and in direct violation of educational decrees. Terrebonne provided one Indian school at Montegut with twenty-three students, and Lafourche provided one Indian school at Golden Meadow, whereas the Catholic, Baptist and Methodist churches enrolled 150 other Indians in private schools. In the director's opinion, every child in Louisiana was entitled to public education, and if parishes insisted on operating within a segregated system while Houma students walked three to four miles or piroqued four to seven miles simply to attend school, they should follow legal standards and provide separate but equal facilities as demanded by *Plessy v. Ferguson*. Moreover, parishes received $18.16 in state funding for every educable Indian child, so Lafourche and Terrebonne were required to provide facilities unless they wanted to return the money.[58]

After 1945 religious organizations and Houma leaders were joined by another vocal group: tribal men who had fought in WWII and acquired an education through military service. Most Houma Indian men were sent to France, where their fluent language skills proved extremely valuable. Immersed into a culture foreign to most Americans, the Houma felt that they had come home in many ways and realized how valuable they were as a bridge between Europeans and Americans. Moreover, military service also offered these men the education denied them in their youth.[59] Yielding under continued attack, the Terrebonne Parish School Board agreed to build a school specifically for Indians but with the stipulation that Methodists run it. The Dulac Indian School was completed accordingly in the summer of 1953, but it only went to the eighth grade.

After that, students had to transfer out of Terrebonne to gain a high school diploma or they could take a general equivalency degree (GED).[60]

Some students did acquire a GED, but quite a few managed to pursue schooling out of state.[61] Close-knit Indian families were committed to their children's education but leery of sending multiple offspring to distant high schools. In response, some parents did what many Indians considered unthinkable: they left traditional communities and moved to the New Orleans area to pass for white and place their children in public schools. Some who relocated were absorbed completely into the city's population, but those who moved to less densely populated Jefferson Parish and Plaquemines Parish maintained family ties, pursued shrimping and trapping economies, and gained good public educations for their children. Houma arrivals covered their ethnic tracks well, but some Indians estimate as many as two thousand relocated to Westwego, Marrero, and other communities along the Mississippi.[62]

The Terrebonne Parish School Board had made it clear that it would be only too happy to supply books and school equipment if religious organizations agreed to run Indian schools, thereby satisfying state and federal requirements but not publicly acknowledging Indian demands. Methodist administrators realized that if they enabled such political maneuvers desegregation would never take place, particularly as they had recently entered into an agreement to administer the "public" school at Dulac. Instead, they chose to force the parish's hand. The MacDonell–Dulac Board closed MacDonell Mission School after the 1953 school term and refused to rent the building to the parish. Moreover, they gave the Terrebonne board warning that the Methodist school at Dulac Indian Mission would close after the spring 1954 term, so the parish could not send students there.[63]

The actions of the MacDonell–Dulac Board might have swayed the Terrebonne Parish School Board, but far more imperative was the May 17, 1954 federal ruling in *Brown v. Board of Education*. In June 1954 the Terrebonne Parish School Board decided to integrate Indian children into white schools, starting at the elementary level. That plan collapsed on September 7, when three fathers of white children appeared before the board and voiced extreme displeasure that Indian students had been registered at the Dularge School. Unless these children were removed immediately, white families would withdraw their children en masse. The school board thus found itself in a very delicate situation. If they maintained segregation they would not only be in violation of federal ruling but moving backward, anathema to a parish that had always prided itself on its progressive school system. On the other hand, if all the white parents withdrew their children from schools there would still be de facto segregation, but with attendant threats of violence and rebellion. The board compromised by withdrawing Indian children from the Dularge school but making sure they had reliable bus transportation to the public Dulac Indian School.[64]

The Terrebonne Parish School Board expanded its Dulac Indian School when the Methodists pulled out of education, but Dulac still only went to the eighth grade in 1957, when the U.S. Supreme Court ordered schools to integrate with all deliberate speed. The board strongly debated the merits of integration but instead chose to maintain the tripartite system. In September 1961 the board selected the preexisting Daigleville School and created a high school specifically for Indians, Daigleville High; the first graduating class in 1962 had five students. That the school board had finally created a high school for Houma students mollified no one in the Indian community. The situation came to a head in March 1963 with *Naquin v. Terrebonne Parish School Board.*[65]

At the beginning of school years 1961 and 1962 Indian parents had engaged in civil disobedience by attempting to register their children at white schools, only to have students turned away. In spring 1963 they took a different path, and a group of nineteen Houma Indian parents filed suit on behalf of their fifty-six children. On August 18, 1963, the United States District Court, Eastern District, New Orleans Division ruled that Indian students had to be admitted to formerly white schools in accordance with federal mandate and that every white and Indian child in the eleventh or twelfth grade had the option to attend the nearest formerly white or Indian school that year. Fall 1963 thus marked the first integrated class in Terrebonne Parish. The judge's ruling also stipulated that the Terrebonne Parish School Board was required to submit a plan for orderly school integration of all other grades on or before August 1, 1964.[66]

On August 13, 1964, the United States District Court read the integration plan proposed by the Terrebonne Parish School Board, made minor amendments, then approved it with the understanding that all changes would be incorporated by September 1965. The legal struggle that began in 1917 with *H.L. Billiot v. Terrebonne Parish School Board* had finally come to fruition, and Indians of Terrebonne Parish now had legal access to quality education that opened the door not only to an accredited high-school diploma but also a college degree.[67]

Legality was one thing, but enforcing court rulings was another matter. In one of the many ironies of Houma history, proponents of integration had the support of a man from whom they would never have expected it: H.L. Bourgeois Jr. On June 17, 1955 H.L. Bourgeois Sr. passed away ten days before his retirement. In December 1962 his son was elected to the Terrebonne Parish School Board, not as superintendent but as a member. A banker by profession, Henry fused education, politics, and a keen business sense, drawing upon all three to further the school board's goals. Well known and respected in the conservative banking community, Bourgeois was the son of a man opposed to integration for decades, and both whites and Indians thought he was a known entity. H.L. Bourgeois Jr. would surely follow the same path as his father.

Both groups would be very surprised. White parents were the most problematic for Bourgeois, but most left his office uneasily calm after he explained that integration was a federal ruling and he had no intention of seeing Terrebonne become another Central High. Others were horrified and enraged when they heard Bourgeois say that he and other school board members would not defy federal mandate and court rulings. In an ironic reversal of the 1916 conversation between his father and H.L. Billiot, Bourgeois informed white parents curtly that the matter was already settled, and they were free to pursue legal means if they chose, but Indian students would integrate. Many such discussions ended with his escorting infuriated parents from his office or slamming the phone down and telling his secretary to hold calls from that person.[68]

Just as Bourgeois worked to make the transition as smooth as possible for students, Houma Indian leaders marshaled their resources. Tom Dion—an activist who later became a major tribal organizer—recruited a handful of students to integrate Terrebonne public schools in fall 1963, and they were followed by larger numbers of Indians in fall 1965. Dion sought students with the highest grades, those most dedicated to their studies, and the most motivated. Detractors of the Houma had traditionally labeled them lazy, sexually immoral, and unintelligent, the sort of people on whom an education would be wasted, and the first Indian students to integrate schools were handpicked specifically because they were the opposite of this stereotype. Pupils attended schools based on proximity, and the majority of Indian students went to South Terrebonne High in Bourg, a little farther than halfway between Indian settlements and the town of Houma.

Public discourse concerning integration was quite civil, but its cordial surface only masked underlying tensions. The Houma had traditionally been extremely sensitive to unflattering remarks or other signs of disdain and usually withdrew from signs of disrespect. There were many such signs in the first months and years of integration. Former students recall that teachers invariably were not unkind, but Indians often felt they were not wanted. One student who had not missed a day of school in ten years was absent for a week due to the mumps, then used her absence as an excuse to permanently leave a school in which she felt out of place. Though violence against female students did not occur, male Indian students were sometimes assaulted by other males—the sons of Tom Dion seem to have been particular targets—and many chose to drop out of school rather than fight every day. Aside from students who were made to feel unwanted, some Indian students were simply not prepared by their previous schooling and quickly floundered.[69]

Other students stayed in high school and exemplified the maxim that dripping water eventually hollows stone, the first several graduating in the spring of 1965. One particularly dark male student was harassed mercilessly on an hourly basis. When a teacher temporarily shielding him from bullying questioned how he could stand such treatment, the young man replied that he had a right to be there and nothing was going to stop him. Indeed, he graduated from South Terrebonne toward the head of his class. Another particularly successful student was Rita Duthu, widely recognized as an exemplary pupil and recruited by teachers to tutor both Indian and white students in algebra. She graduated college, married one of Tom Dion's sons, completed graduate training, and sent her two children to college.[70]

What swiftly ensued in the wake of *Naquin v. Terrebonne Parish School Board* was what racial conservatives had feared for decades. The

Houma entering formerly white schools was the first chink in the wall of segregation, and integration of Indian students was shortly followed by a lawsuit on behalf of African American students. In May 1965 noted Louisiana civil-rights attorney A. P. Tureaud reminded the school board that by law African American children also had to be admitted to white public schools. On June 3, 1965, *Doris Redman et al. v. Terrebonne Parish School Board and C.C. Miller, Superintendent* was filed in order to force black integration, and on April 28, 1966, United States District Court Judge E. Gordon West signed the desegregation order. By fall of 1966 young members of the Houma nation had joined with African Americans and European Americans to form one student body, and present-day school board members maintain Terrebonne was the first system in Louisiana to fully integrate.[71]

In 1973 the Title IV-A Program, the Indian Elementary and Secondary School Assistance Act, began in Jefferson Parish and spread to Lafourche Parish and Terrebonne Parish in 1974, supporting education, health care and cultural enrichment programs. By 2007 the Terrebonne Indian Education Program aided approximately two thousand students, with eleven tutors servicing eight schools. Lafourche had two tutors aiding seven hundred students, a cultural resource specialist, and a data resource specialist. Both Terrebonne and Lafourche had summer camps where Indian students learned both French and Muskhogean words. The number of Houma students completing high school and finishing college had increased dramatically and showed every sign of continuing. Within a few decades the Houma had gone from a nation struggling to produce high school graduates to one producing lawyers, dentists, businesspeople, schoolteachers, engineers, and college professors.[72]

The Houma struggle for education began with their attempted ethnic cleansing in the 1800s and continued with *H.L. Billiot v. Terrebonne Parish School Board*. Lack of access to education crippled the nation in many ways, but it manifested itself most horribly in their inability to defend tribal lands against an onslaught of fur and oil speculators, a theft only aided by the Louisiana legal system. By the 1930s the nation was in very real danger of losing not only its land but also its culture and history. Only their faith in themselves and ability to adapt propelled them forward, but in the following decades Houma leaders, Methodist teachers, concerned citizens, and returning veterans joined forces to first garner education for tribal youths and then compel parish school boards to integrate. It gives some idea of the attitudes against which the nation labored that even as the Terrebonne Parish School Board was ordered to integrate, it continued to refer to the Houma as "so-called Indians" and "a group known as Indians."[73]

Houma integration did not have a perfect ending, nor did the nation expect there to be one.[74] Still, events after 1963 have produced a sense of hope and shared purpose. Though Native American administrators, teachers, and interested parents have made a huge difference, credit is also due to non-Indians. Whereas only a few decades ago the Terrebonne Parish School Board refused to admit Native Americans even existed in the parish, modern administrators and teachers readily discuss the needs and goals of Houma students. Whereas 1933 Terrebonne school board members convinced a Department of the Interior visitor that "so-called" Indians were not his problem, their modern counterparts willingly direct researchers to both Indians and African Americans involved in desegregation and grant free access to school board records. Put simply, there has been a sea change in attitude. When asked why, administrators and teachers explain that holding back any group holds back the whole of society and that it is neither their job nor their desire to maintain mistakes of the past. These are not perfect school systems, but they convey opportunities for young people to reach their potential without fear of being turned away because of their skin color or tribal status. This is what H.L. Billiot wanted so desperately for his sons, and thus his is the final victory.[75]

6

A Paper Genocide

The Fight for Recognition

Challenges have come in many forms for the Houma nation, and with each adaptation their world has expanded or contracted accordingly. Forging political alliances with the French moved them onto an expanded stage, but they saw their position shrink after Spanish arrival and then plummet dramatically in the latter 1700s. By 1900 the Houma world had shrunk to the bayous and marshes of southeastern Louisiana, only to expand again with H.L. Billiot's lawsuit. In the 1960s their political landscape broadened further, as the nation forged alliances with other tribal and nontribal organizations and eventually completed the desegregation effort Billiot had started. Their landscape grew even more beginning in the 1970s, as they applied for federal recognition.

Their bid for recognition made many realize how the Houma had been removed from the historical landscape of southeastern Louisiana and the challenges facing them. The preliminary ruling by the Bureau of Indian Affairs (BIA) that the Houma would not garner federal acknowledgment fractured the nation and created several breakaway groups seeking recognition on their own. The Houma maintained that the BIA had reached its decision under pressure from oil companies, an opinion reinforced by a controversial 2001 *Ethnohistory* article arguing that the nation was extinct.[1]

Throughout their history the Houma had maintained their sense of themselves as a nation even as they interacted freely with other Indian groups, either through alliances or through war. In this sense they were not unique among nations, and in the mid-twentieth century many groups pursued self-determination by coming together via increasingly pan-Indian movements. As one example, in 1944 delegates from diverse tribes came together to form the National Congress of American Indians (NCAI) in Denver. Their goals were to fight termination and assimilation but also to better the general living conditions of Native groups.

In 1961 a Houma elder named Frank Naquin heard about the upcoming Chicago meeting of the NCAI and saw an opportunity to form connections with broader tribal communities. He contacted several young Houma about attending, then started a harried fundraising drive. Unable to gather all the needed money, Naquin mortgaged his home to pay the transportation and housing costs for two young delegates.[2] Helen Gindrat was born in Golden Meadow but raised in New Orleans after the age of ten, while Helen Terrebonne's family was actively involved in several bayou communities.[3] Both women were highly intelligent, driven, and had garnered hard-won educations.

The June 13 to June 20 Chicago conference was a revelation to Gindrat and Terrebonne. The young women had never seen so many Indians together in one place: 450 delegates representing ninety tribes. Participants spoke differently from each other, looked different, and came from different cultural backgrounds, yet all were united by a common sense of purpose. Gindrat was especially moved by the NCAI declaration that it respected federally unacknowledged tribes as much as those already acknowledged, but that full support would be given tribes choosing to pursue recognition.[4]

Helen Gindrat and Helen Terrebonne returned to Louisiana with renewed purpose, realizing how important it was that the nation create a formal organization structure. They and Frank Naquin knew they had several advantages, foremost being that although they certainly identified strongly with localized family groups and were growing to identify with individual settlements, the nation had not abandoned its extensive kinship systems. On the contrary, the nation had long reinforced networks through holidays, family events, meetings during trapping season, and large-scale communal fishing along coastal sandbars after season's end. Upon meeting someone from a different settlement, most Houma immediately determined family relations not only for heritage but also for self-protection; due to previous exploitation, many Houma had developed a great wariness of outsiders and relied only on those they knew they could trust, particularly family members.[5]

Moreover, for several decades new oil and fishing economies that seemingly threatened to shatter long-established band networks by emphasizing a nuclear-family scenario had actually done the opposite. Oil companies were reluctant to hire Houma unless close family members vouched for them. Likewise, insurance companies demanded that fishing boats contain only immediate family members if coverage were to remain affordable.[6] In response, many men kept each other abreast of job opportunities, vouching for relatives who then vouched for others, thus replicating family networks in the new industries. Similarly, female extended family members helped each other concerning jobs in the canneries, thus also replicating kinship networks. Far from destroying traditional family and political networks, new industry reinforced them.

Shortly after the Houma began forging pan-Indian bonds, other members of the nation began organizing on a state level. In 1970 Thomas Dion of Dulac attended a Louisiana Indians meeting in Baton Rouge; integration into Terrebonne public schools had been a group effort, but Dion stood as one of its spearheads, and he spoke at length during planning sessions. Out of this meeting came the establishment of the Louisiana Office of Indian Affairs and the Louisiana Intertribal Council. The Houma and other Louisiana Intertribal Council tribes pressured governor Edwin Edwards to recognize native peoples, and in 1972 he established the Governor's Commission on Indian Affairs. Helen Gindrat continued to reach across tribal boundaries after she became State Commissioner of Indian Affairs in 1980.[7]

Even as they urged Governor Edwards to include native peoples in his vision of a new Louisiana and forged bonds with other Indian nations, the Houma decided to formally reconfigure along a more Eurocentric political model. In 1972 Frank Naquin, Helen Gindrat, and a handful of others organized the Houma Tribe, and the governing board chose adult education as its focus. In 1974 western Houma along Bayou Grand Caillou felt that economic development should be the primary goal of the nation and left to form the Houma Alliance. The two organizations remained on extremely good terms, and by 1978 the Houma Tribe and Houma Alliance leaders decided the two should merge again. Separate organizations would only encourage fracturing, and leaders were also concerned that if they did not present a united front again, the political results would be disastrous. Later events would show their fears to be very prescient.[8]

The Houma Alliance and Houma Tribe merged to form the United Houma Nation, Inc. (UHN) on June 1, 1979, with Kirby Verret (Terrebonne Parish) as chairperson and Helen Gindrat (Lafourche Parish) as vice chairperson. After merger the UHN created a tribal constitution that established guidelines for tribal membership via several criteria, but weighted toward tracing ancestry to a tribal progenitor; a tribal government comprising a chairperson, vice chairperson, secretary, treasurer, and parliamentarian, for a total of fourteen council members elected on staggered two-year terms; and five voting districts. Settlements were extremely concerned about unequal representation but finally agreed to determine council seats by the population of each parish containing Houma communities. Terrebonne received five seats, Lafourche and Jefferson received three seats each, St. Mary received two, and St. Bernard Parish received two.[9]

United Houma Nation meetings were often contentious and very much in the tradition of people following leaders based on force of personality. Still, the Houma consistently pulled together in times of crisis just as they had in the past, and they joined forces to lobby for state recognition. Their efforts bore fruit when Louisiana formally recognized the United Houma Nation in the late 1970s.

While state recognition was gratifying, tribes recognized by the state of Louisiana enjoyed few economic benefits. Moreover, state acknowledgment would not necessarily lead to federal recognition: the process by which the Bureau of Indian Affairs (BIA) admits a unit of Native Americans to a small set of groups it judges to be true tribes. Acknowledgment functions much the same way as for a foreign nation, in that the United States' recognition of another country imparts a stamp of authenticity and opens a number of economic, political, and social opportunities.[10]

In the mid-1970s the Houma invited Janel Curry and Greg Bowman into their community to conduct research for federal recognition. Curry and Bowman were tough-minded investigators who quickly realized they had waded into a historical morass. Accounts of the Houma were few, rarely up to academic standards, and usually said more about their writers than the Indians they described. Sources in French and Spanish were extremely difficult to read and often contradictory. Most "primary" accounts were actually based on earlier initial or secondary accounts, and many original sources were grossly inaccurate.

Many Houma volunteers, just one or two generations from illiteracy, now waded through colonial, territorial, and early state documents that had been incomprehensible to previous anthropologists and government officials. To their dismay, they realized how much tribal fabric was missing. There was nothing about matrilineal kinship patterns, nothing about the Houma who fought in the Natchez War, the American Revolution, and the War of 1812, despite elders hearing these stories when they were children. Tribal genealogists frantically gathered records of grandparents, aunts and uncles as well as second, third, and fourth cousins, many of whom had the same first and last names, street addresses, and villages.

To further complicate matters, while many older Houma had remarkable memories that stretched back generations, they often could not verify those memories via written information. Many who could read family records or had records read to them realized for the first time that birth certificates listed siblings with the same parents as black, white, or Indian, depending on who had been recording vital records that day, and that entire generations of ancestors living down bayous had seemingly never existed. Oral evidence supplied the missing links, but researchers informed Houma elders that BIA officials would only put their faith in formal, written records. By December 1985 researchers had fashioned some order out of chaos, and the United Houma Nation tendered paperwork to the BIA for federal recognition. Submitted records would eventually run to over seventeen feet.

Slowly but increasingly, the UHN had come to sense something was very wrong. Their history made the Houma exquisitely sensitive to personal and cultural slights, and they grew uneasy with the Branch of Acknowledgment and Recognition (BAR) representative's tone of voice when asking questions and the representative's reaction when tribal elders spoke only French. They also felt that the BAR looked at situations and saw main points but missed the underlying meanings tying main points together. For their part, the BAR felt the Houma approached the recognition process with suspicion and defensiveness, and difficulties inherent in any recognition bid were heightened by the UHN's size—8,500 in 1985, eventually swelling to over 17,000 with increased membership drives. More important, the BAR felt the Houma had not exercised due diligence in their original application and left far too many deficiencies. The BAR requested that genealogists with French-language skills determine the exact meaning of "free people of color" and "sauvage" in the context of early Louisiana history and told the Houma they would need additional information to bridge gaps in their original application.[11]

Both the Houma and the BAR grew frustrated with each other, and what might have been a collaborative effort quickly devolved. In 1989 Helen Gindrat voiced her opinion to a Senate Select Committee that the BAR was on a "fishing expedition" and that the UHN's extremely limited financial resources were being decimated by repeated and extraneous information requests. Kirby Verret publicly stated to newspapers and officials that the BIA had requested "minutia that is nearly impossible to come by" and that previous records consisted of accounts written by non-Indians who either had no interest in the Houma or were actively engaged in proving the nonexistence of the tribe.[12]

By 1990 the UHN had grown disillusioned with the recognition process. Years of continuously submitting new documents was bad enough, but the group had disturbing concerns that oil and gas interests might be seeking to derail recognition, lest the nation be in a position to reclaim lost acreage. If these concerns were true, the Houma faced a combined force of the Bureau of Indian Affairs and one of the most powerful lobbying interests in America. Obviously, this would doom the nation, but UHN leaders shifted their focus; knowing that they could also pursue recognition through the courts or U.S. Senate, they pursued the latter option. Kirby Verret persuaded Louisiana's Democratic U.S. senator J. Bennett Johnston to speak before the Senate. Johnston joined interests with Democratic senator John Breaux and Republican representative Billy Tauzin; the latter was elected from the Houma area. With the overwhelming support of both southeastern Louisiana Indians and non-Indians, Johnston introduced legislation on April 5, 1990, to extend federal recognition to the UHN.

On August 7, 1990, the Select Committee on Indian Affairs reviewed testimony and written evidence. Senator Johnston spoke first and gave a history of the nation, an accurate account of Houma migrations and their previous dealings with French, Spanish, and American officials. Johnston was followed by the three representatives from the BAR: Deputy to the Assistant Secretary of Indian Affairs Ronal D. Eden, genealogist Lynn McMillion, and assistant solicitor Scott Keep. Eden took the lead and immediately stated BIA opposition to Houma recognition through the Senate. For the next few minutes, he and McMillion explained that the recognition process ordinarily took about eighteen months and he could say without fear of contradiction that Houma recognition would be decided by May 1992.[13]

The federal representatives also revealed something the UHN had not heard before: the BAR had not started researching the nation's history. Rather, they would contract the research to an outside firm and only verify information given to them.[14] Kirby Verret stated his unhappiness with outside reviewers unfamiliar with Gulf Coast complexities writing the nation's history. In his opinion, the three points hindering the nation in their federal recognition bid were their lack of a formal treaty, their extreme isolation after 1800, and state-segregation and federal-assimilation policies. Only a person well versed in the area's Byzantine history and culture could accurately grasp such nuances.[15]

The final person who spoke was Dr. Jack Campisi, who was working with the UHN to conduct further research. He explained that his people had spent over ten thousand dollars just on an ethnological study for the BIA and that the recognition process placed an almost overwhelming burden on the nation. He argued that the Houma had traditionally shared a common language and history, and that waterways facilitated "an enormous amount of intermarriage between the seven settlement areas. Our research indicated that, while each settlement area had heads of households, those heads of households were related to each other and they met each other, sometimes on a weekly or bi-weekly basis. There was, in a word, an informal council operating by the heads of these settlements."[16]

The Select Committee on Indian Affairs decided to leave the matter to federal officials in light of the fact that, as the BAR assured them, the case would be completely resolved by May 1992. In December 1994 Branch of Acknowledgment and Recognition officials finally issued an initial decision on federal recognition. Though the ruling was technically "preliminary," in practice it served as final judgment unless radical information was uncovered. After eight years of research by both the UHN and BAR and many dealings with the federal agency, the nation knew that "Proposed Finding Against Federal Acknowledgement of the United Houma Nation, Inc." was, in effect, the final ruling.

The BAR ruled that based on its own research the nation would not be federally recognized because of three major deficiencies. In their opinion, the UHN had successfully satisfied criterion (a), (d), (f), and (g) but not (b), (c), and (e).[17] Put another way, the Houma had successfully demonstrated their identification as an American Indian entity since 1900, provided a copy of their governing document and its membership criteria, established that its members were not part of a previously acknowledged tribe, and demonstrated that the UHN had never been terminated. Neither material on the historical Houma of the French and Spanish colonial eras nor establishing their identity as an Indian nation since 1900 was a problem.

The dilemma came when the UHN bridged gaps between the colonial and modern eras. BAR denial was predicated on the Houma inability to prove that (b) the petitioning group had existed as a community from 1699 to the present, (c) the petitioner had maintained political authority over its members since 1699, and (e) the petitioner's members descended from a single historical tribe or from combined historical tribes that had functioned as a single unit. In short, the team's preliminary ruling stated that the modern United Houma Nation, Inc. could not establish connections with the historical Houma recorded in French and Spanish documents.

The Branch of Acknowledgment and Research used a variety of sources and interpretations to reach their decision, but there were two vital issues upon which all arguments hinged. The first was whether the Houma actually migrated down Bayou Lafourche. The second was whether John Swanton had erroneously created an Indian nation called the "Houma" from people who bore no relationship to the historical tribe. The research team argued that the historical Houma had not migrated south but rather had moved northwest and disappeared from the historical record. Likewise, the research team also argued that Swanton had actually created a fictitious tribe on his expedition and convinced a hodgepodge of ethnic mixtures living down the bayous that they were the historical Houma.

That the Houma claimed land along a Bayou Bœuf in the early 1800s was something both the BAR and UHN agreed upon, but they diverged in their opinion of which Bayou Bœuf.

<u>The Early Federal Period Land Claim *By* the "Homas Tribe of Indians" Was Not Located in the Lower Bayous</u>. At some time between 1803 and 1817, a claim was filed by "The Homas Tribe of Indians" to twelve sections of land "on bayou Boeuf, or Black bayou." This claim for land near Natchitoches, in the general Red River area where others of the "petites nations" had established themselves by the time of the American purchase of Louisiana, was denied by the General Land Office in 1817, under the Act of February 27, 1813, on the ground that it did not fall within provisions of the existing laws. It indicates, however, that as of the January, 1817 date of the report to the General Land office in which the claim was included (ASP 1834c, 3:254; ASP 1834c, 3:265, No. 247), Houma Indians apparently were seeking to claim lands in north central Louisiana (ASP, 1834a, 1:349, No. 164). This indicates that the direction of movement of the historical Houma tribe, when it left the Mississippi River parishes, had not been south but rather northwest. One writer has maintained that the denial of this claim violated the Louisiana Purchase Treaty (Curry 1979a, 17).[18]

The BAR interpretation of the Houma claim on Bayou Bœuf was contrary to Louisiana history, geography, and settlement patterns. Louisiana contains several Bayou Bœufs besides that in its southeast, with one about fifty miles from Natchitoches in the northwestern section of Louisiana and another in the state's northeastern quadrant (where there is also another Bayou Lafourche). Louisiana also contains several Bayou Blacks, but the only waterway bearing both names flows close to Houma in the state's southeast quadrant.[19] There is absolutely no indication in the *American State Papers* that this particular Bayou Bœuf/ Black flowed near Natchitoches. On the contrary, passages before and after the Houma claim verify that the geographic area was southeastern rather than northwestern Louisiana. Moreover, hundreds of Acadian family names and other surnames long associated with "the country of

La Fourche" rather than Red River country both precede and follow the claim. In rare instances where land claims outside this immediate area were addressed, they were specifically noted.[20] The Bureau interpretation revealed, at the very least, a shocking lack of familiarity with the geography, culture, demographics, history and genealogies of Terrebonne and Lafourche parishes, even though the BAR claimed to have conducted extensive research in those very areas.[21]

Moreover, the BAR interpretation of a northwestern Houma migration was in direct contradiction to the Janel Curry article cited to validate it. Curry was one of the main researchers arguing that the Houma had relocated southeast to Terrebonne and Lafourche, and she maintained her position in subsequent academic articles and research projects. Indeed, she maintained that argument in the cited article.[22] At no point did she make any reference to a northwestern migration, central Louisiana, northwestern Louisiana, Natchitoches, or Alexandria. Curry did indeed write that the United States' refusal to recognize the Houma claim on Bayou Bœuf violated the Louisiana Purchase, but the passages before and after her statement, the rest of the article, and the absolute consistency in everything else she ever wrote about the Houma make it clear that she referred to the Bayou Bœuf approximately twenty miles from Montegut rather than the one several hundred miles northwest.

In addition, citations in the Bayou Bœuf passage give the misleading impression of multilayered support for BAR interpretation. *American State Papers* "3:254" is simply the front page for the claims section of the Eastern District of Louisiana, and "No. 247" is the numerical heading for that section. The reference "3:265" is the page on which the Houma attempt to claim their land along Bayou Boeuf, and "No. 625" their subsection number. Continuing, "1:349, No. 164" is not actually the first volume of the *American State Papers, Land Claims,* as one would expect given BAR citation method and bibliography. Rather, one must refer to the *American State Papers, Class 10: Miscellaneous,* then locate "No. 164."[23]

Far more disturbing than a confusing citation is what one reads. "No. 164" is a "Description of Louisiana" communicated to Congress by Thomas Jefferson on November 14, 1803, and page 349 contains the passage BAR researchers cited for the Houma's supposed move north: "On the eastern back of the Mississippi, about twenty-five leagues above New

Orleans, are the remains of the nation of Houmas, or red men, which do not exceed sixty persons. There are no other Indians settled on the river, either in Louisiana or West Florida, though they are at times frequented by parties of wandering Choctaws." Twenty-five leagues above New Orleans meant only that some Houma were still living in their Ascension home. The primary document does not preclude that some Houma migrated down Lafourche and in no way indicates that they had relocated to the Natchitoches area by 1803. Ironically, "Description of Louisiana" was used to track Houma movements in *Indian Tribes of the Lower Mississippi Valley and the Adjacent Coast of the Gulf of Mexico* by John Swanton, an ethnologist the BAR later claimed to debunk because of his weak evidence.[24]

The migration passage was a crux of the BAR's proposed finding but not the only in which it dismissed evidence that challenged its ruling. Certainly, there were major gaps in UHN documentation, but the Branch research team rejected strong existing data and instead drew a conclusion in direct contradiction to topography, demography, waterway history, oral history, federal records and previous scholarly research. It did so without any indication there might be an alternative explanation and with the false appearance of multiple lines of evidence converging to support its opinion, even though the cited sources actually contradicted its finding. And this is only one example taken from the preliminary ruling.[25]

The BAR confronted a larger obstacle in challenging John Swanton, given that he was a giant of Southeastern anthropology and thus would be familiar to experts in a way Louisiana culture and history might not. John Reed Swanton visited the Houma on several occasions, first in April 1907. His research indicated that UHN ancestors relocated from Ascension down Bayou Lafourche and absorbed smaller bands of Natives, Euro-Americans and African Americans, though "Houma was always the dominating element." Most important, he recorded that his informants preferred to be called "Indian" to separate themselves from nearby blacks and whites in Jim Crow Louisiana, but their actual name was "Houma," or "Hômas." His discussions with Indians about their histories and recording of words from elderly women speaking the Houma language reinforced his statements.[26] He voiced his theories in three separate works that remain classics in the field: *The Indians of the Southeast-*

ern United States, *The Indian Tribes of North America*, and *Indian Tribes of the Lower Mississippi Valley and the Adjacent Coast of the Coast of Mexico.*

Swanton's approach certainly was a product of its time, with attendant flaws. He displayed little interest in remnant bands and viewed "ideal" aboriginal culture as precontact. He did not travel to Seville or Paris even though many area-specific documents were accessible only in those cities, and he made faint references to sources not in English. His field research was brief, and he did not visit several Houma communities. Since he spoke Muskhogean dialects but not French, he relied on Bob Verret as both guide and translator, thus missing nuances between Houma and non-Houma French or dialects between Indian villages.[27] And yet, however much later scholars disagreed with his personal approach, Swanton's work and personality are still recognized as painstaking and impervious to outside pressure.

The BAR explained away Swanton's findings, and with it the findings of later anthropologists following Swanton's lead, by arguing that informants had actually revealed they were not Houma at all but from the Mobile area. Second, the renowned anthropologist had actually heard Mobilian trade jargon and mistaken it for Houma, which explained away a linguistic link. Last, they maintained that Swanton's field notes were radically different from what he actually published, and that original documents definitively marked the group as non-Houma.

Swanton interviewed a woman of about eighty years of age named "Félicité Billiout," and her life's account would be seminal for two reasons. First, Félicité was the daughter of Rosalie Courteaux, quite possibly the most important figure in United Houma Nation history. Second, her remembrance of her grandfather as a Biloxi medal chief was cited by the BAR as evidence that the UHN could not have descended from the historical Houma. Swanton continued, "Her grandmother, whose Indian name was Nuyu'n, but who was baptized 'Marion' after her removal to Louisiana, was born in or near Mobile; her grandfather, Shulu-shomon, or, in French, Joseph Abbé, and more often called 'Couteaux' was a Biloxi medal chief; and her mother 'an Atakapa from Texas.'"[28]

Something was definitely lost from Félicité to Verret to Swanton, as her description of events would be impossible given the tribes listed. Swanton does not record the relationship of her grandparents to her mother, but

Joseph Abbé (or "Tacalobé," among a plethora of other names) and Marion gave birth to Rosalie Tacalobé (known as Rosalie Courteau), who in turn married Jacques Billiot and produced Félicité along with half a dozen male progenitors of the United Houma Nation.[29] Based on this passage, neither the most important figure in UHN history nor her parents were Houma. Rather, Joseph was from the Biloxi tribe, Marion an unknown tribe in Alabama, and their daughter from a completely unrelated tribe in Texas.

The account given by Swanton via Verret via Félicité, later used by the BAR to argue that there was no biological link between the UHN and the historical Houma, is, of course, impossible. Swanton probably assumed that Félicité Billiot had described her paternal grandparents and her mother; he did not conduct genealogical research and would not have known the family line from Félicité to Rosalie to Joseph. Whatever the reason, this description was obviously not viable, yet the BAR referred to it often and consistently labeled Rosalie's grandfather a "Biloxi medal chief" without asking any further questions.[30] He is listed as a member of that nation in some nineteenth-century land-sale documents, but Joseph was illiterate and certainly not writing his own history.[31] In its proposed ruling the BAR maintained that Swanton had actually received the information from her brother Bartholemy Billiot rather than from his sister Félicité, and that the ethnologist also recorded their father was a Chitimacha chief. The Branch did not address that Bartholemy's account would be as impossible as his sister's.[32]

The second point on which the BAR contested Swanton was his linguistic evidence. The ethnologist recorded about eighty words from an elderly woman, which he then verified with another elderly female; though Swanton did not give their names, his description indicates neither was Félicité Billiot. He noted slight deviations, which he thought resulted from errors of memory or dialectical variations but did not affect the meaning or basic pronunciation of terms. Satisfied with the words' validity, he compared them to Choctaw and Bayougoula, noted differences versus similarities, and, after careful analysis, determined these words were actually Houma.[33] His interpretation would be supported in 1940 by Victor Naquin, recognized as the leader of Isle de Jean Charles, who told a BIA visitor that "his grandmother spoke 'Indian' and that it is his understanding it was 'Houma-Choctaw.'"[34]

Swanton's conclusion was that the Houma had been an offshoot of the "*Chakchiuma*, or *saktchi-homa*, as it is more correctly spelled," who in turn had been related to the Choctaw and the Chickasaw, which would explain the similarity in roots and slight variation in some full words. Linguistic evidence led him to this conclusion, though other points also indicated similarities. He particularly noted a female elder's discussion of a red-crawfish war totem. Swanton had read Dumont de Montigny's 1753 account of his eighteen years in Louisiane, *Memoires Historiques sur la Louisiane*, in which the military man and engineer observed the Houma using a red crawfish as their war symbol.[35]

The BAR refuted Swanton's linguistic judgment and said his recordings were either Choctaw or Mobilian jargon, a trade language used throughout the coast and interior.[36] Their interpretation was shocking given Swanton's deep knowledge of Southeastern linguistics and his many groundbreaking publications on the topic. True, he had visited the Houma before his major works on Southeastern languages appeared, but even his earliest publications on the region displayed a clear, critical attitude in addressing the relationships between tribes and their languages.[37] To defend its position, the BAR drew upon renowned linguist Emanuel J. Drechsel's work and asked him to review Swanton's notes and publications.

Dr. Drechsel enjoyed a position as one of the world's leading experts on Mobilian trade jargon. The BAR relied heavily upon his opinion in their proposed finding but did not include his last section, which reads:

Allow me to add two points. First, I should emphasize that I make my arguments from the perspective of having studied Mobilian Jargon and that I am not an expert on Choctaw . . . Secondly, I am very much concerned that the above not be interpreted improperly in any petition for the United Houma Nation for federal recognition. Please note that *my interpretation of Swanton's linguistic data does not in any fashion question the Native American ancestry of the Houma people.* If they did not speak Choctaw as their *first* language around the turn of the century, they did speak *some* other Native American language as their mother tongue. This conclusion is justified for a simple sociolinguistic reason: like other Southeastern

Indians, the Houma would never have provided Swanton with a list of Mobilian Jargon or Choctaw as a second language unless they spoke some Native American language in the first place. Thus, there is absolutely *no doubt in my mind about their status as Native Americans; the Houma can draw on a Native American ancestry as much as other Southeastern Indian communities* [italics in the original].[38]

The BIA's omission of Drechsel's last section dramatically changed how readers might interpret his writing. Later research by other specialists revealed that the scholarly opinions he provided the BIA had been taken out of context from his broader work and cropped, thus giving a false impression of his argument.[39] Unrelated linguists would later support Swanton's findings.[40]

The last point on which the BAR attempted to discredit Swanton was its account of his field notes. Researchers maintained they could not make the anthropologist's notes correspond to his three books that reference the Houma. In a press release after the 1994 initial findings report, team leader Holly Reckord stated that her group had conducted research on a deeper level than previous anthropologists or historians and thus discovered whom the UHN actually were. Attempting to reconcile BAR findings with Swanton's interpretation, "bureau researchers debunked Swanton's theories. They found even his field notes of interviews with elders contradicted what he had written in his report." Her group had "performed ground-breaking new research to determine the group's origins and cracked a historical mystery that historians and anthropologists had not been able to solve in 100 years."[41]

Swanton's Houma notes, now lodged at the Smithsonian archives, are difficult to read and written in spidery shorthand that seems almost a code, but they are certainly decipherable and in no way contradicted the ethnologist's final interpretation. Equally nonsensical was the BAR claim that, in contradiction to his books, Swanton's field notes actually "support a theory of diverse origins for the group, very similar to the history of the group advanced by the Bureau of Indian Affairs researchers."[42] In reality, he repeatedly said in published works that the Houma had absorbed diverse bands—Bayougoula, Acolapissa, Biloxi, Chitimacha, Washa, Chawasha, whites, and blacks—but that the Houma had always remained dominant. Swanton's statements are buttressed by Houma oral tradition, newspaper interviews with tribal leaders, a 1936 letter to the BIA by an assistant United States attorney, and a series of ensuing researchers.[43] The difference was that Swanton, the Houma, and later scholars argued that outsiders were pulled into the Houma nation, whereas the BAR team argued that the UHN were a hodgepodge of ethnic groups with only the thinnest veneer of Indian ancestry.

The most puzzling issue was why the BAR thought Swanton lied about his material. If there were innocent transcription errors, surely he must have read his works and thus caught gross errors if they had existed, particularly since three of his best-known books examine the Houma and all maintain the same interpretation. If these errors were not innocent, and he truly did "create" the Houma nation, what motivation did Swanton have? Continuing, if Swanton were willing to jeopardize his scholarly integrity in order to create a tribe for some unknown motive, why did he not destroy his notes and rewrite them to match his final interpretation? Last, if Swanton's interpretation were so unreliable, then what becomes of the hundreds of recognition cases that relied on his opinion and what happens to tribes already federally recognized, at least in part, based on his research? If Swanton had truly acted as claimed, he was either utterly incompetent or a charlatan. Nothing in his background indicates either of these possibilities, and the BAR team that claimed to have debunked his theories gave no explanation as to why he would have acted the way they said he did.

In the BAR interpretation, the major kin groups of whom Swanton spoke were actually African American and German (the Billiots), German, French, and unidentified Indian (the Verdins), and a small nuclear family of Biloxi (the Courteauxs). While these groups had intermarried to the extent that 84 percent of the modern UHN now had some Indian ancestry according to the "Proposed Finding," the BAR argued that it could only specifically identify one family and two unrelated women with Native American ancestry, and in official documents from the 1800s they were labeled "Indian" rather than "Houma." Thus, in their opinion, there was no link between the historical Houma and the modern United Houma Nation, Inc.[44]

The federal recognition process would have been complicated under any circumstances, but possible acknowledgment made some non-Houma nervous for one very important reason: the nation's bayou history centered on oil lands. On July 30, 1921, U.S. Congressman Whitmell P. Martin sent a letter to Charles Burke, commissioner of Indian Affairs. M. Ernest Coycault of New Orleans, a Creole man married to a Houma-Indian woman, had written Martin about the possibility of claims against the government. In August he received a reply that there were no funds available with which to begin an investigation.[45] Coycault then wrote U.S. Representative Carl Hayden of Arizona, who forwarded the letter to Commissioner Burke in December 1921 along with a note saying that Coycault "desires legislation to be passed authorizing that suit be filed in the court of Claims for the value of the lands formerly occupied by these Indians." Burke replied that he had no information about the Houma in his office other than Bulletin 30, Part 1, Bureau of Ethnology, which said that the Houma were believed to be extinct. They had not signed treaties and no funds were held in trust, so they were the responsibility of Louisiana.[46]

Beginning in the 1930s Charles and Maurice Billiot sent a flurry of letters to federal officials, the majority of which were pleas to stop land grabs and return former Houma territory to the nation.[47] These pleas were routinely dismissed. The Houma believed that opponents to recognition feared that the UHN would reclaim oil-rich lands. A successful bid would have many repercussions, not least of which how it would endanger mineral-severance taxes by which Louisiana garnered tens of millions of dollars a year from oil companies; according to one UHN member, Lafourche and Terrebonne severance taxes in 1998 alone produced twenty million dollars for the state.[48]

From the Houma perspective, pressure from oil companies through Washington and Louisiana lobbyists had factored into their denial, and if the nation seemed suspicious or paranoid as a group, they had reason to be. In 1993 a small group of tribal citizens filed a federal suit against the Louisiana Land and Exploration Company (LLE), over vociferous objection from UHN leadership. Steve Cheramie, Sidney Verdin, and colleagues attempted to use the 1790 Nonintercourse Act, which nullified sale of Indian lands unless conducted through a United States treaty;

strictly interpreted, the act excludes states, businesses, and private individuals from buying Indian lands. In the 1970s attorneys Barry Margolin and Tom Tureen had used the Nonintercourse Act to recover traditional lands in the Northeast and successfully argued that the act applied even in cases where states had separated from states.

While using the Nonintercourse Act was successful in the Northeast, it was an error of such epic proportions in Louisiana as to be suicidal. Legal ramifications in an area passing through successive European hands and other complications associated with the locale were very much an issue, but the main problem was that a small element of the Houma had deliberately made a tribal enemy of one of Louisiana's most powerful corporate entities and one of the nation's most powerful oil and gas companies. LLE developed as a modern corporate entity in the 1920s while buying large tracts of land and leasing them to trappers. By 1925 it controlled almost six hundred thousand acres in coastal Louisiana and began a shift to oil and gas exploration that year. In 1927 the company changed its name from Border Research Corporation to Louisiana Land and Exploration Company, and in 1928 it began a long-standing relationship with Texaco. LLE continued to expand and diversify, quickly becoming a multistate and multinational corporation that wielded not only great power but also great wealth; in 1980 company profits were $1.075 billion. At the time of the UHN petition LLE was not only a major player on the Louisiana and American political scenes but also the largest owner of wetlands in the continental United States.

Steve Cheramie and colleagues had antagonized the Louisiana Land Corporation at the worst possible time. The UHN had not garnered recognition and was relying on a reservoir of local and state goodwill, which dried up quickly in the lawsuit's wake. Far more important, even though the lawsuit was dismissed in court, the LLE moved from concern about its interests to an aggressive defense precisely when the Houma were most vulnerable in the recognition process. The BAR was still evaluating research and material in 1993 when LLE lawyers began taking depositions on how the UHN were not true Indians and finding loopholes in their arguments. Whether lawyers communicated it directly or indirectly, both the BAR and UHN were very much aware that oil industry lawyers would closely examine their findings. Thus, the usually tense atmosphere of the recognition process grew considerably more so with the understanding that corporate lawyers concerned about losing billions of dollars would scrutinize every judgment, question every source that did not agree with their stance, and quite likely enter into a lawsuit. If the Houma seemed paranoid about possible oil-industry machinations in the review process, they had reason. Their worst fears seemed justified the following year, when the BAR decided against them in its preliminary ruling.[49] Houma response came in 1996 when they filed a rebuttal to the report.

Another point the Houma felt worked against them was their size, as UHN recognition would have been extremely expensive for the federal government. The UHN had 8,500 members in 1985, but in succeeding years membership swelled to 17,000, and, according to 1993 estimates by the Congressional Budget Office, a recognized tribe of that size would cost the federal government approximately $53,700,000 in annual health and education outlays; this was not even factoring possible lost revenues on oil lands.[50] Precisely this issue had been raised in 1988 concerning the Lumbee tribe of 40,000 members, as one reason Assistant Secretary Ross Swimmer gave for opposing their recognition was the $30,000,000 to $100,000,000 in federal monies the tribe would require each year.[51]

At the same time the United Houma Nation was countering resistance from outside forces, they also endured attack from within. Internal confrontations stemmed not only from general tribal politics but also tensions produced by the recognition process. Divisions started in 1988 when a group of Indians led by UHN Secretary Reggie Billiot challenged the tribal leadership, which they felt was heavy-handed and unresponsive. Tensions and heated words quickly escalated, with both sides accusing the other of trying to wrest political control of the nation. After its challenge was quashed by UHN leadership, the Billiot faction began corresponding with the BIA about political matters. As told to a reporter by Reggie Billiot, the BIA had told him that it would be easier for smaller groups to garner recognition than the large UHN.[52]

Interpretations diverged at that point, as one side maintained that federal officials helped them understand their true identity and encouraged separate application simply to increase their chances of recognition; they firmly believed there was no ulterior BAR motive and certainly no attempt to fracture the group.[53] UHN members recall a very different version of events, beginning with Bureau officials speaking to an assembled tribal group but afterward speaking privately about separate application with Billiot and a few of his followers. They insist the BAR deliberately convinced an ambitious faction that they stood a much greater chance of acknowledgment after seceding and trying for separate recognition, in the time-honored tradition of the U.S. government not only dividing and conquering but also creating friendly chiefs. In their opinion, the BIA planned to use one group to rule against the other and thus deny recognition to both.

Factionalism escalated in January 1995 when two groups broke away from the United Houma Nation and took almost two thousand members with them: the Biloxi, Chitimacha Confederation of Muskogees (BCCM) under the leadership of Reggie Billiot and the Pointe-au-Chien Indian Tribe (PACIT) under the leadership of Steve Cheramie, who later took the last name of "Risingsun."[54] Some people claimed they were tricked into leaving the UHN and later came back, but the splinter groups continued to shift and subdivide. By June 2004 the two initial groups had realigned themselves into the Pointe-au-Chien Indian Tribe, the Isle de Jean Charles Band of the Biloxi Chitimacha Confederation of Muskogees, the Bayou Lafourche Band of the Biloxi Chitimacha Confederation of Muskogees, and the Grand Caillou Dulac Band of the Biloxi Chitimacha Confederation.[55] All groups agreed to apply for acknowledgment separate from the UHN but with final ruling at the same time. Though separate entities, each followed the same basic philosophy in their tribal histories: they were not and never had been Houma but rather a collection of Biloxi, Chitimacha, Choctaw, Acolapissa and Atakapa who had migrated into the area and interbred with whites, blacks, and Houmas.

The United Houma Nation now found itself caught between the devil and the deep blue sea. If they attacked the breakaway tribes then they would be no better than the people who had been attacking them for decades, people who scoffed and claimed that the "Indians" were motivated by ignorance and greed. Moreover, the squabbling and open attacks would destroy the one weapon the nation had always maintained in the face of adversity: their dignity. However bad things had been in the past, Houma ancestors had always been able to withdraw from white scorn and maintain their sense of themselves. The thought of outsiders laughing and pointing while Houma factions ripped each other apart for scraps from the federal government brought a cold shudder to members of the nation.

The other possibility was no less disagreeable. If they did not refute breakaway groups' claims, the UHN would endure defeat in the recognition process; the BAR would use one group to destroy the others, all the while claiming it had explicitly followed federal guidelines. Of this there was no doubt. They firmly believed the BAR was collecting negative interviews given to local and national newspapers by the splinter groups, though even that could be tolerated. What enraged UHN leaders the most were what they felt were aggressive actions to deliberately torpedo the UHN in their recognition bid by both former Houma members and other Louisiana tribes. One example of this was the 1992 drive by Coushatta Barry Langley to defeat Houma recognition through letters to legislators, meetings with the governor, and media releases to turn public perception against the UHN.[56]

One last point gnawed at Houma elders, who had been told for decades they did not exist. Opponents such as H.L. Bourgeois had claimed the "Houma" were actually racial mongrels ignorant of their own history and deluded by whites such as Swanton or, alternatively, charlatans deliberately trying to adopt a Native identity. Reggie Billiot had been not only the UHN secretary but also the Native American liaison with Terrebonne Parish's Department of Economic and Community Development. In his latter capacity he testified at the 1990 Senate committee on Houma recognition, "I am a native. I am a member of the Houma Nation also."[57] That this man had played such an active role in the UHN but could so easily switch his heritage indicated one of two things to outsiders. Either the "Houma" were actually simpleminded people easily led by a few words from whites, be that Swanton or the BIA, or they were a morally bankrupt group eager to reinvent themselves at the slightest possibility of gain. Much as UHN members hoped this reflected on just Billiot, they knew outsiders would generalize about their group based on the actions of a few.

In 1996 the nation made one last-ditch effort to bypass Department of Interior officials by appealing to Senator John Breaux to speak on their behalf for legislative recognition. Given that the BAR process was still in play, he refused. Representative Billy Tauzin agreed to speak but only on certain conditions. The major caveat was that the UHN give up land claims they had maintained for years.[58] This would be a bitter pill to swallow, and the nation's leaders thought long and hard. Would the elders understand that injustices of their youth had been forgotten and forgiven simply because it was expedient? Assuredly not, and tribal leaders dreaded sacrificing these people on the chessboard of politics. On the other hand, if the nation did not garner recognition, it would not only not regain traditional lands but also lose the potential benefits recognition carried. The loss would thus be twice as great.

When discussing their options, both UHN leaders and politicians knew that the 1993 lawsuit against Louisiana Land and Exploration Company had poisoned the waters. Many people now questioned Houma motivation and theorized that they wanted recognition simply to reclaim land or erect a casino. The only way to diffuse suspicion was to eradicate any appearance of economic gain. Tauzin stressed that congressional recognition would still be a slow process, as it would first go through committee and then to both the House and the Senate.

After much debate the UHN agreed to forfeit claims on traditional lands, and on June 18, 1996 Representative Tauzin introduced H.R. 3761 to grant federal recognition.[59] As it turned out, land claims were a moot point, as the bill stalled in committee. Former tribal chairman Kirby Verret pleaded with the breakaway groups to remember that "We are the same people. Remember when we could not go to school because we are Houma Indians? Now some people say they are not Houma Indians and they have taken a real long name and claim to be something else. A tribe is a large family. Even the ones who claim to be different from us are still our relatives! How can we separate our blood? We can not."[60]

Whether the BAR truly used one faction against another is a question only the federal agency can answer. Members of the smaller groups did not believe they were being used as pawns, nor did they believe the UHN would be denied recognition based on other tribes also applying. In a 2003 interview Ronald Courteaux, council member for the Grand Caillou Dulac Band of the Biloxi-Chitimacha Confederation and tribal office administrator; Audrey Westerman, genealogist for the Biloxi Chitimachas; and Marie Marlene Verret-Foret, chairperson of the Grand Caillou

Dulac Band of the Biloxi-Chitimacha Confederation addressed their history, as did Albert Naquin in a separate interview. Naquin was Chief of the Isle de Jean Charles Band of the Biloxi-Chitimacha Confederation. All maintained that they bore the UHN no ill will but that they had spent decades being told who they were and would now tolerate such conduct from neither Indians nor non-Indians.[61]

Various threads of the recognition movement came together in *United Houma Nation, Inc. v. Texaco.* In 1997 several dozen human remains were uncovered on the grounds of a Texaco plant near Larose, Louisiana; the graves had possibly resided in a mound once, but the area had been leveled. The Chitimacha tribe had lived in the area but so had later waves of Houma, and the area retained a strong UHN presence. Testing by R. Christopher Goodwin and Associates of New Orleans established the archaeological site as between 1350 and 1500 CE, before Houma arrival. The United Houma Nation sued Texaco to gain the burial remains, but the court ruled for the oil company. As a result of NAGPRA guidelines Texaco returned burial remains to the Chitimacha, who were living in the area at time of burial and, just as important, federally recognized. Discussing the matter at length and valuing courtesy above all, the Chitimacha invited UHN, PACIT and BCCM members not only to the reburial ceremony but also to speak.[62]

In recounting *United Houma Nation, Inc. v. Texaco*, UHN Principal Chief Brenda Dardar Robichaux freely expressed her anger. From her perspective, the primary goal had been ensuring the bodies were treated with respect in a way other Indian sites and bodies in southern Louisiana had not been. She thus doubly appreciated both that the Chitimacha had repatriated the bodies and that they had invited UHN members to the reburial ceremony. Still, she remained unhappy with *how* the case had been decided; the court ruling was partially predicated on the Houma not existing as a federally recognized tribe and, oil lawyers argued, not existing at all. The judge's ruling had included the statement, "As discussed supra, the National Historic Preservation Act process defines participants as consulting parties and interested persons. UHN is neither a consulting party nor a local government nor a federally recognized Indian tribe and thus is 'the public' for these purposes and may merely comment upon the plan."[63]

United Houma Nation, Inc. v. Texaco illustrated why the Houma felt they were under assault from oil companies, and their opinion was only reinforced in 2001 when Dr. Dave Davis published "A Case of Identity: Ethnogenesis of the New Houma Indians" in *Ethnohistory*, one of the most respected journals in its field. Davis had been Texaco's chief academic support, and in his article he now argued that the Houma were an amalgam of whites and blacks, with perhaps a light mixture of Indian groups, who had adopted Indian identity to escape Jim Crow persecution. The historical Houma were long extinct and the modern UHN a group of pretenders, hence his designation of "new Houma Indians."[64]

"A Case of Identity: Ethnogenesis of the New Houma Indians" set off a firestorm among those concerned with recognition and sparked comments that this was a prime example of "paper genocide." Brenda Dardar Robichaux immediately called Dr. Jack Campisi and Dr. William Starna, who were working on the Houma recognition appeal. All noted how similar the article was to the BAR's preliminary judgment not only in theory and approach but in the facts used to construct arguments—in particular, with a lengthy series of factual errors. They were immediately suspicious that something other than scholarly research was at play and contacted the editors of *Ethnohistory*.[65]

Journal editors were at first extremely reluctant to be drawn into controversy. Davis's credentials were impressive, and scholarly research produces differing opinions by its nature. Campisi explained that the author had testified as an expert witness for Texaco and filed an affidavit that the Houma did not exist, that Davis was hardly an objective scholar, and that he now used a respected journal to peddle opinions likely financed by Texaco.[66] *Ethnohistory* eventually agreed to publish a counterargument to Davis's article, with him giving a rejoinder.

In its Fall 2004 edition the journal published Campisi and Starna's "Another View on 'Ethnogenesis of the New Houma Indians'" and Davis's "Response to Campisi and Starns [sic]." Campisi and Starna addressed fourteen major parallels between the BAR's and Davis's findings and systematically dismantled his initial article. Completely setting aside the issue of whether Davis had sold his academic integrity to Texaco, his article had been rife with errors, a series of which duplicated mistakes in the BAR report. To use only their first example, Davis had duplicated an error that La Salle was the first European to meet the Houma in 1682, whereas he had actually sailed past them in a fog. Davis gave the same explorer and date for the first meeting that the BAR had, an inaccuracy appearing in no other text and easily corrected if Davis had looked at a primary document of La Salle's voyage or any secondary account of Louisiana or Houma history other than the BAR findings.[67] In his rejoinder Davis offered no credible explanation for the series of duplicative errors.

Houma interpretation of Davis's work was that it was a modern addition to the "ethnic cleansing" literature of the nineteenth and twentieth centuries, only this time deliberate rather than accidental. But the context had changed. Whereas school and federal officials once had free rein to argue that the Houma were simply racial mongrels scurrying to hide their true identity, a well-educated nation and its colleagues now argued its history from a position of strength. What illustrated the Houma sense of political fair play so well was that, whereas they maintained a grudging respect for BAR officials, they held Dave Davis in absolute contempt. Even in situations where they felt outright treachery was at play, as in what they believed was the divide-and-conquer policy using the BCCM and PACIT, they freely admitted that the BAR played the chess game of politics well. Davis was denied even the respect reserved for a wily adversary. To the Houma, he had sold himself to the oil companies first in *United Houma Nation v. Texaco, Inc.* and then in "A Case of Identity." Moreover, they believed that he had lifted material directly from the BAR's preliminary report while selling his integrity. Their disdain only increased in coming years when Davis took a position as a senior vice president at R. Christopher Goodwin & Associates, Inc., which had been involved in the *Texaco* case. From the perspective of the Houma, Davis's paper genocide had failed, and the nation that had always treasured its dignity above all else held him as a figure beneath scorn.

The bid for federal recognition had taken up much of the tribe's energy and time since the mid-1970s, but as of January 2020 the Bureau of Indian Affairs still has not issued its final ruling on the United Houma Nation. Perversely, in 2008 they ruled against the Pointe-au-Chien Indian Tribe and the Biloxi, Chitimacha Confederation of Muskogees, Inc., two groups whose members had broken away from the United Houma Nation in a bid for recognition. "The BIA pointed out the oddity of their contention by noting that the vast majority of the splinter tribes' members were enrolled in the UHN prior to the BIA's negative proposed finding of the UHN petition."[68] Leaders of the splinter groups had maintained in a 2003 interview that the BIA had been trying to help them discover who they really were, whereas members of the UHN firmly believed that the organization had engaged in a time-honored tradition of the federal government dividing and conquering Indian peoples. Whichever the correct interpretation was, the end result was that former members of the United Houma Nation had broken away and sought recognition on their own, and they were now denied not only recognition but also reentry to the UHN.

The United Houma Nation may eventually garner federal recognition, or it may not, but one may be certain that the nation will continue no matter what judgment comes. Bruce Duthu, a Houma fisherman's son turned law professor and Ivy League scholar, has been writing about this topic for decades, and his words are as true now as they were in 1997: "If the Houma do gain federal recognition of tribal status, it will likely be perceived by the tribe as good news long overdue. It will also play an important, but certainly not pivotal role in determining the paths the Houma chart for themselves into the next century."[69]

Conclusion

The Sea of Galilee

By the beginning of the twenty-first century the Houma nation had successfully navigated a constantly changing series of political and economic landscapes for three hundred years. In 1999 a French delegation traveling through the United States met with the Houma Tribal Council and presented Principal Chief Brenda Dardar Robichaux with a medal from their government. The date marked the three hundredth anniversary of the nation's first meeting with a French delegation, and Dardar Robichaux thus became the first Houma medal chief since colonial times. The post-1699 period had been a hectic political era for the Houma, and the past forty years among the most hectic of all. From a nation maintaining its political structure through an informal council of village elders, the Houma had reorganized and stepped onto a pan-Indian stage financed by one man's 1961 mortgage. In the next decades the Houma deepened their ties with other Indian and non-Indian groups, successfully integrated public schools, and began a quest for formal acknowledgment on both state and federal levels. Through it all the Houma maintained their history, their ability to adapt, and their dignity.

In 2001 "A Case of Identity: Ethnogenesis of the New Houma Indians" had clearly illustrated that the twenty-first century would present its own challenges. But challenges come in many forms, and in August and September 2005 nature tested the qualities that had sustained the Houma for centuries.[1] In less than a month, two of the worst hurricanes ever to make landfall in the United States struck opposite sides of Louisiana. The effect on the Houma was predictably devastating, but the two storms also produced a surprising echo of past history and illustrated why the nation continues to survive as a people.

On August 29, 2005, Hurricane Katrina made landfall in extreme southwest Mississippi, close to the state line. Houma settlements to the storm's west benefited from its slight jog eastward; because of prevailing tidal patterns, Katrina actually pulled water away from Indian villages. Communities thus suffered wind but little water damage. Area residents allowed themselves a breath of relief as the eye passed, until levees inside New Orleans and along the southernmost Mississippi gave way. Lower Jefferson Parish and Plaquemines Parish were almost completely flooded, and all of St. Bernard Parish was under water. Plaquemines Parish stood on the other side of Barataria Bay from bayou communities and thus had contained several hundred Indian residents; many Houma had settled around small Venice and even smaller communities named the Half-Way House, Tiger Pass, Spanish Pass, Stryker's Woods and the Village. Now, those and settlements farther upriver stood twelve feet under water and the Village had been scoured away.[2]

Houma leaders estimated that approximately four thousand UHN members had lost their homes to Katrina. Some fled the state, but the majority sought refuge with relatives in southernmost Lafourche Parish and Terrebonne Parish. Even worse than the initial storm, however, was that lifetimes spent along the Gulf Coast led many Houma to believe that another hurricane was on the way, the deepest fear of a region staggering from Katrina. Though Terrebonne and Lafourche had escaped the worst flooding, shingles and entire roofs had been ripped from bayou homes, and people desperately tried to place coverings before a second hurricane hit. Hordes of Indians and Cajuns swarmed across the landscape to lift boats from roads and yards, patch roofs, clear debris, and feed the hungry. They worked together, they worked separately, but above all they worked in a desperate race against the clock. Hurricane season would not end until November 30, and folk belief holds that the most ferocious tempests arrive in September.

On September 24, 2005, the worst fears of southern Louisiana were realized as a Category 5 hurricane named Rita gathered speed over warmer-than-average Gulf waters and rammed the Louisiana–Texas border. In little under four weeks Louisiana had been hit by two of the most powerful hurricanes ever to strike the United States. Katrina and Rita hit opposite sides of the state, but the sister storms had two different effects on the Houma. Whereas Katrina collapsed levees but pulled water away from bayou Houma settlements to her west, Rita's storm surge pushed nine feet of water into those same communities to her east; prevailing winds and currents made all the difference. Almost every levee in Terrebonne Parish was topped and many were breached. It was as if the element that had protected the Houma for centuries now rose up and attacked.

The combined impact of Katrina and Rita was like a boxer stunning an opponent with one blow and then launching a series of crippling punches. An additional five thousand Houma lost their homes or possessions to Rita; between the two storms, the displaced comprised almost half the nation. Several days after the second hurricane, winds and natural tidal patterns pushed and pulled floodwaters back to the Gulf, leaving a thick layer of mud over floors and walls. Many were stunned by the scale of human suffering, and people who had lived through several hurricanes faced a level of chaos greater than they had ever seen. Younger people were able to fend better for themselves, but many elders could not speak English fluently enough to communicate well in the resulting melee. Moreover, some suffered from Alzheimer's and searched desperately for family members decades gone.[3]

Several factors kept the Houma from descending into pandemonium. The first was their previous experience with hurricanes. A UHN child born in January 1988 had lived through Hurricanes Georges, Frances, Opal, Juan, and Andrew hitting southeastern Louisiana as well as a number of floods caused by distant hurricanes. People descended on their settlements at the first sign of lowering water. Communal workgroups quickly began salvaging residences while the homeless stayed with family or friends. The psychological effects of getting back to dwellings quickly and rebuilding among friends and family members were vitally important.

Moreover, the UHN enjoyed the advantage of a strong collective network. Bilingual tribal members stayed with elders and translated for them with monolingual English speakers. Older people gathered children and made sure they were safe. Tribal members on higher ground invited dozens of relatives and friends into their homes, while those unable to fit inside pitched tents on lawns. Strong leadership—political, religious, social—asserted itself and absorbed the twin hurricanes into the cultural fabric of a water-based nation. A dense and extended network of friends and relatives not only provided basic needs but also assured tribal members that they would conquer this hurricane as they had conquered others.[4]

Tribal leaders put aside differences, remained calm, and projected an image of stability. On October 10, 2005, United Houma Nation Principal Chief Brenda Dardar Robichaux and Chairman of the Pointe-au-Chien Indian Tribe Charles Verdin spoke together on the *Democracy Now!* radio program and presented a remarkably unified front. These political leaders working together after being at loggerheads for years was a slightly surreal experience, but one that showed why southern Louisiana Indians have endured. Robichaux and Verdin knew each other very well, and both their personalities and communication styles meshed nicely as they voiced community needs and expressed gratitude to other Indian and non-Indian groups for their aid. Both were extremely proactive in seeking help, and from the interview one would have no idea that these two leaders stood on opposing political sides.

Modern psychology maintains that elements of one's personality already exist during times of disaster, though different facets surface during crisis. Conversely, a Houma elder once explained that no one person is 100 percent of what he or she might be, and that during catastrophe *le Bon Dieu* gives grace that simply does not exist in one's everyday life; thus, the Sea of Galilee that He calmed was as much a terrified mind as a body of water. Whichever interpretation one prefers, after Katrina and Rita members of the Houma nation helped friends and family, strangers, and people they might have loathed under regular circumstances. If disaster reveals the true nature of an individual, so too does it reveal the character of a nation, and Houma Indians working together after two hurricanes revealed the very attitude that critics said had destroyed them.

H.L. Bourgeois and other detractors had argued that tribal patterns of offering refuge to other groups—European, African, Native—was the major reason the *Shâkti Humma* had drowned as a nation and become "so-called Indians." After Katrina and Rita the Houma did not offer formal adoption to those in need, but as both a nation and as individuals they certainly offered food, clothing, shelter, and comfort to their own citizens, to non-Indian residents of southeastern Louisiana, and to members of the PACIT and BCCM. They did this when half their own nation was homeless and the entire region overwhelmed with New Orleans survivors, and when the most powerful country in the world had seemingly left its own people to die. Horrible as Katrina and Rita were, they forced the Houma to once again affirm what they had always been: an interconnected people with not only an extremely strong will to survive but an exceptionally strong will not to let others perish. The Houma did not die as a nation in 1700, 1800, 1900, or 2005 any more than they denied aid to those in need.

The combined effect of the two storms also sparked another relocation of Indians, not on the scale of previous movements but certainly in a noticeable demographic shift. Specifically, Indians who had relocated to the parishes of St. Bernard, Jefferson, and Plaquemines left after they were flooded out, moving back to Terrebonne and Lafourche; moreover, most Indians from down the bayou returned home after floodwaters receded, but others relocated farther up near friends and family. By 2007 the storms had sparked a cultural resurgence the nation could not have foreseen. With New Orleans–based Houma coming back to the bayou landscape and the United Houma Nation keeping tallies of who needed help, tribal identity was reinforced and strengthened. As a secondary consequence, the UHN and various Indian units with whom they had been at loggerheads forged a renewed sense of common cause, of reaching across political boundaries in a small pan-Indian movement.

Katrina and Rita might at first seem tangential to the Houma narrative as two powerful but isolated storms. When one looks at them in the context of a broader history, however, one sees that these hurricanes and their aftermath illustrate this book's thesis. That is, Katrina and Rita were only the latest of many storms (albeit physical in this case) to strike the nation between 1699 and 2005. Likewise, rather than destroying the tribe, they revealed the Houma's strengths, particularly how the nation successfully navigated a constantly changing series of political and social landscapes between 1699 and 2005.

Iberville's March 20, 1699 entrance into the Houma village transformed the tribe in ways neither he nor they could have known. Both sought to form alliances with the other and use those alliances against their traditional enemies. For the Houma, this meant the Bayougoula, a hated rival for territory. For their part, the French were always on the lookout for Native alliances against a traditional enemy, albeit in their case English colonists to the east. Likewise, both groups misunderstood the other. Ever the political animal, Iberville carefully watched the interactions between the Houma and the Bayougoula who spoke for him and noted that the Houma viewed the Bayougoula "as Frenchmen, because they brought us into their homes." Placed in the broader context of Lower Mississippi Valley indigenous cultures, however, it would be more accurate to say that the Houma viewed the Frenchmen as Indians. According to tribal protocol, alliances formed earlier in the year when tribal ambassadors sang the calumet for them were only reinforced when Iberville's party physically entered the village.[5] All diplomatic accoutrements such as parley in front of the temple, the ceremonial giving of food, and formal exchange of presents were those that tribes in the Lower Mississippi Valley traditionally made with other tribes. Moreover, the formal and lengthy speeches were very much in keeping with ceremonial norms of behavior along the Mississippi Gulf.[6]

Thus, 1699 marks the year in which the Houma stepped onto a world political stage. Though politically active before, the nation had formed alliances and waged war only with other tribes, and conflicts with the Bayougoula had erupted mainly over local hunting grounds. Post 1699 they engaged with other powers on a more intercontinental level and, tragically, were pulled into global conflicts. Living on a bend of the Mississippi with paths stretching back through the hills, the nation occupied a strategic position geographically. Moreover, by forming close alliances with the French, the Houma reaped the benefits of trade and, just as important, kept other tribes from reaping those benefits. Conversely, by forming alliances with the French the Houma made sworn enemies of tribes supporting the English exactly when tensions were exacerbating. Only a few hundred miles to their southeast the English and their allies attacked Mobile, St. Augustine, and Mission San Luis, whereas several hundred miles east the French, Spanish, and their allies besieged Charleston.

Adding to colonial-inspired conflict was the Carolina hunger for deerskins and slaves, which spurred the Creeks and Chickasaws ever farther west and into Tunica homelands. Themselves under attack, the Tunica sought to save themselves by first settling with and then rising against the Houma. By 1710 they had routed their host nation. In no way can Tunica attack and Houma removal to the south be viewed as simple treachery or an isolated event. On the contrary, these events must be viewed as part of a new, more international landscape. Adopting the Tunica was the Houma's attempt to rebuild tribal population after a devastating epidemic that was likely introduced by Europeans. When seeking refuge, the Tunica would surely have pleaded their case based on Chickasaw aggression.

Thus, the period after 1699 reflects the Houma not only willingly stepping onto a broader political and social stage but also being pulled into a broader historical narrative, whether they chose it or not. This trend would only speed up in coming decades. At almost the same time the nation settled along Bayou St. John, French settlers from Mobile arrived and immediately began acquiring land along the waterway. Just as important, after the 1718 founding of New Orleans not only epidemics but also alcohol began flooding the region. Thus, there was a very strong push from Bayou St. John. The pull of Ascension was that the area on the Mississippi's eastern bank offered a wonderful mix of transportation routes and natural bounty, and it was free of the competition for land and resources that had necessitated their previous two moves. Moreover, the rich, dark soil stretched hundreds of feet down, and the area's position in the Mississippi Valley Flyway and the region's abundant rivers, lakes, and bayous ensured excellent food supply. Bayou Lafourche intersected with the Mississippi just upstream from the Houma settlements and offered entrance to bayous on the Mississippi's west bank.

Their new Ascension location was perfect for the Houma, far enough to protect them from the corrosive effects of New Orleans society but close enough that they could easily get to the city. Moreover, village locations along the Mississippi guaranteed that they would encounter river traffic as people went up or down the mightiest waterway in North America. The nation grew more wedded to the French politically as they regularly parleyed with colonial officials. Just as important, the fledgling city of New Orleans came to rely heavily on tribal foodstuffs. Houma traders maintained a particularly robust position because of their strong agricultural history, familiarity with the geography of the Bayou St. John–New Orleans area, excellent relations with French politicians, and ideal position on transportation routes. They shipped large amounts of cereal, fish, game, and medicinal herbs to the markets of New Orleans and in return reaped the benefits of trade. Indeed, they grew so wedded to the French that they allied with that colonial power in both the Natchez War of 1729 and the Chickasaw War of 1739.[7] All these factors ensured that the Houma maintained the more international outlook they had practiced since 1699, choosing and absorbing various elements of French culture and working with the Crown against other colonial powers.

The poet John Haines wrote, "To live by a large river is to be kept in the heart of things." Fortunately for the Houma, they lived in an increasingly global landscape and controlled an area rich in natural resources. Unfortunately for the Houma, they lived in an increasingly global landscape and controlled an area rich in natural resources. In the 1720s the French Crown brought German farmers to the fertile landscape and settled them just downstream from the nation. Then the 1763 Treaty of Paris excluded the French from the Lower Mississippi Valley and divided the nation's land between Spain and England. Over the next decades the Spanish began bringing in increasingly large numbers of settlers, both Acadians and Canary Islanders. The combined effect of these international arrivals was devastating to the Houma, as settlers proved to be not only excellent farmers but skilled and reliable soldiers.

The Houma had flourished since 1699 precisely because the world they lived in had become more global. Houma agriculturalists, hunters, traders, and politicians had formed alliances with the French for over half a century and reaped the benefits. That world no longer existed. Unable to play the Spanish and English against each other after the American Revolution and, worse, surrounded by rapidly increasing numbers of settlers, the Houma saw their status spiral downward. Canary Islanders and Cajuns now supplied foodstuffs and soldiers, the very areas in which the nation had proven so valuable. In short, the nation had gone from being vital to colonial expansion to being an obstacle to colonial expansion. They had two choices. They could relocate as they had done in the past and hopefully maintain autonomy, or they could lose their status along the Mississippi River and quite likely face extermination.

The period between 1762 and 1850 is crucial in the history of the Houma. Tribal history maintains one version of events while the Bureau of Indian Affairs maintains something quite different. While no one disputes that the historic Houma split into bands and left Ascension, oral tradition maintains that two bands moved back upriver and were lost to history, presumably removed to Oklahoma with other tribes. The people claiming to be modern-day Houma say that their band moved down Bayou Lafourche, eventually settling on smaller bayous in Terrebonne Parish and Lafourche Parish. The Branch of Acknowledgment and Recognition (BAR) maintains that the historical Houma were absorbed into other tribes, with the modern United Houma Nation an amalgam of various Native bands, European, and Africans. Determining the authenticity of this claim is at the crux of the modern Houma campaign for federal recognition.

Between 1762 and 1850 the Houma created a new world—physically and culturally—for themselves along the bayous of southeastern Louisiana. Elders brought animal and plant lore with them, but healers immediately tested the new flora and fauna they saw around them. Food gatherers quickly devised fish weirs, nets, and animal traps with which to control their environment. Farmers gauged the difference in water tables and how that affected crops. Knowledge gathered in their first years in the new environment was quickly memorized and passed on to succeeding generations, and that education endures today. The Houma "encountered nature and transformed it into a decidedly cultural entity. They remade the land in fact and in the mind."[8] Indeed, it was the Houma's very ability to change their environment that made their land so tempting for incoming Euro-American settlers. Later arrivals not only adopted Indian crops but also appropriated cleared Indian fields and villages. When the Houma were eventually driven from natural levees and forced ever lower down waterways, it was competition for cleared land in conjunction with competition for high ground itself that was the deciding factor.

At many points in their history the Houma acted as decisive agents in their own narrative. At other points, like all people, survival in the face of extreme change was enough to qualify as victory. After 1865 the subtle castes and intricate racial structure stemming from a fused Gallic, Iberian, and American system gave way under Reconstruction. Even though Louisiana Natives were sometimes referred to as *gens des libres*, there had been little confusion between them and free people of African descent in the colonial era because of observed social norms. Faced with a destroyed racial order, Louisiana's white ruling class now sought to regain control by dividing the state into exclusively white versus non-white binaries. Given Jim Crow mores and colonial records that unfortunately referred to both Indians and emancipated blacks as free people of color, the struggle the Houma faced beginning in the late 1800s is obvious. At least on paper, they had ceased to exist. Terrebonne and Lafourche officials welcomed this lie of silence because it allowed them to maintain an artificial social and racial structure. On their part, many Houma embraced the lie because remaining down bayous and maintaining a low profile offered relative peace and a chance of a livelihood.

Thus, *H.L. Billiot v. Terrebonne Parish School Board et al.* must be examined not only in its own right but also in light of broader historical themes. The Houma navigated Jim Crow and survived at a time when their land was being stolen by fur trappers, the state, and oil companies. H.L. Billiot's rebellion against this system and attempt to integrate his children in 1916 was one man's individual action, but it took place amid broader historical movements. Likewise, the Indian integration of Terrebonne Parish schools in 1964 must be looked at in the context of a broader historical narrative. For roughly two hundred years after French arrival the nation had formed both alliances and conflicts with various colonial powers—French, English, and Spanish. In all of their dealings with outside powers the Houma had maintained a strong sense of their own identity but also worked closely with outsiders when it helped them successfully navigate a changing world. This continued after American arrival. Shifts in racial classification after the Civil War took the nation by surprise but did not cripple them. On the contrary, in coming decades they worked closely with other tribes, various anthropologists, historians, non-Houma Methodists, and various members of the Catholic Church. *H.L. Billiot* and *Naquin*, like Katrina and Rita, must be interpreted not as individual moments of crisis or triumph but as broader examples of how the Houma successfully navigated a series of political and economic landscapes for over three hundred years while retaining their sense of identity.

In October 2017 I was reminded of how the Houma are still writing their history when I received an email and then a phone call from Adam Crepelle, a young Houma lawyer pursuing a master of laws degree at the University of Arizona. Smart, funny, and unfailingly polite, Adam was writing an article on tribal recognition and wanted to check facts and sources from some of my previous works.[9] We spent a pleasant hour discussing family histories and friends in common, as well as other people with whom he should touch base. I emailed him some material from this book as we spoke, after which he was kind enough to send two references on the Houma that I hadn't read. Glancing at my watch and realizing I had about five minutes left to get to class, I made a quick goodbye with him and gathered my things. As I hurried down the hall, I thought about what a fool H.L. Bourgeois had been. Almost one hundred years ago to the day, a twelve-year-old named Harry Billiot had been denied entry to a school a few hundred feet from his home, and with him the entire Houma nation. What a colossal waste of potential, and how much Harry and others like him might have achieved if things had been different. Rounding a corner as I pondered this bitter thought, however, I remembered a Tolstoy quote, that patience and time are the two greatest warriors. It struck me then that Adam Crepelle and others like him are not a new generation of Houma so much as an old generation with new skills. For over three hundred years the nation had absorbed the best of foreign cultures, survived the worst, and lived to pass along those lessons. Different as they might be in time and place, the Houma of 1699 and the Houma of today would probably recognize each other in many respects. Names had changed, faces had changed, languages and religions had changed, but the Houma nation's survival in a constantly changing world and its sense of itself as a nation have not.

Notes

INTRODUCTION

1. Fortunately, later historical interpretations have fleshed out some early records, though more for other tribes than for the Houma. Kathryn Braund's *Deerskins and Duffels* is an excellent work to which I owe a great debt, as is Micheline E. Pesantubbee's *Choctaw Women*.
2. Guevin, "Ethno-Archaeology."
3. An anonymous reviewer suggested I include more information on sources examining the Houma nation, while another reader suggested I cut what references I had. Both reviewers made excellent points, so I will take the middle ground and direct interested readers to a previous article I published, "The Houma Nation: A Brief Overview of the Literature." That article provides more material and more interpretation than I can give in this introduction.
4. I would also enthusiastically recommend several other works that touch upon similar themes, such as Katherine Osburn's *Choctaw Resurgence in Mississippi*, Clara Sue Kidwell's *Choctaws in Oklahoma*, and Donna Akers's *Living in the Land*.

1. "HE AND I SHALL BE BUT ONE"

1. D'Iberville, *Iberville's Gulf Journals*, 67. Two members of the Quinipissa tribe also stood with the Houma, but I excluded them from my sentence given that this is the only reference Iberville makes to them. Related to the Bayougoula, these Quinipissa members likely helped during this first meeting, but Iberville only notes that they also stood on the shore.
2. Albrecht, "Origin and Early Settlement," 49. Andrew Albrecht draws his information from both Swanton and Adair but deserves credit for his own interpretation. For further reading on the subject of emerging tribes in the Lower Mississippi Valley, see Ethridge and Shuck-Hall, *Mapping the Mississippian*.
3. Swanton, *Indian Tribes*, 29; see Brown and Hardy, "What is Houma?," 521–48, particularly 546.
4. Bayougoula ("bayou people" or "river people") territory stretched to the south of the Houma, and their main village was on the Mississippi's west bank in modern Iberville Parish. They formed close political and cultural associations with the nearby Quinipissa and Mougoulacha. Though the Bayougoula's Musk-

hogean dialect was similar to the Houma's, both tribes were extremely defensive about hunting territory and were in constant rivalry with each other. Interested readers should examine Swanton, *Indian Tribes* for a nice historical overview on the Bayougoula (274–79) and on the Quinipissa and Mougoulacha (279–81).

5. Folklore in Baton Rouge maintains the city was founded on the site of an *istrouma* (*istra huma* or, more accurately, *iti huma*) or *bâton rouge*, which divided Houmas to the north and Bayougoulas to the south. Red was a war color; ergo, to cross this red marker was an invasion and declaration of war. Pénicaut stated this in his writings. However, Iberville recorded that a stream actually served as the boundary line between the two tribes. See d'Iberville, *Iberville's Gulf Journals*, 65. European interpretation of the red stick as a dividing marker was possibly a misreading of lower Mississippi Natives; the pole served as a totemic symbol for the Houma. In this interpretation, the color was likely a manifestation of the tribe's color of *huma*, or red. Andrew Albrecht placed the red stick in a broader context, noting that the Chakchiuma erected tall poles with hanging tribal paraphernalia; wind blowing through the objects was interpreted by prophets as a spiritual voice warning that a tribal member had just been killed. Thus, for the Houma, the pole would have had overtones of the supernatural as well as of tribal and military organizations. "In other words, it symbolized not only the tribal unity of the people but also the particular place which they considered their home and which they were willing to defend against encroaching neighbors . . . at the Red Pole site which represented the southernmost outpost of the Houma territory." See Albrecht, "Origin and Early Settlement," 55, 56.

6. For more information, see Kane, *Plantation Parade*. A journalist and popular author, Harnett Kane examined how the former Houma territory later became an extraordinarily wealthy area with the arrival of plantations, a wealth tied to the area's geography and geology. Based on Iberville's journal, the village's location was close to modern Fort Adams, Mississippi.

7. Pierre Le Moyne d'Iberville (1661–1706) and his younger brother Jean-Baptiste Le Moyne de Bienville (1680–1767) are two of the major figures of Louisiana history, and they maintained close relations with the region's Indians. Born in Montreal to a prominent family with strong military ties, the two were major colonizers in the Lower Mississippi Valley and extraordinarily complicated men. Rather than go into the lengthy explanation one of my reviewers suggested, I will make a comparison with two figures better known to people outside the region: Imagine that George Washington and Thomas Jefferson were brothers and spent their lives working closely together, and that most of their ten other brothers became major military and political leaders. That gives some idea of the importance of the two Frenchmen in the Lower Mississippi Valley.

8. Cox, *Journeys of Réné Robert*, 1:165, 167.

9. For further reading, see Patricia Galloway, "Sources," 11–40. As Iberville found when he entered the Lower Mississippi Valley, many of Tonty's statements proved to be highly inaccurate. To be fair to Tonty, however, his "accounts" had been wildly embroidered by publishers.

10. D'Iberville, *Iberville's Gulf Journals*, 60, 79.

11. D'Iberville, *Iberville's Gulf Journals*, 46–48.

12. D'Iberville, *Iberville's Gulf Journals*, 67–68.

13. D'Iberville, *Iberville's Gulf Journals*, 79, 68.

14. D'Iberville, *Iberville's Gulf Journals*, 68. For further explanation on the ritual significance of gift giving, see Braund, *Deerskins and Duffels*, 27.

15. D'Iberville, *Iberville's Gulf Journals*, 68.

16. D'Iberville, *Iberville's Gulf Journals*, 61.

17. D'Iberville, *Iberville's Gulf Journals*, 69; Swanton, *Indian Tribes*, 43.

18. D'Iberville, *Iberville's Gulf Journals*, 63.

19. D'Iberville, *Iberville's Gulf Journals*, 122.

20. Fort Maurepas is present-day Ocean Springs, Mississippi.

21. D'Iberville, *Iberville's Gulf Journals*, 69.

22. D'Iberville, *Iberville's Gulf Journals*, 63.

23. D'Iberville, *Iberville's Gulf Journals*, 70.

24. Gravier, *Gravier's Voyage*, 144.

25. D'Iberville, *Iberville's Gulf Journals*, 86, 112–13.

26. These children were named Saint-Michel, Pierre Huet, Gabriel Marcal, Jean Joly, Jacques Charon, and Pierre Le Vasseur. See Higginbotham, *Fort Maurepas*, 85.

27. Pénicaut, *Fleur de Lys*, 68; d'Iberville, *Iberville's Gulf Journals*, 176–77.

28. Pénicaut, *Fleur de Lys*, 73–74, 78–79.

29. D'Iberville, *Iberville's Gulf Journals*, 86, 93.

30. Du Ru, *Journal of Paul du Ru*, 5.

31. Du Ru, *Journal of Paul du Ru*, 7.

32. Du Ru, *Journal of Paul du Ru*, 8–9.

33. Du Ru, *Journal of Paul du Ru*, 26.

34. Gravier, *Gravier's Voyage*, 144.

35. Du Ru, *Journal of Paul du Ru*, 28, 27.

36. Du Ru, *Journal of Paul du Ru*, 26, 30.

37. Gravier, *Gravier's Voyage*, 145.

38. Du Ru, *Journal of Paul du Ru*, 32.

39. Du Ru, *Journal of Paul du Ru*, 45.

40. Du Ru, *Journal of Paul du Ru*, 47.

41. Given that the Ouga whom Iberville had met died in the epidemic two months before du Ru's arrival, the Ouga whom Gravier refers to must have been the deceased man's successor, the younger man Iberville met when he first encountered the Houma in 1699; Gravier, *Gravier's Voyage*, 144, 145.

42. Gravier, *Gravier's Voyage*, 145.

1. The Pearl forms the modern boundary between Louisiana and Mississippi, just east of New Orleans.
2. De La Harpe, *Historical Journal*, 14.
3. Braund, *Deerskins and Duffels*, 32.
4. Bienville to Pontchartrain, August 12 and September 1, 1709, in Rowland and Sanders, *Mississippi Provincial Archives*, 3:133.
5. There has been some excellent scholarship written on this topic, but one of the best is Micheline Pesantubbee's *Choctaw Women in a Chaotic World*. Pesantubbee covers some of the same historical ground as other authors but does a very nice job of explaining how slavers' incursions affected the daily cultural fabric of tribes under attack.
6. D'Iberville, *Iberville's Gulf Journals*, 122.
7. Pénicaut, *Fleur de Lys*, 129–30. Pénicaut maintained that Houma emigration was bloodless and that the nation removed in 1709; de La Harpe, *Historical Journal*, 54. La Harpe maintained that the Houma moved after a 1706 attack in which half the tribe was killed.
8. For a comprehensive history of the waterway, see Freiberg, *Bayou St. John*. Like most things around New Orleans, Bayou St. John enjoyed a number of different names and only took its modern pronunciation after Americans moved into the area. The Houma and other Muskhogean tribes called it "Choupicatcha" or "Soupitcatcha" and Bienville later named it "Bayou St. Jean" after his patron saint. Paddling up the waterway in late 1699, he saw a trail after 5 ½ miles that his Bayougoula guides said connected Choupicatcha with an open area of high ground next to the great river. Bienville made a mental note of the elevation and there, in nineteen years, he founded La Nouvelle Orleans.
9. Freiberg, *Bayou St. John*, 10–11.
10. Giraud, *History of the French*, 1:190–91; d'Artaguette to Pontchartrain, February 12, 1710, in Rowland and Sanders, *Mississippi Provincial Archives*, 2:53; d'Artaguette to Pontchartrain, February 20, 1710, in Rowland and Sanders, *Mississippi Provincial Archives*, 2:59. Caveat: the Mississippi Provincial Archives and Giraud both refer to the Bayou St. John locale as "Biloxi," but this site is unrelated to the Gulf Coast settlement of the same name. Moreover, some translations state that colonists were sent there to grow maize or corn. Given colonial needs, their original crop was European wheat.
11. Martin, *History of Louisiana*, 413–14. An annotated map of land ownership along Bayou St. John is attached between those pages in the volume at Hill Memorial Library, Louisiana State University. I later found another version of this map at the Historic New Orleans Collection and included it as one of my illustrations for this work. See map 2 in chap. 2; Freiberg, *Bayou St. John*,

32; Maduell, *Census Tables*, 21. LaVigne is also listed in the census as "Rivard" and "Rivarri."

12. Maduell, *Census Tables*, 21.

13. Swanton, *Indian Tribes*, 289–90. Swanton cites La Harpe, who passed the villages in 1718, and Charlevoix, who passed the locale in January of 1722.

14. Just as there is a welter of names for the main players in Houma history, so is there a welter of names assigned to areas where they have lived. Suffice it to say that in 1804 the United States divided Orleans Territory (modern Louisiana) into twelve subdivisions, with "Acadia" being one. In 1807 the region was further subdivided; "Ascension Parish" was formed from Acadia, with the new parish sitting on both the east and west banks of the Mississippi. The name stemmed from a church established at modern Donaldsonville in 1772, La Iglesia de la Ascensión de Nuestro Señor Jesús Christo de La Fourche de Los Tchitimacha. The term "Ascension" was not used as a political designation by colonial officials or the Houma while they lived there, but the (political, not religious) parish name has become so associated with the locale that I have chosen it as the most convenient term for the rest of this work.

15. Charlevoix visited the villages on January 3, 1722; he noted in *Histoire et description générale*, 3:436 that there were two Houma villages, one on the eastern bank and another a quarter of a league inland. Lieutenant Crenay, "Carte de la Louisiane par de M. le Baron de Crenay, Lieut. Pour le Roy et Commandant a la Mobile, 1733" records the smaller village on the west bank and the larger on the east. The former was on the point of land that steamboat pilots later named Houmas Point, while the latter, Grand Village, would become the site of Houmas House Plantation. To offer one more contradiction, d'Anville's "Carte de la Louisiane" shows three Houma villages, but all are on the east bank. Map 1 in chap. 1 is the d'Anville map.

16. Attending this council meeting were the "Chaqtos, the Taouchas, the Apalaches, the Tinnsas, the Mobiliens, the Tomez, the Gens des Forches, the Chactaw, the Pascagoulas, the Oumas, the Tonicas, the Chaouchas, the Natchez, the Chicachas, the Nassitoches, the Yatacez, the Alibamons, the Canapuches and others." Pénicaut, *Fleur de Lys*, 206.

17. Sauvole to unnamed recipient, August 4, 1701, in Rowland and Sanders, *Mississippi Provincial Archives*, 2:13.

18. Maduell, *Census Tables*, 88.

19. "Indian Remains and Relics," *Donaldsonville Chief*, July 12, 1884. One site was slightly above Donaldsonville on the west bank's Evan Hall Plantation, while the other was slightly below Donaldsonville on the east bank's Clark Plantation, adjacent to modern Houmas House Plantation; Guevin, "Ethno-Archaeology" 84–85.

20. Le Page du Pratz, *History of Louisiana*, 1:148; Barnett, *Natchez Indians*, 33, 35.

21. Usner, *Indians, Settlers, and Slaves*, 85.

22. French, "History of Louisiana," 96.

23. French, "History of Louisiana," 99–101.

24. Périer to Maurepas, March 18, 1730, in Rowland and Sanders, *Mississippi Provincial Archives*, 1:64, 71; editor's analysis of the letter on p. 71. Galloway, *Mississippi Provincial Archives*, 4:33. Vols. 4 and 5 were begun by Rowland and Sanders in 1927.

25. "Memoir on Indians by Kerlérec, December 12, 1758," in Galloway, *Mississippi Provincial Archives*, 5:212.

26. Gravier, *Gravier's Voyage*, 143; d'Iberville, *Iberville's Gulf Journals*, 69.

27. Swanton, *Indians of the Southeastern*, 140.

28. "Census of the Indians in Louis Judice's District, September 5, 1768," in Papeles Procedentes de Cuba, 187A, Archivo General de las Indias, n.p., microfilm reel 2. Judice Papers, Center for Louisiana Studies, University of Louisiana at Lafayette.

29. Swanton, *Indians of the Southeastern*, 82–83, 95.

30. M. de Kerlérec, December 12, 1758, in Galloway, *Mississippi Provincial Archives*, 5:212.

31. Usner, *American Indians*, 44–45. Absorption of survivors was common throughout the Southeast, and one can easily draw parallels with the Houma. While the Catawba also stand as an example of different bands coming together, a particularly nice discussion of absorption along the Atlantic seaboard is Bowne, *Westo Indians*, 25. Eric Bowne succinctly examines not only Westo absorption of bands between 1656 and 1680 but also what these Indians brought to the larger group.

32. "Statement about the Church in Louisiana," *Mississippi Provincial Archives*, 2:572; Father Raphael to Abbe Raguet, September 15, 1725, in *Mississippi Provincial Archives*, 2:509.

33. Bolton, *Athanase de Mézières*, 1:238–39, n351.

34. Marchand, *Story of Ascension Parish*, 26.

3. A DUCK'S NESTING PLACE

1. Brasseaux, *Comparative View of French*, 96. The Houma were not the only nation to parley with the French concerning these rumors. The Biloxi, Chitimacha, Choctaw, Arkansas and "Natchez" (probably the Chickasaw) also met with d'Abbadie.

2. Hutchins, *Historical Narrative*, 9–10.

3. Brasseaux, *Comparative View of French*, 113. Houma actions stood in stark contrast to those of the Tunica, who attacked British people traveling upriver in 1784. See Alvord and Carter, *Critical Period*, 285–87.

4. General Gage to Conway, June 24, 1766, in Carter, *Correspondence of General Thomas*, 1:93.

5. Aubrey to French Ministry, February 4, 1765, in Alvord and Carter, *Critical Period*, 431.

6. Instructions from Ulloa, March 14, 1767, in Houck, *Spanish Regime in Missouri*, 1:11–12.

7. "Census of the Indians in Louis Judice's District, September 5, 1768," in Papeles Procedentes de Cuba, 187A, n.p., microfilm reel 2.

8. O'Reilly to Arriaga, October 17, 1769, in Kinnaird, *Spain in the Mississippi*, part 1, 2:101.

9. O'Reilly to Arriaga, October 17, 1769, in Kinnaird, *Spain in the Mississippi*, part 1, 101–2.

10. O'Reilly to Arriaga, October 17, 1769, in Kinnaird, *Spain in the Mississippi*, part 1, 102–3.

11. Arena, "Land Settlement Policies," 53. To give a brief overview, the *Laws* were a series of 148 ordinances that built upon earlier Spanish edicts concerning behavior and settlement in the Americas. Previous codes dating back to the Laws of Burgos in 1512 underwent constant refining. The last revision of the *Recopilación* was published in 1681. These codes applied both to Spaniards and Natives, particularly as the two groups affected each other.

12. I have written about the Houma nation's link with New Orleans foodways elsewhere and thought it best not to belabor that point in this book. Interested readers should see d'Oney, "Harvest of Life," 50–55.

13. The district took its name from La Fourche des Chetimaches, sometimes called Rivière des Chetimaches. Adding to the locale's confusing terminology, "La Fourche des Chetimaches" applied to both the district and the waterway. Likewise, "Lafourche" would come to be the preferred term for the bayou but also apply to a series of political designations. In 1807 the American territorial legislature split what is now the state of Louisiana into nineteen parishes and with it the area once administered by Judice. The section directly along the Mississippi became Ascension Parish, while the area running southward toward the Gulf was named "Interior Parish." In 1812 the latter was renamed "Lafourche Interior Parish" but in 1822 the western section was designated "Terrebonne Parish," the parish sharing its name with the main waterway running through it. In 1853 what remained of Lafourche Interior was renamed "Lafourche Parish." The Houma eventually traveled south along modern-day Bayou Lafourche to the point where present-day Bayou Terrebonne split from it. Some remained along the larger waterway and thus in modern-day Lafourche Parish, while others filtered down the smaller waterway and through Terrebonne Parish.

14. For more information, see Brasseaux, House, and Michot, "Pioneer Amateur Naturalist," 71–103. In the first pages of their article the authors give a wonderful overview of Judice's life and his experiences in the region.

15. Marchand, *Story of Ascension Parish*, 24.

16. John Thomas to John Stuart, December 12, 1771, in National Archives of the UK. Deep thanks to Cindy Stark at the New York State Archives, where I tried to look at the microfilm. When the finding aid proved completely unreliable, she searched diligently through the reels and emailed the letter and citation to me, then spoke with me several times over the phone to make sure I had what I needed.

17. John Stuart, in charge of English trade in the Southeast, devised a series of nineteen articles in conjunction with Governor Johnstone. The first is that "no Indian trader by himself or substitute, or servant, shall sell or give to any Indian any spirituous liquor of any kind whatsoever." This and the other eighteen articles are in Alden, *John Stuart*, 341–43; Farmar to Stuart, December 16, 1765, in Alvord and Carter, *New Regime*, 128.

18. Robertson to Johnstone, New Orleans, September 2, 1765, in Robertson, *Lieutenant-General Royal Engineer*, 16–17.

19. Robertson to Johnstone, New Orleans, September 2, 1765, in Robertson, *Lieutenant-General Royal Engineer*, 17.

20. Robertson to Johnstone, New Orleans, September 2, 1765, in Robertson, *Lieutenant-General Royal Engineer*, 17–18.

21. John Thomas to John Stuart, December 12, 1771, in National Archives of the UK.

22. Brasseaux, *Founding of New Acadia*, 79. See p. 93 for a map of Acadian settlements. In both this book and his contribution to Uzee, *Lafourche Country*, Brasseaux mined the voluminous Papeles Procedentes de Cuba archives. After reviewing both his writings and his original sources, I concur with Carl's opinions. Given that I rely so much on his interpretation, however, I have chosen to cite him instead of referencing the original letters. Readers interested in the original documents should mine his notes in these two works for the complete list of Papeles Procedentes de Cuba letters and folios from which he drew and which I reviewed in writing this book. They make for fascinating reading.

23. Brasseaux, *Founding of New Acadia*, 182; Brasseaux, "Acadian Life," 37; Campisi, "Houma," 635.

24. Brasseaux, "Acadian Life," 37.

25. Lee, "Historic Houma of Louisiana," 136. In constructing her passage, Lee draws upon the Papeles Procedentes de Cuba and cites her source as "February 5, 1775; AGI, Cuba, legajo 189-B, folders 266–7." I drew upon both her Papeles Procedentes de Cuba material and her interpretation in this paragraph.

26. Lee, "Historic Houma of Louisiana," 136–37. In constructing the incident with the Pascagoula, Dayna Bowker Lee drew upon two sources. The first is Acosta's letter in Kinnaird, *Spain in the Mississippi*, 2:227. This presents the event from the Pascagoula side. The second source is a letter from Judice in the Papeles Procedentes de Cuba, which she cites as "May 18, 1775: AGI, Cuba,

legajo, 180-B, folders 270–1." This presents the incident from the Houma perspective. The quote used in this paragraph comes from Lee's translation of the event as recorded by Judice. In my passage I draw upon her source documents, her translation, and her interpretation.

27. Din, *Canary Islanders of Louisiana*, 15–16, 19, 30.

28. Din, *Canary Islanders of Louisiana*, 69–70.

29. Because Spain did not want to set a precedent of aiding colonies against a European power, they entered the war not as allies of the colonies but as coaggressors. See Haarmann, "Spanish Conquest of British," 108.

30. Gayerré, *History of Louisiana*, 125–26. In one of the many intricacies of Lower Mississippi Valley politics, Gálvez served in northern Africa with O'Reilly after the latter had left Louisiana.

31. Gayerré, *History of Louisiana*, 126.

32. Gayerré, *History of Louisiana*, 127, 129. Fort Panmure was close to the former site of Fort Rosalie, on a river bluff at the modern town of Natchez, Mississippi.

33. For more information on the battles and what they meant in the context of the Lower Mississippi Valley, see Haynes, *Natchez District*.

34. Gayerré, *History of Louisiana*, 126.

35. De Kerlérec, "Rapporte de Chevalier," 1:75.

36. Brasseaux, "Acadian Life," 37. As with note 22, in this passage I rely both on Dr. Brasseaux's sources and his interpretation.

37. Brasseaux, "Acadian Life," 37.

38. Brasseaux, *Founding of New Acadia*, 183.

39. A piastre was worth about five livres. This type of Spanish silver coin had been used freely even during the French colonial period, and its use continued into the Iberian colonial era; Brasseaux, *Founding of New Acadia*, 193–94.

40. Brasseaux, *Founding of New Acadia*, 184.

41. Brasseaux, *Founding of New Acadia*, 184.

42. Claiborne, *Houmas Land Claim*, 3–4; Hart, *Exposition of the Houmas*, 5–6. Subsequent transfers of land produced ugly legal battles between Euro-Americans and voluminous paperwork before courts finally ruled in 1866. Lacking original petitions, grants, acts of sale from the Houma, or acts of conveyance to Conway, heirs to the estate had to make do with a supposed copy of the conveyance from the Houma to Conway and Latil as well as a supposed copy of Unzaga's grant. Court proceedings and related documents are Byzantine, but two good secondary sources are Gautreau, *Pre-Emption Entries* and "Memorial of the Representatives," both from the 1830s.

43. "Census of the Indians in Louis Judice's District, September 5, 1768," in Papeles Procedentes de Cuba, 187A: n.p., microfilm reel 2. Primary and secondary accounts of the land transaction display not only a variety of spellings in this

man's name but also in the names of other participants. This use of multiple names is very typical of the era's records.

44. Claiborne, *Houmas Land Claim*, 4; Toombs, *Report*, 2, 3.
45. Louis Judice to Unzaga, October 1, 1775, in Papeles Procedentes de Cuba, 189B: 284–85.
46. Louis Judice to Unzaga, October 1, 1775, in Papeles Procedentes de Cuba, 189B: 284–85.
47. Louis Judice to Unzaga, October 1, 1775, in Papeles Procedentes de Cuba, 189B: 284–85.
48. Hutchins, *Historical Narrative*, 39.
49. Hutchins, *Historical Narrative*, 40. The 1752 Jean Baptiste Bourguignon d'Anville map that serves as the first image in this book does indeed indicate the existence of Bayou Lafourche and Bayou Terrebonne, but Hutchins apparently was not familiar with it.
50. Hutchins, *Historical Narrative*, 40; Tom Dion, interview. Dion recorded that his ancestors had hunted the lower bayous even when in Ascension.
51. Lee, "Historic Houma of Louisiana," 140. See her original source as given: "1776, AGI, Cuba, legajo 189-B, no folder number."
52. My interactions with many tribal members when I was living in Houma reinforced how common this account is, cropping up in discussion after discussion. Swanton presumably heard it from Indians in 1907, after which he recorded it in *Indians of the Southeastern*, 140, and *Indian Tribes*, 291. For a formal oral interview recording this migration, see Dion, interview.
53. Lowrie and St. Clair Clarke, *American State Papers*, 2:432. Bayou "Terrebonne" here is noted as "Darbonne," which it was often also called until the mid-1800s.
54. Lowrie and St. Clair Clarke, *American State Papers*, 2:433.
55. De Sinclair, "Correspondence of Laussat," 115.
56. Claiborne to Henry Dearborn, April 4, 1806, in Rowland, *Official Letter Books*, 3:347.
57. An unavoidable fact of historical research is that many people privilege the written record over oral history. Insulting as this might be to keepers of the oral tradition, the look to colonials and Americans as more reliable sources is something with which native peoples must unfortunately contend. In this case, however, which is more reliable is a moot point given that both oral tradition and Judice's letters support each other.
58. Swanton draws the same conclusion in *Indian Tribes*, 291: "The records leave us in doubt when the bulk of the tribe moved from Ascension into Terre Bonne parish, and possibly it was a drift rather than a regular migration."
59. Lee, "Historic Houma of Louisiana," 142; Dardar, *Women-Chiefs*, 28.
60. Din, *Canary Islanders of Louisiana*, 80–81.
61. Comeaux, "Louisiana's Acadians," 146–47.

4. A KINGDOM OF WATER

1. One finds various years for when the final separation of Bayou Lafourche from the Mississippi took place. 1903, 1905, and 1906 are all given in sources as the date for the damming of the bayou, based on what stage of the closure one notes. The year given here is the first in which the bayou was "officially" closed, as noted in a 1955 site marker.

2. Watkins, "History of Terrebonne Parish," 12–14. Watkins notes on p. 10 that Bayou Dularge was once known as Bayou Black and that readers should bear that in mind when looking at maps.

3. One of the most succinct examinations of this "Second Expulsion" is in Comeaux, "Environmental Impact," 147; Carl Brasseaux argues in *Acadian to Cajun*, 10–11, that the theory of the Second Expulsion is greatly overblown. Even he, though, notes that there was large-scale movement from the river parishes to Terrebonne and Lafourche parishes.

4. Given that the same words are used to describe bayous and parishes, a bit of explanation is in order. Please see note 13 in chap. 3 for a more complete explanation, but in brief: On March 31, 1807, the American territorial legislature created nineteen political divisions called parishes. One was Ascension Parish, along the river. By 1853 modern-day Lafourche Parish and Terrebonne Parish had also emerged in their present forms. Bayou Lafourche is the main waterway flowing through Lafourche Parish. Likewise, Bayou Terrebonne flows through the middle of a town called Houma, in modern-day Terrebonne Parish. The Lafourche and Terrebonne parishes stretch along the Gulf of Mexico from east to west, and the United Houma Nation recognizes them as its homeland.

5. Marchand, *Flight of a Century*, 20.

6. Becnel, *Barrow Family*, 23, 43–45; see Davis, *Traînasse*, 349–59. Davis gives an excellent overview of the history of these smallest of waterways and the effects they had on economy and erosion. I have seen this word spelled as "trenasse" rather than traînasse but have chosen the latter spelling for this work.

7. De Caro and Jordan, *Louisiana Sojourns*, 399.

8. Martin, *Anatole's Story*, 106–7. The distance between the two communities today is about twenty-three miles by driving and twelve miles as the crow flies.

9. The Houma's relationship with water came up in each one of the oral interviews I conducted with tribal members and lodged at the T. Harry Williams Center, Louisiana State University. To list only two, the interviews with Father Roch Naquin and Brenda Dardar Robichaux were particularly revealing in that respect.

10. See La Vente to Pontchartrain, March 2, 1708, in Rowland and Sanders, *Mississippi Provincial Archives*, 2:31 and "Census of Louisiana by de La Salle," August 12, 1708, in Rowland and Sanders, *Mississippi Provincial Archives*, 2:32.

Father La Vente argued that "It is necessary to issue an ordinance to forbid the French of Mobile from taking Indian women as slaves and especially from living with them under the same roof in concubinage." La Salle echoed this in his census when he recorded "60 Canadian backwoodsmen who are in the Indian villages situated along the Mississippi River without any permission from any governor, who destroy by their wicked, libertine lives with Indian women all that the missionaries of foreign missions and others teach them about the divine mysteries of the Christian religion."

11. Duclos to Pontchartrain, December 25, 1715, in Rowland and Sanders, *Mississippi Provincial Archives*, 2:207.

12. United Methodist Church of Dulac, "Remembrance of Our Church History," 9. The document is uncatalogued, so interested researchers must ask the archivist to locate it; Baade, "Louisiana's Laws," 3, 7–9, 10. Baade's paper contains the translated Royal Order of December 16, 1792.

13. Albert Naquin, interview.

14. Swanton, *Indian Tribes*, 292.

15. Albert Naquin, interview.

16. Roch Naquin, interview.

17. Ancelet, Edwards, and Pitre, *Cajun Country*, 69–70.

18. This researcher lived in Houma, Louisiana (the parish seat of Terrebonne) for almost a year in the late 1990s, and it was made extremely clear to him at churches, banks, groceries, libraries, social events, the gym, and dozens of other places that there was an extremely strong concept of Indians versus non-Indians. As one Terrebonne Parish matron sniffed when she found out where I was going the next day, "I don't know what kind of a man would marry into that group of people, those Sabines. As far as we're concerned those men stopped being white as soon as they had children with those women." "Sabine," the term this woman used, is an ethnic slur considered highly offensive by the Houma.

19. "Certificate of Burial."

20. Uzee, "Father Charles M. Menard," 375. For further reading, please see Menard, "Annales de l'Eglise." Those not able to access the archives can access Philip Uzee's translation in serial form at the *Bayou Catholic*, a serial from the Diocese of Houma-Thibodaux.

21. Montegut was named for Gabriel Montegut, a plantation owner in the area, and did not acquire this name until 1889. Before that the Euro-American name was "Le Terrebonne," confusing given that a bayou and parish also had the same name. Even more confusing is that Bayou Terrebonne was sometimes called Bayou "Darbonne."

22. Certification and Abstract Document, Birth-Baptismal Record, Diocese of Houma-Thibodaux, Office of Archives, Thibodaux, Louisiana. Baptismal Register of St. Joseph Church, 4:20. Abstracted October 6, 1986.

23. Baudier, *Catholic Church in Louisiana*, 416.

24. Pelletier, *Ile Jean Charles*, 5. This is a privately printed history of Isle de Jean Charles; Guidry, *Le Terrebonne*, 7, 8. In gauging whether Joseph was Houma Indian or from the town of Houma, my conversations with members of the Duthu Indian family confirm that this Joseph is the ancestor of several modern members of the UHN.

25. Guidry, *Le Terrebonne*, 7, 8.

26. Swanton, *Indian Tribes*, 28–29.

27. De Sinclair, "Correspondence of Laussat," 115.

28. Kane, *Bayous of Louisiana*, 120–21.

29. Roch Naquin, interview; Mrs. Joseph Naquin, interview. Mr. Bordeaux is sometimes called "Boudreaux" by younger people, but in talking to those who knew him or were closer to his time, "Bordeaux" is given consistently.

30. Pelletier, *Ile Jean Charles*, 17–18.

31. The following interviews were conducted by Janel Curry and Bruce Duthu and are in the possession of the latter: Mr. and Mrs. Charles Billiot, February 21, 1978 and August 21, 1978; Cyril Billiot, July 26, 1978; Jimmy and Albertifle Courteaux, July 20, 1978. Thanks to Bruce Duthu for letting me listen to them. Ruth Underhill made reference to the Houma telling her about the land grant when she was in the community during the 1930s. Ruth Underhill to Frank Speck, October 22, 1938, series 1, folder 4 (16c3), Frank G. Speck Papers, American Philosophical Society; Fischer, "History and Current Status," 220. The Atchafalaya River is here given as the western boundary, but some oral histories indicate the boundary line ran along Bayou Black to the point where it connected with other waterways and emptied into the river.

32. Lowrie and St. Clair Clarke, *American State Papers*, 3:265.

33. Burns, "Spanish Land Laws," 573.

34. Lowrie and St. Clair Clarke, *American State Papers*, 2:95.

35. *Compendium of the Enumeration*, 3:60–62.

36. DeBow, *Seventh Census*, 1:473.

37. Kennedy, *Population [. . .] Eighth Census*, 1:188–95. Indian statistics are on pp. 192–93, while the final tally of "whites," "free colored," and "slave[s]" is on p. 194.

38. Walker, *Ninth Census*, 1:35.

39. Department of the Interior, *Statistics [. . .] Tenth Census*, 1:544–45, 587.

40. Department of the Interior, *Report [. . .] Eleventh Census*, 1:963, 397, 401.

41. Merriam, *Twelfth Census*, 1:541–42.

42. Department of Commerce, *Thirteenth Census*, 773, 777.

43. Department of Commerce, *Fourteenth Census*, 388, 391.

44. Department of Commerce, *Fifteenth Census*, 992.

45. Department of Commerce, *Sixteenth Census*, 332, 334.

46. Department of Commerce, *Report [. . .] Seventeenth Decennial Census*, 18–81, 18–97, 18–71, 18–76, 18–75, xvi.

47. The Houma were absolutely not alone in their experience, and readers may examine other works that address similar themes. Brian Klopotek touches upon this issue for other Louisiana Indian tribes in *Recognition Odysseys.* The Houma are sometimes compared to the Lumbee, and Malinda Maynor Lowery's *Lumbee Indians in the Jim Crow South* is an outstanding examination of similar events in North Carolina. Christopher Arris Oakley addresses some of the same issues Lowery does but expands his focus to include other North Carolina tribes in *Keeping the Circle.* One of the strongest works on the topic is Andrew Denson's *Monuments to Absence.* Nor is this issue confined to the Southeast: Daniel Mandell's *Tribe, Race, History* and Jean M. O'Brien's *Firsting and Lasting* are outstanding examples of this same practice in another region.

The more one reads about Natives and ethnic identity, the more one realizes that erasing Indians from the official record and thus from memory was a constant rather than an exception. In this respect the Houma's experience is definitely part of a broader trend. On the other hand, their experience reflects their own particular history with surrounding communities.

48. Brasseaux, *Acadian to Cajun,* xii.

49. Baudier, *Catholic Church in Louisiana,* 584.

50. For more on the status of swamps as both reality and imagined space, see Wilson, *Shadow and Shelter.*

51. Pierce, "Historical and Statistical Collections," 603; *Biographical and Historical Memoirs of Louisiana,* 1:23.

52. Cole, "In Fair Terrebonne," 61.

53. Speck, "Social Reconnaissance," 137, 138.

54. Wendt, "Brother Martin of the Bayous."

55. Martin, *Anatole's Story,* 187.

56. To give just one example among many, very common shortenings of *Petit Jean* ("Little John," or "John Jr.") are "Tijan'," "Tijean," or "T-Jean." With how people use "dit" names in a variety of ways (on checks and mailboxes, etc.), it is very easy to believe that these are birth names. Michael Dardar, the unofficial Houma tribal historian, publishes under the name "T-Mayheart" to honor his father.

57. "Land Sale-Jean Billiot to Touh-la-bay alias Courteau of Beloxy Nation," *Terrebonne Life Lines* 17, no. 4: 297. Taken from OA Book A no. 51; COB 1 p. 71, Conveyance Department, Terrebonne Parish Courthouse, Houma LA.

58. "Land Sale-Toup-la-bay to Alexandre Verdun," *Terrebonne Life Lines* 17, no. 4: 298. Taken from bk. E, no. 837, pp. 108, 109, 3/526, Conveyance Department, Terrebonne Parish Courthouse, Houma LA.

59. "Probate of Tacolabe," trans. Elton Oubre, annotated by Audrey B. Westerman, *Terrebonne Life Lines* 17, no. 4, 299–306. Name of the deceased son given on pp. 303 and 304. Taken from bk. 10, Civil Suits & Probate Records 109–

27, Probate 115, Conveyance Department, Terrebonne Parish Courthouse, Houma LA.

60. Martin, *Orleans Term Reports*, 1:65.

61. Louisiana's Indian peoples were reaffirmed to be free in *Ulzere v. Poeyfarré.*

62. Lowrie and St. Clair Clarke, *American State Papers*, 2:433. Her first name is sometimes listed as "Marianne" and her last as "Enerise" and "Iris." For further reading, see "The Indians of Terrebonne and Lafourche Parishes," *Terrebonne Life Lines* 20, no. 3 (Fall 2001), 165. Marie Nerisse is very likely the woman referred to as "Mariane Erice" in *H.L. Billiot v. Terrebonne*, no. 22567. To add another layer of obfuscation, the school board argued that she was black, but witnesses claimed she was Spanish.

5. "SO-CALLED INDIANS"

1. Struggling to accommodate and organize—and control—diverse elements of their new society, the French and Spanish regimes in Louisiana developed a complex racial order which, while not always recognized by people in their daily lives, was rigid as defined by law: Mulattoes (the offspring of a European and an African), quadroons (European and a mulatto), griffes (mulatto and African), metifs (white and quadroon), marabons (mulatto and griffe), and meameloucs (European and metif). Despite the seeming precision with which complex terms were used, however, there was quite a bit of overlap where Native Americans were concerned. Both French and Spanish records referred to Indians of the Lower Mississippi Valley as "Indiens," "sauvages," or "gens de couleur libres." See Forbes, *Africans and Native Americans*, 129; Nash, "Hidden History of Mestizo," 17–22.

2. I would like to stress that my use of the word "bastard" is not a personal choice on my part but rather a legal designation. Louisiana law made sharp distinctions between illegitimate children and bastards, as I will address later in the chapter.

3. One might question whether a "white versus everyone else" mentality truly existed given that *Plessy v. Ferguson* allowed Chinese people to ride in white cars. Justice Harlan made special note of this in his dissent, but this exception does not negate the general trend of Louisiana law during the time. Indeed, Harlan noted the exception specifically because it contradicted the general flavor both of the ruling and of where he judged Louisiana law was moving. The Chinese population in the state was so small at this time that Chinese exclusion or inclusion was a nonissue, though it might very much have been an issue if the population had been higher.

4. *State v. Treadaway*, 508.

5. Some excellent scholarship has been written on social conflict as it pertains to Louisiana schools, but a wonderful starting point is vol. 18 of Wade, *Louisiana*

Purchase Bicentennial Series. Edited by Michael Wade, its forty articles examine the state's educational history from a number of perspectives.

6. *Acts of the First*, 62.

7. Watkins, "History of Terrebonne Parish," 134.

8. *H.L. Billiot v. Terrebonne*, no. 7876, pp. 1, 2, 3. "17th District" is given on the court record's first page, while "20th District" is given on all subsequent pages, but the docket number remains the same. The twentieth district later became the seventeenth, and another cover was placed over the proceedings in an attempt to preserve them. Thanks to Robert Boudreaux and Wendy Chauvin for explaining this discrepancy; TPSBM 3:15.

9. *H.L. Billiot v. Terrebonne*, no. 22567, 1–2.

10. Even within the court records, there are inconsistencies. Marie Lejunie is also referred to as Marie Lajourne. In another instance, the record maintains that Billiot suffered $1,000 in damages while another part of the court case maintains he suffered $2,000 in damages.

11. *H.L. Billiot v. Terrebonne*, no. 22567, 2.

12. *H.L. Billiot v. Terrebonne*, no. 22567, 5.

13. *H.L. Billiot v. Terrebonne*, no. 22567, 6.

14. *H.L. Billiot v. Terrebonne*, no. 22567, 5, 6, 8.

15. *H.L. Billiot v. Terrebonne*, no. 22567, 8, 19.

16. *H.L. Billiot v. Terrebonne*, no. 22567, 6, 18, 20, 22.

17. *H.L. Billiot v. Terrebonne*, no. 22567, 25.

18. *H.L. Billiot v. Terrebonne*, no. 22567, 26, 31.

19. *H.L. Billiot v. Terrebonne*, no. 22567, 20–22, 27.

20. *H.L. Billiot v. Terrebonne*, no. 22567. This appeal may be found in the archives of the Supreme Court of the State of Louisiana, New Orleans, Louisiana. The Louisiana Supreme Court ruling is also contained in the Terrebonne Parish Courthouse with the original trial proceedings.

21. Terrebonne Parish School Board, *School Board Minutes*, 3:154. Hereafter TPSBM.

22. TPSBM 3:152, 154, 169, 264, 292, 560; Bourgeois, "Four Decades of Public," 67.

23. One hesitates to use the word "delightful" to describe a thesis on the muskrat industry, but interested readers should see Boscareno, "Rise and Fall." It gives a wonderful overview of the topic.

24. Chatterton, "Muskrat Fur Industry," 194. Though he wrote for a popular audience, Harnett Kane gave an excellent overview of the trapping lifestyle, the people involved with it, and the effects on Louisiana culture in chap. 5 of *Bayous of Louisiana* titled "M'sieu Mus'rat and His People," 102–22.

25. Fischer, "History and Current Status," 220.

26. These were very dark days for the nation and still produce a great deal of rage. In the late 1990s and early 2000s I was fortunate enough to be invited into many Houma homes to visit, and the conversation invariably became uncomfortable when land losses to the fur and oil industries came up. Speakers—

especially older speakers—usually became very agitated. Listening to Houma elders, one realized how close to the surface this history was and what an incredibly traumatic time of loss this was for the nation.

27. "The Musk Rat," originally printed in the *Houma Courier* on December 19, 1925. *Houma Daily Courier* reprint December 06, 2006.

28. In the 1930s Eugene Dumez wrote several letters to federal officials concerning the Houma nation's education and economy. See Dumez to Indian Office, April 27, 1931, and Dumez to Hon. Commissioner of Indian Affairs, September 11, 1934. Both in National Archives, Indian Office Files, file 25436, box 150.

29. "Frederic Querens to Commissioner of Indian Affairs, January 9, 1933, in National Archives, Indian Office Files, 1932, file 43488, box 150.

30. Commissioner C. J. Rhoads to Mr. Frederic C. Querens, January 20, 1933; Commissioner C. J. Rhoads to Hon. John Barton Payne, January 20, 1933. Both in National Archives, Indian Office Files, 1932, file 43488, box 150.

31. Ruth Underhill to Frank Speck. October 22, 1938, in Frank G. Speck Papers, American Philosophical Society. series 1, folder 4 (16c3); Ann Fischer, "History and Current Status," 220, 226.

32. *Digest of the Civil Laws*, title 4, chap. 1, art. 1 and 2, p. 24.

33. Elements of forced heirship were revised in the 1990s, and this created an uproar in the state. Even today, though, many elements of forced heirship remain, albeit under different terms.

34. *Digest of the Civil Laws*, title 4, chap. 1, art. 1 and 2, p. 24.

35. "The Will of Alexandre Verdun," Bk. E, no. 829, 94–96: 3/531, in Terrebonne Parish Courthouse, Houma LA. The will is translated and annotated in *Terrebonne Life Lines* 3, no. 1 (Spring 1984), 17–20.

36. Articles 220, 221, 224, 226, and 227 in Upton and Jennings, *Civil Code*, 33–35; Curry, *Reports of Cases Argued*, 542–48. Though *Reports of Cases Argued* is a good overview of the proceedings, the original court documents are enlightening as a reflection of Louisiana attitudes in race relations and inheritance law. These documents can be found at *Robinet v. Verdun's Vendees*, 1–7. The numbering system is repetitive and unclear, but see pages 1–11, 21, 36, and 41–46.

37. United Methodist Church of Dulac, *A People Named Houmas*, 9.

38. TPSBM 3:384.

39. Both letters are quoted in their entirety in Downs and Whitehead, "Houma Indians," 4–5. See this article for citations to the original documents in the National Archives.

40. Nash, "Indians of Louisiana," 11.

41. W. Carson Ryan Jr. to Mr. David Billiot, October 13, 1934; W. Carson Ryan Jr. to Mr. Eugene Dumez, September 26, 1934; David Billiot to President Roosevelt, May 31, 1934; and David Billiot to Gov. O. K. Allen, August 6, 1933. All in National Archives, Indian Office Files, file 25436, box 150.

42. Speck, "Social Reconnaissance," 139, 141, 145, 142.

43. Harrington, "Among Southern Indians," 657–58. These pages were detached from the *Southern Workman* and are housed in the Rare Books Collection, University Libraries Division of Special Collections, University of Alabama. Thanks to Donelly Lancaster for sending me a copy of this source and helping me with the citation.

44. Paul Fickinger to Harvey Meyer, March 5, 1940, in National Archives, Indian Office Files, file 48363, box 260. Ruth Underhill responded to Meyer's previous report at the request of federal officials. This box contains a typed, unsigned paragraph which is probably Underhill's original response to Meyer's report. Fickinger inserted an edited version of this in his letter to Meyer and stated that it was her response. This response was inserted into several letters sent from Fickinger's office regarding the Houma and includes Underhill's opinion of Bourgeois. Interestingly, Fickinger and others who quote Underhill always leave out the phrase "(which apparently nobody read)", a reference to the fact that people seemed to have been talking about the Houma without reading her report on them.

45. TPSBM 2:117.

46. Woman's Missionary Council of the Methodist Episcopal Church, South, *Eighth Annual Report*, 280–81. Yearly reports from the Women's Missionary Council were graciously copied and sent to me by Tracey Del Duca, archivist at the General Commission on Archives and History, United Methodist Church, Madison NJ; United Methodist Church of Dulac, *A People Named Houmas*, 12.

47. "If I can help my people, that's what I want to do." Slind-Flor, "If I Can Help," 1A–2A.

48. Martin, *Anatole's Story*, 106.

49. "Wesley House," 8. The school was also sometimes called the French Mission School or just Wesley House. Depending on the source, spelling for the home varies between "McDonell" and "MacDonell."

50. Martin, *Anatole's Story*, 166–67.

51. Roy, "Indians of Dulac," 57.

52. Woman's Missionary Council of the Methodist Episcopal Church, South, *Twenty-Ninth Annual Report*, 199. Yearly reports from the Women's Missionary Council were graciously copied and sent to me by Tracey Del Duca, archivist at The General Commission on Archives and History, United Methodist Church, Madison NJ.

53. Bourgeois, "Four Decades of Public," 70. Both the *Associated Press* dispatch and Bourgeois's response are on the same page; the moniker "so-called Indian" is an anthropological term for groups with some claim to Indian ancestry. In its original context the term is not pejorative. Ann Fischer of Tulane's Anthropology Department used it in reference to the Houma, and she was very friendly with the tribe. Still, when used by members of the Terrebonne Parish School Board, it hardly seems an anthropological term.

54. TPSBM 4:242, 281, 282.
55. TPSBM 4:287.
56. TPSBM 4:287–88.
57. TPSBM 4:288.
58. Beatty, *Louisiana Educational Survey*, 2–3.
59. Francis and Francis, interview; Michael Dardar, oral communication with the author, October 8, 2007.
60. Spicker, Steiner, and Walden, *Survey of Rural Louisiana*, 20.
61. Ella Mae Charlton, "Eva Dean Paves the Way," July 13, 1958, 10–11. Article found in the vertical file at MacDonell United Methodist Children's Home, Houma, Louisiana.
62. Robichaux, interview; Slind-Flor, "If I Can Help," 2A.
63. TPSBM 5:293.
64. TPSBM 5:414–15, 445.
65. TPSBM 7:259.
66. Roy Parfait, interview; *Naquin v. Terrebonne*, 5. Though many pages of this document are unnumbered, the material in this paragraph comes from the section dated August 13, 1964. For a more detailed examination of this court case, see Krupa, "'So-Called Indians' Stand," 171–94.
67. *Naquin v. Terrebonne*, sec. dated August 13, 1964.
68. H.L. Bourgeois Jr., interview.
69. Billiot, interview; Clyde Dion, interview.
70. Rita Duthu Dion, interview by Bruce Duthu. The original is in the possession of Bruce Duthu, who let me listen to the tape; Howard Dion and Rita Dion, interview.
71. TPSBM 2:147, 322.
72. Robichaux, interview.
73. TPSBM 7:259.
74. I am well aware that Lafourche Parish is overlooked in this chapter, but the two parishes had marked differences in terms of Houma education. Moreover, the records at the Terrebonne Parish School Board are more detailed than those in Lafourche; there were court cases, and the underlying body of literature is much richer for Terrebonne Parish. Aside from this, it would have been very difficult to construct a narrative that constantly switched back and forth between the parishes. This is not to downplay the struggles of those Houma in Lafourche Parish.
75. I would once again like to thank the Lafourche and Terrebonne school boards. Every person with whom I came in contact went out of their way to give me free access to records and to create a quiet area for my research. They graciously gave of their time in helping me understand nuances of parish and state educational history, asked older family members about their memories, and directed me to other sources outside their archives.

1. See Davis, "Case of Identity," 473–94.
2. Though Naquin is listed as "Joseph" in some documents relating to the conference, relatives and friends consistently refer to him as "Frank," so that is the name used here.
3. "Houma Heroine."
4. Miller, *Forgotten Tribes*, 188.
5. Curry-Roper, "Cultural Change," 238. Curry is referred to as "Janel Curry," "Janel Curry-Roper," or "Janel Roper-Curry" in her publications. I refer to her as "Janel Curry" in the chapter for the sake of continuity but give her name in citations as they appear in each work; Campisi, *Brief History*, 7–8.
6. Campisi, *Brief History*, 8.
7. Curry, "History of the Houma," 23. See notes 98 and 99 for Curry's sources.
8. "Indians Plan Merger Talks."
9. "Houma Indians Unite"; Campisi, *Brief History*, 9.
10. A number of sources give good, concise descriptions of the process. See "Branch of Acknowledgement and Research" and "Federal and State Recognition" in Davis, *Native America*, 78–79, 195–97.
11. Memo from Elizabeth Shawn Mills to Lynn McMillion, "Documenting Ethnic Identity of Early 'Mixed' Families in Lower Louisiana," January 23, 1992; Memorandum from Miriam R. Miller to Lynn McMillion, "Marie Gregoire, Femme Sauvage," August 28, 1992. Both in the Bureau of Indian Affairs Archives in Washington DC.
12. Miller, *Forgotten Tribes*, 195, 194–95. I pull from Gindrat and Verret quotes that Miller used, and readers should consult notes 109 and 106 for his original sources.
13. Inouye, *Houma Recognition Act*, 12, 14.
14. Inouye, *Houma Recognition Act*, 13.
15. Inouye, *Houma Recognition Act*, 16.
16. Inouye, *Houma Recognition Act*, 33.
17. "Summary under the Criteria 83.7" in Department of the Interior, *Proposed Finding*, 1.
18. "Historical Report" in Department of the Interior, *Proposed Finding*, 44. *By* is erroneously italicized in the original.
19. Davis, *Rivers and Bayous*. See pages 52–61 for the Red River of northwestern Louisiana chapter, 21–29 for the chapter on the Ouachita–Black River of northeastern Louisiana, and 121–28 on Bayou Lafourche.
20. Lowrie and St. Clair Clarke, *American State Papers*, 3:265. This is the page of the Houma claim on the bayou. See preceding and following pages for geographic references and references to other claimants with Acadian names.
21. This error is repeated in the findings. See "Appendix, Historical Indian Tribes in Louisiana, Background Paper" in Department of the Interior, *Proposed Finding*, 45.

22. See Curry, "History of the Houma," 16–17.
23. To those who will check this note, please do not assume that because "ASP 1834C, 3:254; ASP 1834C, 3:265, No. 247" refers to volume 3 that "ASP, 1834a, 1:349, No. 164" refers to volume 1. There is no "No. 164" listed on that page, and the section encompassing page 349 begins on page 305 with the designation of "No. 135" for the entire section and the title "Land Claims in the Michigan Territory." To test whether the wrong volume had been cited, this author checked page 349 of all volumes of the ASP, Land Claims. Only three volumes refer to Louisiana on that page. Volume 2, page 349 is a list of Euro-American settlers; the beginning of the section on page 348 notes that all claims were "for the county of Point Coupée and part of the county of Iberville," neither of which were around Natchitoches. Volume 6, page 349 (No. 974) does indeed mention a land claim in Louisiana, but it is a claim by John C. Williams to land purchased in East Feliciana. Aside from the second half of a land claim in Peoria, Illinois, that is the only entry on that page. Volume 8, page 349 is part of a section from pages 348–50 addressing land and property claims on the Mississippi River, on Lake Borgne, and in New Orleans, with no mention of Indians. "No. 164" actually appears in Volume 2 but refers to Indians around the Great Lakes, so the only logical conclusion is that the BAR referred to the *Miscellaneous* volume. My thanks to the reference and government documents librarians at the New York State Library in Albany.
24. Description of Louisiana communicated to Congress by Thomas Jefferson, November 14, 1803, American State Papers: Miscellaneous 1, no. 164, p. 349.
25. For further commentary on how claims were organized in the *American State Papers* and how the Houma claim could not have been around Natchitoches despite the BAR interpretation, see Miller, *Forgotten Tribes*, 164.
26. Swanton, *Indian Tribes*, 292.
27. See Kroeber, "Work of John," 1–9. Also see Swanton's obituary in Fenton, "John Reed Swanton."
28. Swanton, *Indian Tribes*, 292.
29. See "Land Sale-Jean Billiot to Touh-la-bay alias Courteau of Beloxy Nation," "Land Sale-Toup-la-bay to Alexandre Verdun," and "Probate of Tacalobe," in *Terrebonne Life Lines* 17, no. 4 (Winter 1998), 297, 298, 299–306.
30. For the BAR interpretation of Courteaux, see "Anthropological Report" and "Genealogical Report" in Department of the Interior, *Proposed Finding*, 19, 38–42.
31. See "Land Sale-Jean Billiot to Touh-la-bay alias Courteau of Beloxy Nation," "Land Sale-Toup-la-bay to Alexandre Verdun," and "Probate of Tacolabe" in *Terrebonne Life Lines* 17, no. 4 (Winter 1998), 297, 298, 299–306. Please see chap. 5 of this book for a more detailed discussion of this topic.
32. "Genealogical Report" in Department of the Interior, *Proposed Finding*, 41.
33. Swanton, *Indian Tribes*, 27–29.

34. Harvey Meyer to Commissioner of Indian Affairs, February 20, 1940, in National Archives, Indian Office Files, file 48363, box 260.

35. Swanton, *Indian Tribes*, 29.

36. "Summary under the Criteria 83.7" in Department of the Interior, *Proposed Finding*, 4–5, 27. "Historical Report, the United Houma Nation, Inc." and "Appendix, Historical Indian Tribes in Louisiana" in Department of the Interior, *Proposed Finding*, 57, 11.

37. See Swanton, *Indian Tribes*, 7–39. This overview of regional tribes illustrates Swanton's linguistic perspective, as do his many later works on Native languages along the Gulf Coast.

38. Campisi and Starna, "Another View," 786. The full letter Emanuel Drechsel wrote to Virginia DeMarce, dated October 3, 1993, is in Campisi's possession.

39. Campisi and Starna, "Another View," 786; Miller, *Forgotten Tribes*, 178.

40. Brown and Hardy, "What is Houma?" 521–48. Interested readers may also compare Brown and Hardy's article to Speck, "Some Comparative Traits."

41. The first quote is from a BIA press release (December 1994) and the second from a debriefing paper from Holly Reckord to the Secretary (November 1984), both quoted in Campisi and Starna, "Another View," 785.

42. BAR press release, quoted in Campisi and Starna, "Another View," 785.

43. Swanton, *Indian Tribes*, 292; "Houma Heroine"; J. Fair Hardin to the Commissioner of Indian Affairs, February 15, 1936, in National Archives, Indian Office Files, file 25436, box 150. See also any number of published works but particularly those by Frank Speck, Janel Curry, and Michael Dardar.

44. "Summary under the Criteria 83.7" in Department of the Interior, *Proposed Finding*, 9, 10, 25.

45. H.P. Martin to Charles Burke, July 30, 1921; E.B. Meritt to H.P. Martin, August 1921. Both in National Archives, Indian Office Files, 1921, file 62897, box 150.

46. Carl Hayden to Charles Burke, December 3, 1921; Charles Burke to Carl Hayden, December 9, 1921. Both in National Archives, Indian Office Files, file 97649, box 266.

47. Maurice Billiot to J.M. Stewart, October 17, 1938; J.M. Stewart to Marice [sic] Billiot, November 10, 1939; Maurice Billiot to Ruth Underhill, June 28, 1929; Ruth Underhill to Land Division, U.S. Indian Office, August 2, 1939; J.M. Stewart to Marice [sic] Billiot, September 1, 1939; A.H. McMullen to Commissioner of Indian Affairs, received October 1, 1940; J.M. Stewart to A.H. McMullen, October 14, 1940. All in National Archives, Indian Office Files, file 48363, box 260.

48. Dardar, "Istrouma," 54.

49. Miller, *Forgotten Tribes*, 201.

50. Dardar, "Istrouma," 226–28.

51. Miller, *Forgotten Tribes*, 70.

52. Goldsmith, "Group Breaks Away," 21.

53. Courteaux, Foret, and Westerman, interview; Albert Naquin, interview.

54. Goldsmith, "Group Breaks Away," 21.

55. Hackenburg, "Tribes Celebrate State Recognition," 1A, 9A.

56. Langley, "Non-indigenous, Non-aborigine Group."

57. Inouye, *Houma Recognition Act*, 23.

58. Goldsmith, "Rep. Tauzin Introduces Bill."

59. Goldsmith, "Rep. Tauzin Introduces Bill."

60. See Miller, *Forgotten Tribes*, 201n124. I pull Verret's quote from Miller's work, and readers should consult the author's note for the original source.

61. Courteaux, Foret, and Westerman, interview; Albert Naquin, interview.

62. "Indians Can't Stop Plant," *Franklin Banner-Tribune*. June 9, 1998, p. 2.

63. *United Houma Nation v. Texaco*, 10; Brenda Dardar Robichaux, oral communication with the author, February 18, 1997.

64. Davis, "Case of Identity," 473–94.

65. Brenda Dardar Robichaux, oral communication with the author, June 16, 2003.

66. Brenda Dardar Robichaux, oral communication with the author, June 16, 2003.

67. Campisi and Starna, "Another View," 780. For the BAR and Davis interpretations, see "Summary under the Criteria 83.7" and "Anthropological Report" in Department of the Interior, *Proposed Finding*, 6–7, 11. See also Davis, "Case of Identity," 474, 479. Interested readers should read and compare both works in their entirety.

68. Crepelle, "Standing Rock," 175.

69. Duthu, "Houma Indians of Louisiana," 436.

CONCLUSION

1. See Davis, "Case of Identity."

2. For more information on Katrina as well as Houma communities below New Orleans, see Dardar, "Tales of Wind," 27–34.

3. Dardar, "Tales of Wind," 32.

4. For further reading on the role of hurricanes in Houma history, please see my previous article, "Watered by Tempests."

5. D'Iberville, *Iberville's Gulf Journals*, 46–48.

6. D'Iberville, *Iberville's Gulf Journals*, 69, 79.

7. Le Page du Pratz, *History of Louisiana*, 1:148.

8. Kidder, "Making the City Inevitable," 20.

9. See Crepelle, "Standing Rock," 141–86.

Bibliography

UNPUBLISHED WORKS

Ann Champagne, et al. "Remembrance of Our Church History." Unpublished manuscript. Diocese of Houma-Thibodaux Archives, Thibodaux LA.

Baade, Hans W. "Louisiana's Laws and the Creole Family in History." Paper presented at French Creole Family in Louisiana: A Symposium, Cabildo, New Orleans, October 18, 1980.

Beatty, Willard W. "Education of Louisiana Indians." Sec. 9 of *Louisiana Educational Survey, Survey of Elementary and Secondary Education*. Louisiana Educational Survey Commission, Law Building, Louisiana State University, Baton Rouge, 1942.

Campisi, Jack. "A Brief History of the Houma People." Unpublished manuscript, Wellesley College.

"Certificate of Burial for L. Joseph." Burial Register of Ascension Catholic Church. Vol. ASC-4, p. 238, no. 254. Donaldsonville LA: Catholic Diocese of Baton Rouge Archives.

de Sinclair, Henri Delville, trans. "Correspondence of Laussat, 1803–1804, to Spanish Officials Relative to the Cession of Louisiana; Memoirs and Correspondence of Clément de Laussat." New Orleans: Survey of Federal Archives in Louisiana, Works Projects Administration of Louisiana, 1940. Located at Louisiana State University Special Collections, Baton Rouge LA.

Guidry, Sherwin. *Le Terrebonne: A History of Montegut*. Self-published, 1971.

Menard, Charles M. "Annales de l'Eglise de St. Joseph, Psse. Lafourche, Etat de la Louisiane." Archives of St. Joseph Cathedral, Thibodaux LA.

Pelletier, Father Gérard J. *Ile Jean Charles*. New Orleans, 1972.

United Methodist Church of Dulac. *A People Named Houmas*. Dulac Community Center, Dulac LA.

"Wesley House, The MacDonell Methodist Center." Typed manuscript. Vertical file, MacDonell Methodist Children's Home, Houma LA.

PUBLISHED WORKS

Acts of the First Session of the Fifth Legislature of the State of Louisiana, Begun and Held in the City of New Orleans. New Orleans: J. C. de St. Rome, State Printer, 1821.

A Digest of the Civil Laws Now in Force in the Territory of Orleans, with Alterations and Amendments Adapted to its Present System of Government. Title 4, chap. 1, art. 1 and 2, p. 24. Printed by Bradford and Anderson, Printers to the Territory, 1808.

Albrecht, Andrew. "Origin and Early Settlement of Baton Rouge." *Louisiana Historical Quarterly* 28, no. 1 (January 1945): 48–68.

Alden, John R. *John Stuart and the Southern Colonial Frontier: A Study of Indian Relations, War, Trade and Land Problems in the Southern Wilderness, 1754–1775.* London: H. Milford, 1944.

Alvord, Clarence, and Clarence Carter, eds. *The Critical Period, 1763–1765.* Springfield: Trustees of the Illinois State Historical Library, 1915.

———. *The New Regime, 1765–1767.* Springfield: Illinois State Historical Society, 1916.

Akers, Donna. *Living in the Land of Death: The Choctaw Nation, 1830–1860.* East Lansing: Michigan State University Press, 2004.

Ancelet, Barry Jean, Jay D. Edwards, and Glen Pitre. *Cajun Country.* Jackson: University Press of Mississippi, 1991.

Arena, C. Richard. "Land Settlement Policies and Practices in Spanish Louisiana." In *The Spanish in the Mississippi Valley, 1762–1804,* edited by John Francis McDermott, 51–60. Urbana: University of Illinois Press, 1974.

Baudier, Roger. *The Catholic Church in Louisiana.* New Orleans: A. W. Hyatt, 1939.

Barnett, Jim. *The Natchez Indians.* Natchez: Division of Historic Properties, Mississippi Department of Archives and Property, 1998.

Becnel, Thomas A. *The Barrow Family and the Barataria and Lafourche Canal: The Transportation Revolution in Louisiana, 1829–1925.* Baton Rouge: Louisiana State University Press, 1989.

Bibb, George M. *Report from the Secretary of the Treasury, Communicating (in Compliance with a Resolution of the Senate) Information in relation to the Claim to Land in the State of Louisiana, Called the "Houmas Claim."* Washington DC: Department of the Treasury, Government Printing Office, January 13, 1845.

Billiot, Marie. Interview by J. Daniel d'Oney, 2003. Recording. Houma Indian Series, collection 4700.1573, tape 3154. Louisiana and Lower Mississippi Valley Collections, Louisiana State University Libraries, Baton Rouge LA.

Biographical and Historical Memoirs of Louisiana, Embracing an Authentic and Comprehensive Account of the Chief Events in the History of the State, A Special Sketch of Every Parish and a Record of the Lives of Many of the Most Worthy and Illustrious Families and Individuals. In Three Volumes. Chicago: Goodspeed, 1892.

Bolton, Herbert Eugene, ed. *Athanase de Mézières and the Louisiana-Texas Frontier, 1768–1780, Documents Published for the First Time, from the Original Spanish and French Manuscripts, Chiefly in the Archives of Mexico and Spain; Translated into English; Edited and Annotated, By Herbert Eugene Bolton.* 2 vols. Cleveland: Arthur H. Clark, 1914.

Bourgeois, H.L. "Four Decades of Public Education in Terrebonne Parish." Master's thesis, Louisiana State University, 1938.

Bourgeois, H.L., Jr. Interview by unknown interviewer, 1983. Terrebonne Oral History Project (Memories of Terrebonne: Archives of the Terrebonne Parish Police Jury's Oral History Program), labeled but not numbered. Terrebonne Parish Public Library, Houma LA.

Boscareno, Jared. "The Rise and Fall of the Louisiana Muskrat, 1890–1960: An Environmental and Social History." Master's thesis, University of New Orleans, 2009. University of New Orleans Theses and Dissertations (992).

Bowne, Eric. *The Westo Indians: Slave Traders of the Early Colonial South*. Tuscaloosa: University of Alabama Press, 2005.

Brasseaux, Carl A. "Acadian Life in the Lafourche Country, 1766–1803." In *The Lafourche Country: The People and the Land*, edited by Philip Uzee, 33–42. Lafayette: Center for Southwestern Studies, University of Southwestern Louisiana, 1985.

———. *Acadian to Cajun: Transformation of a People, 1803–1877*. Jackson: University of Mississippi Press, 1992.

———, ed. and trans. *A Comparative View of French Louisiana, 1699 and 1762: The Journals of Pierre Le Moyne d'Iberville and Jean-Jacques-Blaise d'Abbadie*. Lafayette LA: Center for Louisiana Studies, 1979.

———. *The Founding of New Acadia: The Beginnings of Acadian Life in Louisiana, 1765–1803*. Baton Rouge: Louisiana State University Press, 1987.

Brasseaux, Carl, H. Dickson House, and Thomas C. Michot. "Pioneer Amateur Naturalist Louis Judice: Observation of the Fauna, Flora, Geography, and Agriculture of the Bayou Lafourche Region, Louisiana, 1772–1786." *Louisiana History: The Journal of the Louisiana Historical Association* 45, no. 1 (Winter 2004): 71–103.

Braund, Kathryn E. Holland. *Deerskins and Duffels: Creek Indian Trade with Anglo-America, 1685–1815*. Lincoln: University of Nebraska Press, 1993.

Brown, Cecil, and Heather K. Hardy. "What is Houma?" *International Journal of American Linguistics* 66, no. 4 (October 2000): 521–48.

Burns, Francis P. "The Spanish Land Laws of Louisiana." *Louisiana Historical Quarterly* 11, no. 4 (October 1928): 557–81.

Campisi, Jack. "Houma." In *Southeast*, edited by Raymond D. Fogelson, 632–41. Vol. 14 of *Handbook of North American Indians*. Washington DC: Smithsonian Institution Scholarly Press, 2004.

Campisi, Jack, and William A. Starna. "Another View on 'Ethnogenesis of the New Houma Indians.'" *Ethnohistory* 51, no. 4 (Fall 2004): 779–91.

Carter, Clarence, ed. *The Correspondence of General Thomas Gage*. 2 vols. New Haven CT: Yale University Press, 1931.

Courteaux, R., M. Foret, and A. Westerman. Interview by J. Daniel d'Oney, 2003. Houma Indian Series, collection 4700.1582, tapes 3161.1–2. Louisiana and Lower Mississippi Valley Collections, Louisiana State University Libraries, Baton Rouge LA.

Chatterton, H. J. "The Muskrat Fur Industry of Louisiana." *Journal of Geography* 43, no. 5 (1944):185–95.

Claiborne, John. *The Houmas Land Claim; A Letter from John Claiborne, Esc., to the Hon. C. T. Bemiss.* New Orleans: Delta Mammoth Job Office, 1859.

Cole, Catharine [Martha Reinhard Smallwood]. "In Fair Terrebonne." July 17, 1892. Reproduced in *Terrebonne Life Lines* 18, no. 1 (Spring 1999): 59–68. Submitted by Lorraine Wise.

Comeaux, Malcolm. "Louisiana's Acadians: The Environmental Impact." In *The Cajuns: Essays on Their History and Culture*, edited by Glenn R. Conrad, 142–60. Lafayette: Center for Louisiana Studies, University of Southwestern Louisiana, 1978.

Compendium of the Enumeration of the Inhabitants of the United States, as Obtained at the Department of State, from the Returns of the Sixth Census, by Counties and Principal Towns. Published, by Authority of an Act of Congress, under the Direction of the Secretary of State. Washington DC: Thomas Allen, 1841. Reprint, New York: Norman Ross, 1990. Page references are to the 1990 edition.

Conrad, Glenn R., ed. *Cross, Crozier and Crucible: A Volume Celebrating the Bicentennial of a Catholic Diocese in Louisiana.* Chelsea MI: BookCrafters, 1993.

Cox, Isaac, ed. *The Journeys of Réné Robert Cavelier as Related by His Faithful Lieutenant, Henri de Tonty; His Missionary Colleagues, Father Zenobius Membré, Louis Hennepin, and Anastasius Douay; His Early Biographer, Father Christian LeClercq; His Trusted Subordinate, Henri Joutel; and His Brother, Jean Cavalier; Together with Memoirs, Commissions, etc.* New York: A. S. Barnes, 1905.

Crepelle, Adam. "Standing Rock in the Swamp: Oil, the Environment, and the United Houma Nation's Struggle for Federal Recognition." *Loyola Law Review* 64, no. 1 (2018): 141–83.

Curry, Jan. "A History of the Houma Indians and Their Story of Federal Nonrecognition." *American Indian Journal* 5 (February 1979): 8–28.

Curry-Roper, Janel M. "Cultural Change and the Houma Indians: A Historical and Ecological Examination." In *A Cultural Geography of North American Indians*, edited by Thomas E. Ross and Tyrel G. Moore, 227–41. Boulder CO: Westview Press, 1987.

Curry, Thomas. *Reports of Cases Argued and Determined in the Supreme Court of the State of Louisiana.* Vol. 14. New Orleans: Benjamin Levy, 1840. Reprinted with annotations by Thomas Curry. St. Paul MN: West, 1911. Page references refer to the 1911 version.

d'Anville, Jean Baptiste Bourguignon. "Carte de la Louisiane, Par le Sr. d'Anville, Dressee en Mai 1732." d'Anville Map Collection, Hill Memorial Library, Louisiana State University.

Dardar, Michael T. Mayheart. *Istrouma: A Houma Manifesto.* Shreveport LA: Cahiers du Tintamarre, 2014.

———. "Tales of Wind and Water: Houma Indians and Hurricanes." *American Indian Culture and Research Journal* 32, no. 2 (2008), 27–34.

———. *Women-Chiefs and Crawfish Warriors: A Brief History of the Houma People.* New Orleans: United Houma Nation; New Orleans: Centenary College, 2000.

Davis, Dave. "A Case of Identity: Ethnogenesis of the New Houma Indians." *Ethnohistory* 48, no. 3 (Summer 2001): 473–94.

———. "Response to Campisi and Starns [sic]." *Ethnohistory* 51, no. 4 (Fall 2004): 793–97.

Davis, Donald. *Trainasse.* Annals of the Association of American Geographers 66, no. 3 (September 1976), 349–59

Davis, Edwin Adams, ed. *The Rivers and Bayous of Louisiana.* Baton Rouge: Louisiana Education Research Association, 1968.

Davis, Mary, ed. *Native America in the Twentieth Century: An Encyclopedia.* New York: Garland, 1994.

DeBow, J. D. B., *The Seventh Census of the United States: 1850. Embracing a Statistical View of Each of the States and Territories, Arranged by Counties, Towns, Etc.* Washington DC: Robert Armstrong, Public Printer, 1853. Reprint, New York: Norman Ross, 1990. Page references are to the 1990 edition.

de Caro, Frank A., and Rosan Augusta Jordan, eds. *Louisiana Sojourns: Travelers' Tales and Literary Journeys.* Baton Rouge: Louisiana State University Press, 1998.

de Charlevoix, Pierre-Francois-Xavier, S. J. *Histoire et description générale de la nouvelle France, avec le journal historique d'un voyage fait par ordre du roi dans l'Amérique Septentrionale.* 6 vols. Paris: Rollin Fils, 1744.

de Kerlérec, Chevalier. "Rapporte de Chevalier de Kerlérec, governeur de la Louisiane française sur les peuplades des vallées du Mississipi et du Missouri." Vol. 1 of *Compte rendu congrés internationale des Américanistes.* Quebec City: Dussault et Proulx, 1907.

de La Harpe, J. B. Bénard. *The Historical Journal of the Establishment of the French in Louisiana.* Edited and translated by Glenn C. Conrad, John Cain, and Virginia Koenig. Lafayette: Center for Louisiana Studies, University of Southeastern Louisiana, 1971.

Denson, Andrew. *Monuments to Absence: Cherokee Removal and the Contest Over Southern Memory.* Chapel Hill: University of North Carolina Press, 2017.

Department of Commerce, Bureau of the Census. *Thirteenth Census of the United States: Taken in the Year 1910.* Vol. 2, *Population: 1910.* Washington DC: Government Printing Office, 1913.

Department of the Interior, Bureau of Indian Affairs. *Proposed Finding against Federal Acknowledgment of the United Houma Nation, Inc.; Notice.* Part 4. Federal Register, vol. 59, no. 245. Washington DC: Bureau of Indian Affairs, 1994.

Department of the Interior, Census Office. *Statistics of the Population of the United States at the Tenth Census (June 1, 1880), Embracing Tables of the Population of States, Counties, and Minor Civil Divisions, with Distinction of Race,*

Sex, Age, Nativity and Occupations. Washington DC: Government Printing Office, 1883. Reprint, New York: Norman Ross, 1990. Page references are to the 1990 edition.

——. *Report on Population of the United States at the Eleventh Census: 1890*. Washington DC: Government Printing Office, 1895. Reprinted, New York: Norman Ross, 1990. Page references are to the 1990 edition.

d'Iberville, Pierre Le Moyne. *Iberville's Gulf Journals*. Edited and translated by Richebourg Gaillard McWilliams. Tuscaloosa: University of Alabama Press, 1981.

Dion, Clyde. Interview by J. Daniel d'Oney, 2003. Recording. Houma Indian Series, collection 4700.1572, tape 3153.1. Louisiana and Lower Mississippi Valley Collections, Louisiana State University Libraries, Baton Rouge LA.

Dion, Howard, and Rita Dion. Interview by J. Daniel d'Oney, 2003. Recording. Houma Indian Series, collection 4700.1574, tape 3155.1. Louisiana and Lower Mississippi Valley Collections, Louisiana State University Libraries, Baton Rouge LA.

Dion, Tom. Interview by unknown interviewer, ca. 1982. Terrebonne Oral History Project (Memories of Terrebonne: Archives of the Terrebonne Parish Police Jury's Oral History Program), labeled but not numbered. Terrebonne Parish Library, Houma LA.

Din, Gilbert C. *The Canary Islanders of Louisiana*. Baton Rouge: Louisiana State University Press, 1988.

Donaldsonville Chief. "Indian Remains and Relics." July 12, 1884. Vol. 13, no. 45.

d'Oney, J. Daniel. "Harvest of Life." *Louisiana Cultural Vistas* 19, no. 3 (Fall 2008): 50–55.

——. "The Houma Nation: A Brief Overview of the Literature." *Louisiana History* 47, no. 1 (Winter 2006): 63–90.

——. "Watered by Tempests: Hurricanes in the Cultural Fabric of the United Houma Nation." *American Indian Culture and Research Journal* 32, no. 2 (2008), 11–26.

Downs, Ernest C., and Jena Whitehead. "The Houma Indians: Two Decades in a History of Struggle." *American Indian Journal* 2 (March 1976): 2–18.

du Ru, Paul. *Journal of Paul du Ru [February 1 to May 8, 1700], Missionary Priest to Louisiana*. Translated by Ruth Lapham Butler. Chicago: Caxton Club, 1934.

Duthu, Bruce. "The Houma Indians of Louisiana: The Intersection of Law and History in the Federal Recognition Process." *Louisiana History* 38, no. 4 (Fall 1997): 409–36.

Ethridge, Robbie, and Sheri Shuck-Hall, eds. *Mapping the Mississippian Shatter Zone: The Colonial Indian Slave Trade and Regional Instability in the American South*. Lincoln: University of Nebraska Press, 2009.

Fenton, William N. "John Reed Swanton 1873–1958." *American Anthropologist* 61, no. 4 (August 1959), 663–68.

Fischer, Ann. "History and Current Status of the Houma Indian." In *The American Indian Today*, edited by Stuart Levine and Nancy O. Lurie, 212–35. Baltimore MD: Penguin, 1968.

Forbes, Jack. *Africans and Native Americans: The Language of Race and the Evolution of Red-Black People.* Urbana: University of Illinois Press, 1993.

Francis, Mary, and Antoine Francis. Interview by J. Daniel d'Oney, 2003. Recording. Houma Indian Series, collection 4700.1578, tape 3157.1. Louisiana and Lower Mississippi Valley Collections, Louisiana State University Libraries, Baton Rouge LA.

Freiberg, Edna B. *Bayou St. John in Colonial Louisiana, 1699–1803.* New Orleans: Harvey Press, 1980.

French, Benjamin Franklin, ed. "History of Louisiana, Translated from the Historical Memoirs of M. Dumont." In *Historical Memoirs of Louisiana, from the First Settlement of the Colony to the Departure of Governor O'Reilly in 1770, with Historical and Biographical Notes, Forming the Fifth of the Series of Historical Collections of Louisiana.* New York: Lamport, Blakeman, and Law, 1853.

Galloway, Patricia Kay, ed. *Mississippi Provincial Archives, French Dominion.* Vols. 4–5. Baton Rouge: Louisiana State University Press, 1984. Vols. 4 and 5 begun by Rowland and Sanders in 1927.

———. "Sources for the La Salle Expedition of 1682." In Daniel Usner, *La Salle and His Legacy: Frenchmen and Indians in the Lower Mississippi Valley*, 11–40. Jackson: University Press of Mississippi, 1982.

Gautreau, Henry W., Jr. *Pre-Emption Entries on the Backlands of New River, Louisiana, in Conflict with the Houmas Land Claim.* Gonzales LA: East Ascension Genealogical and Historical Society, 1995.

Gayerré, Charles. *History of Louisiana: The Spanish Domination.* New York: William J. Widdleton, 1867.

Giraud, Marcel. *A History of French Louisiana.* Vol. 1, *The Reign of Louis XIV, 1698–1715*, translated by Joseph Lambert. Baton Rouge: Louisiana State University Press, 1974.

Goldsmith, Sarah Sue. "Group Breaks Away to Seek Recognition on Own." *Baton Rouge Advocate*, June 23, 1996, 21. Baton Rouge LA.

———. "Rep. Tauzin Introduces Bill to Grant Houmas Federal Recognition." *Baton Rouge Advocate*, June 23, 1996, 19.

Gravier, James. *Gravier's Voyage Down and Up the Mississippi, 1700.* In *Early Voyages Up and Down the Mississippi, by Cavelier, St. Cosme, Le Sueur, Gravier, and Guignas. With an Introduction, Notes, and an Index by John Gilmary Shea*, edited and translated by John Gilmary Shea, 115–63. Albany: Joel Munsell, 1861.

Guevin, Bryan. "The Ethno-Archaeology of the Houma Indians." Master's thesis, Louisiana State University, 1979.

Haarmann, Albert W. "The Spanish Conquest of British West Florida, 1779–1781." *Florida Historical Quarterly* 39, no. 2 (October 1960): 107–34.

Hackenburg, Liz. "Tribes Celebrate State Recognition." *Daily Comet*, July 5, 2004.

Harrington, M. Raymond. "Among Louisiana Indians." In *The Southern Workman*, 656–61. Hampton VA: Hampton Institute Press, ca. 1908. Hoole Rare Books Collection, University of Alabama Libraries.

Hart, Frederick Weber, Romanta Tillotson, Nathan Clifford, United States Department of the Treasury, United States Supreme Court, and United States Department of Justice. *Exposition of the Houmas Land Claim, and of the Second Section of the Missouri Land Bill, Approved June 2, 1858*. Washington DC: Government Printing Office, 1859.

Haynes, Robert V. *The Natchez District and the American Revolution*. Jackson: University Press of Mississippi, 1976.

Higginbotham, Jay. *Fort Maurepas: The Birth of Louisiana*. Mobile AL: Colonial Books, 1968.

H.L. Billiot v. Terrebonne Parish School Board et al. No. 22567, 143 La. 623. In vol. 79 of *The Southern Reporter, Permanent Edition, Comprising the Decisions of the Supreme and Appellate Courts of Alabama and the Supreme Courts of Florida, Louisiana and Mississippi, with Key-Number Annotations, July 27–December 14, 1918*. St. Paul MN: West, 1919.

H.L. Billiot v. Terrebonne Parish School Board et al. No. 7876. 20th Judicial District Court, Parish of Terrebonne, Terrebonne Parish Courthouse, Houma LA.

Houck, Louis, ed., *The Spanish Regime in Missouri: A Collection of Papers and Documents [. . .]*. 2 vols. Chicago: R. R. Donnelley and Sons, 1909.

"Houma Heroine." *Dixie*, November 9, 1980, 39. Vertical file, Louisiana Room, Archives and Special Collections, Ellender Memorial Library, Nicholls State University, Thibodaux LA.

"Houma Indians Unite in Merger Ceremony," *Houma Daily Courier and The Terrebonne Press*, Sunday, May 13, 1979, 16. Vertical file, Louisiana Room, Archives and Special Collections, Ellender Memorial Library, Nicholls State University, Thibodaux LA.

Houstoun, Matilda Charlotte. "Cruising the Marshes and Coast." In *Louisiana Sojourns: Traveler's Stories and Literary Journeys*, edited by Frank de Caro and Rosan Augusta Jordan, 399–404. Baton Rouge: Louisiana State University Press, 1998.

Hutchins, Thomas. *An Historical Narrative and Topographical Description of Louisiana, and West-Florida [. . .]*. Facsimile of the 1784 edition, with an introduction and index by Joseph G. Tregle Jr. Floridiana Facsimile and Reprint Series. Gainesville: University of Florida Press, 1968.

"Indians Plan Merger Talks." *Houma Daily Courier and Terrebonne Press*, June 14, 1978, 1, 14. Vertical file, Louisiana Room, Archives and Special Collections, Ellender Memorial Library, Nicholls State University, Thibodaux LA.

Inouye, Daniel. *Houma Recognition Act: Hearing before the Select Committee on Indian Affairs, United States Senate, One Hundred First Congress, Second Session [. . .].* Washington DC: Government Printing Office, 1990.

Kane, Harnett. *The Bayous of Louisiana.* New York: William Morrow, 1943.

———. *Plantation Parade: The Grand Manner in Louisiana.* New York: William Morrow, 1945.

Kennedy, Joseph G. *Population of the United States in 1860; Compiled from the Original Returns of the Eighth Census, under the Direction of the Secretary of the Interior.* Washington DC: Government Printing Office, 1864. Reprint, New York: Norman Ross Publishing, 1990. Page references are to the 1990 edition.

Klopotek, Brian. *Recognition Odysseys: Indigeneity, Race, and Federal Tribal Recognition in Three Louisiana Indian Communities.* Durham: Duke University Press, 2011.

Kidder, Tristram R. "Making the City Inevitable: Native Americans and the Geography of New Orleans." In *Transforming New Orleans and Its Environs: Centuries of Change,* edited by Craig E. Colton, 9–21. Pittsburgh PA: University of Pittsburgh Press, 2000.

Kidwell, Clara Sue. *The Choctaws in Oklahoma: From Tribe to Nation, 1855–1970.* Norman: University of Oklahoma Press, 2007

Kinnaird, Lawrence, ed. *Spain in the Mississippi Valley, 1765–1794.* In *Annual Report of the American Historical Association, 1945. In Four Volumes.* Washington DC: Government Printing Office, 1946–49.

Kroeber, A. L. "The Work of John R. Swanton." In *Essays in Historical Anthropology of North America: Published in Honor of John R. Swanton in Celebration of His Fortieth Year with the Smithsonian Institution.* Washington DC: Smithsonian Press, 1940.

Krupa, Kimberly. "'So-Called Indians' Stand Up and Fight: How a Jim Crow Suit Thrust a Louisiana School System into the Civil Rights Movement." *Louisiana History: The Journal of the Louisiana Historical Association* 51, no. 2 (Spring 2010): 171–94.

Langley, Barry. "Non-indigenous, Non-aborigine Group Seeking Federal Recognition as a Native American Indian Tribe." May 1992. Vertical file on the United Houma Nation, Chitimacha Cultural Center, Charenton LA.

Lee, Dayna Bowker. "The Historic Houma of Louisiana: 1699–1835." *Southern Studies* 8, no. 3–4 (1997): 119–55.

Le Page du Pratz, Antoine. *The History of Louisiana, or Of the Western Parts of Virginia and Carolina: Containing a Description of the Countries that Lye on Both Sides of the River Mississippi: With an Account of the Settlements, Inhabitants, Soil, Climate and Products.* 2 vols. London: T. Becket and P. A. de Hondt, 1763.

Lowery, Malinda Maynor. *Lumbee Indians in the Jim Crow South: Race, Identity, and the Making of a Nation.* Chapel Hill: University of North Carolina Press, 2010.

Lowrie, Walter, and Matthew St. Clair Clarke, eds. *American State Papers: Documents, Legislative and Executive, of the Congress of the United States, in Relation to The Public Lands.* 9 vols. Washington DC: Gales and Seaton, 1832–61. Reprint, Greenville SC: Southern Historical Press, 1994. From an original set owned by the State Historical Society of Wisconsin.

Maduell, Charles R., Jr., comp. and trans. *The Census Tables for the French Colony of Louisiana from 1699 through 1732.* Baltimore: Genealogical Publication, 1972.

Mandell, Daniel R. *Tribe, Race, History: Native Americans in Southern New England, 1780–1880.* Baltimore: Johns Hopkins University Press, 2011.

Marchand, Sidney. *The Flight of a Century (1800–1900) in Ascension Parish, Louisiana.* Baton Rouge: J. E. Ortlieb, 1936.

——. *The Story of Ascension Parish, Louisiana.* Baton Rouge LA: J. E. Ortlieb, 1931.

Martin, François-Xavier. *The History of Louisiana, from the Earliest Period.* New Orleans: James A. Gresham, 1882.

——. *Orleans Term Reports: or Cases Argued and Determined in the Superior Court of the Territory of Orleans.* Annotated edition. St. Paul MN: Samuel M. Stewart, 1913.

Martin, Polly Broussard. *Anatole's Story.* Gretna LA: Pelican Press, 2002.

McDermott, John Francis, ed. *The Spanish in the Mississippi Valley, 1762–1804.* Urbana: University of Illinois Press, 1974.

"Memorial of the Representatives of Wade Hampton, For the confirmation of their claims to land in Louisiana." Document no. 144 in *Public Documents Printed by Order of the Senate of the United States, Second Session of the Twenty-Fifth Congress,* vol. 3. Washington DC: Blair and Rives, 1838.

Merriam, William. *Twelfth Census of the United States, Taken in the Year 1900.* Washington DC: United States Census Office, 1901.

Miller, Mark Edwin. *Forgotten Tribes: Unrecognized Indians and the Federal Recognition Process.* Lincoln: University of Nebraska Press, 2004.

Naquin, Albert. Interview by J. Daniel d'Oney, 2003. Recording. Houma Indian Series, collection 4700.1578, tape 3159.2. Louisiana and Lower Mississippi Valley Collections, Louisiana State University Libraries, Baton Rouge LA.

Naquin, Joseph, Mrs. Oral interview by unknown interviewer, ca. 1976. Recording. Terrebonne Oral History Project (Memories of Terrebonne: Archives of the Terrebonne Parish Police Jury's Oral History Program), reel 105. Terrebonne Parish Public Library, Houma LA.

Naquin, Roch. Interview by J. Daniel d'Oney, September 30, 1996. Recording. Houma Indian Series, collection 4700.0841, tape 1210. Louisiana and Lower Mississippi Valley Collections, Louisiana State University Libraries, Baton Rouge LA.

Naquin v. Terrebonne Parish School Board. Civil Case 13291, Record Group 21, ELA 56. Records of U.S. District Courts, Eastern District of Louisiana, New Orleans Division. National Archives at Fort Worth.

Nash, Gary. "The Hidden History of Mestizo America." In *Sex, Love, Race: Crossing Boundaries in North American History*, edited by Martha Hodes, 10–32. New York: New York University Press, 1999.

Nash, Roy. "The Indians of Louisiana in 1931." Indian Office Files, file 25436, box 150. National Archives Building, Washington DC.

National Archives of the UK. *Public Record Office, Colonial Office, Class 5 Files: Part 1, Westward Expansion, 1700–1783*. Edited by Randolph Boehm, compiled by Linda Womanski and Randolph Boehm. Microfilm, reel 6, frame 0412. Reproductions from the Manuscript Division, Library of Congress.

Oakley, Christopher Arris. *Keeping the Circle: American Indian Identity in Eastern North Carolina, 1885–2004*. Lincoln: University of Nebraska Press, 2005.

O'Brien, Jean M. *Firsting and Lasting: Writing Indians Out of Existence in Southern New England*. Minneapolis: University of Minnesota Press, 2010.

Osburn, Katherine. *Choctaw Resurgence in Mississippi: Race, Class, and Nation Building in the Jim Crow South, 1830–1977*. Lincoln: University of Nebraska Press, 2014.

Parfait, Roy. Interview by J. Daniel d'Oney, 2003. Houma Indian Series, collection 4700.1579, tape 3161.1. Louisiana and Lower Mississippi Valley Collections, Louisiana State University Libraries, Baton Rouge LA.

Papeles Procedentes de Cuba. Papers. Archivo General de las Indias. Microfilm. Reel 2. In Judice Papers, Center for Louisiana Studies, University of Louisiana at Lafayette.

Pénicaut, André. *Fleur de Lys and Calumet: Being the Pénicaut Narrative of French Adventure in Louisiana*. Translated and edited by Richebourg Gaillard McWilliams. Baton Rouge: Louisiana State University Press, 1953.

Pesantubbee, Micheline E. *Choctaw Women in a Chaotic World: The Clash of Cultures in the Colonial Southeast*. Albuquerque: University of New Mexico Press, 2005.

Pierce, G. W. "Historical and Statistical Collections of Louisiana—Terrebonne." *De Bow's Review* 11, no. 6 (1851): 601–11.

Ruth Underhill to Frank Speck. October 22, 1938. Frank G. Speck Papers. Ser. 1, folder 4 (16c3). American Philosophical Society.

Robertson, Archibald. *Lieutenant-General Royal Engineers. His Diaries and Sketches in America, 1762–1780*. Edited with an introduction by Harry Miller Lydenberg. New York: New York Public Library, 1971.

Robichaux, Brenda Dardar. Interview by J. Daniel d'Oney, 2003. Houma Indian Series, collection 4700.1581, tape 3163.1. Louisiana and Lower Mississippi Valley Collections, Louisiana State University Libraries, Baton Rouge LA.

Robinet v. Verdun's Vendees. MS. 106. Docket 3546. Historical Archives of the Supreme Court of Louisiana, Eastern District 1813–46. Earl K. Long Library, University of New Orleans.

Rowland, Dunbar, ed. *Official Letter Books of W.C.C. Claiborne, 1801–1816*. 6 vols. Jackson: Mississippi Department of Archives and History, 1917.

Rowland, Dunbar, and Geoffrey Sanders, eds. and trans. *Mississippi Provincial Archives, French Dominion*. Vols. 1–3. Jackson: Press of the Mississippi Department of Archives and History, 1927–32. Reprint, New York: AMS Press, 1973. Page references are to the 1973 edition.

Roy, Edison Peter. "The Indians of Dulac: A Descriptive Study of a Racial Hybrid Community in Terrebonne Parish, Louisiana." Master's thesis, Louisiana State University, 1959.

Sennegy, Rene de [M. Aldric Lettin de la Perchardiere]. *Une paroisse louisianaise. St. Michel, du comité d'acadie*. Translated and edited by Pearl Mary Segura. New Orleans: M. Capo, 1877.

Slind-Flor, Victoria. "If I Can Help My People, That's What I Want to Do." Profile of John Billiot. *West Bank Guide*, February 24, 1985, 1A–2A. Houma-Thibodeaux Diocese Archives, Houma LA.

Speck, Frank. "A Social Reconnaissance of the Creole Houma Indian Trappers of the Louisiana Bayous." *American Indigena* 3 (1943): 135–46.

———. "Some Comparative Traits of the Maskogian Languages." *America Anthropologist* 9, no. 3 (1907): 470–83.

Spicker, Jean R., Halk R. Steiner, and Rupert Walden. *A Survey of Rural Louisiana Indian Communities*. Baton Rouge: Inter-Tribal Council of Louisiana, 1977.

State v. Treadaway et al. 126 La. 300, 52 So. 500. In *The Southern Reporter, Volume 52, Permanent Edition, with Key-Number Annotations, Containing all the Decisions of the Supreme Courts of Alabama, Florida, Louisiana, Mississippi, May 14–August 13, 1910*, 508. St. Paul LA: West, 1910.

Swanton, John R. *The Indians of the Southeastern United States*. Washington DC: Smithsonian Institution Press, 1979.

———. *Indian Tribes of the Lower Mississippi Valley and the Adjacent Coast of the Coast of Mexico*. New York: Dover, 1998. Reprint of Bureau of American Ethnology Bulletin no. 43. Washington DC: Government Printing Office, 1911.

Terrebonne Parish School Board, Terrebonne Parish School Board Minutes. Terrebonne Parish School Board Building, Houma LA.

Toombs, Mr. *Report. [To Accompany Bill S. 307] The Select Committee to whom was Referred the Memorial of Residents and Owners of Lands in the Parishes of Ascension and Iberville, Louisiana, Praying the Repeal of the "Act to Provide for the Location of Certain Confirmed Private Land Claims in the State of Missouri, and for Other Purposes," to Whom, Also, Were Referred the Protest of the Owners of the Houmas Grant, Have Had the Same under Consideration, and Report*. Washington DC: Government Printing Office, 1860.

Ulzere v. Poeyfarré. 468, 8 Mart. (O. S.) 155. La. (1820). New Orleans: Roche Brothers, 1820. Annotated ed., St. Paul MN: West, 1913. Page references are to the 1913 edition.

United Houma Nation v. Texaco Inc. Discovery Gas Transmission, L. L. C. and Goodwin and Associates, Inc. United States District Court, Eastern District of

Louisiana. Civil Action no. 97–4006. Reproduction from vertical file on the United Houma Nation, Chitimacha Cultural Center, Charenton LA.

Upton, Wheelock S., and Needler R. Jennings. *Civil Code of the State of Louisiana; with Annotations*. New Orleans: E. Johns, 1838.

Usner, Daniel. *American Indians in the Lower Mississippi Valley: Social and Economic Histories*. Lincoln: University of Nebraska Press, 1998.

————. *Indians, Settlers, and Slaves in a Frontier Exchange Economy: The Lower Mississippi Valley before 1793*. Chapel Hill: University of North Carolina Press, 1992.

Uzee, Philip. "Father Charles M. Menard: The Apostle of Bayou Lafourche." In Conrad, *Cross, Crozier and Crucible: A Volume Celebrating the Bicentennial of a Catholic Diocese in Louisiana*, 375–87. Chelsea MI: BookCrafters, 1993.

————, ed. *The Lafourche Country: The People and the Land*. Lafayette: Center for Southwestern Studies, University of Southwestern Louisiana, 1985.

Wade, Michael, ed. *The Louisiana Purchase Bicentennial Series in Louisiana History*. Vol. 18 of *Education in Louisiana*. Lafayette: Center for Louisiana Studies, University of Southwestern Louisiana, 1999.

Walker, Francis. *Ninth Census, Volume I. The Statistics of the Population of the United States, Embracing the Tables of Race, Nationality, Sex, Selected Ages, and Occupations*. Washington DC: Government Printing Office, 1872. Reprint, New York: Norman Ross, 1990. Page references are to the 1990 edition.

Watkins, Marguerite. "History of Terrebonne Parish to 1861." Master's thesis, Louisiana State University, 1939.

Wendt, Lloyd. "Brother Martin of the Bayous." December 21, 1947. Vertical file, Archives and Special Collections, Ellender Memorial Library, Nicholls State University, Thibodaux LA.

Wilson, Anthony. *Shadow and Shelter: The Swamp in Southern Culture*. Jackson: University Press of Mississippi, 2006.

Woman's Missionary Council of the Methodist Episcopal Church, South. *Eighth Annual Report of the Woman's Missionary Council of the Methodist Episcopal Church, South, for 1917–1918*. Nashville TN: Publishing House of the Methodist Episcopal Church, South, n.d.

————. *Twenty-Ninth Annual Report, 1939*. Nashville TN: Publishing House of the Methodist Episcopal Church, South, [1939/40?].

Index

Page numbers in italics indicate illustrations.

schools for, xvii. *See also* African Americans; free people of color; mulattoes; people of color; slaves

Blue (waterway), 54

Boisbrian, Monsieur, 10

Bordeaux, France, 84

Bordeaux, François, 64, 81, 159n29

Border Research Corporation. *See* Louisiana Land and Exploration Company

Bourbons, 80

Bourgeois, H.L.: death of, 104; on Houma's existence, 129; on Indian identity, 88, 98, 138, 164n53; objection to Indian students, 82, 83, 87, 94, 98; as research source, xx, 145; Ruth Underhill's assessment of, 96, 164n44

Bourgeois, H.L., Jr., 104

Bourg LA, 105

Bowker, Dana Lee, 50, 51, 154n26

Bowman, Greg, 112

Bowne, Eric, 152n31

Branch of Acknowledgment and Recognition: discrediting of John Swanton's research, 120, 122, 123, 124; on Houma history, 121, 132, 133, 143; on Houma migration and land claims, 117–18; and recognition of Indian tribes, 113–19, 126–30. *See also* U.S. government

La Bras Coup. *See* Tonty, Chevalier Henry de

Brasseaux, Carl, xx–xxi, 154n22, 157n3

Breaux, John, 114, 129–30

Brittany, 83–84

Brown v. Board of Education, 102–3

Bureau of Ethnology, 125

Bureau of Indian Affairs: authority of, 90, 94, 95; on education of Indian children, 101; Frank Speck's meeting with, 96; and Houma history, 121, 123, 124, 142–43; and recognition of Indian tribes, 109, 112–15, 127, 128, 129, 133–34. *See also* U.S. government

Burke, Charles, 125

Caddo Lake, 89

Cahabanooze, 39

Caillouet, Rev. Abel, 100

Cajuns, xx, 96, 136, 142

Calabée, 41, 46–47, 50, 155n43

Calcasieu Parish, 70

Campisi, Jack, 115, 132

Canada, 2, 3, 7, 31, 39, 61, 157n10

Canary Islanders, xxi, 42, 43, 51, 142

Cantrelle plantation, 49, 64

Capuchin Order, 28. *See also* priests

Caribbean, 2, 29, 39

Carolinians, 18, 19, 140

"A Case of Identity" (Davis), 132, 133, 135

Catawba Indians, 152n31

Catholic Church, 58–59, 62, 97, 98, 101, 144

Catholicism: of Acadians, 39; Houma's attitude toward, xvii, xix, xxii, 12, 14–15, 28, 52, 53, 61–63, 76; similarity to Houma religion, 11, 60; threat to Carolinians, 18

Cbiasson (surname), 59

Cedar Grove School, 96

Central High School, 104

Chaisson (surname), 59

Chakchiuma, 1, 122, 148n5

Charleston SC, 18, 140

Charon, Jacques, 149n26

Chauvin, Jean Baptiste, 44

Chawasha Indians, 123

Cheramie, Steve, 125, 126, 128

Cherokee Indians, xix

Chicago, 110

Chickasaw Indians: as English allies, 18, 19, 27; at Fort Bute, 37; French children adopted by, 10; French relationship with, 24–25, 151n16, 152n1;

National Congress of American Indians (NCAI), 109–10
National Historic Preservation Act, 131
Native Americans: absorption of other tribes, 28, 152n31; in colonial conflicts, 18, 25, 26, 46; demographic records on, 69–71, 160n47; education of, 79, 81, 83, 86, 87, 96–101, 107; English relations with, 37, 154n17; French relations with, 29, 58; land rights of, 35, 68–69, 93, 125–26; racial classification of, 60–61, 75–76, 88, 92, 93, 161n1; recognition of, 107, 110, 112, 116, 124, 129, 131, 166n10; reservation vs. "civilized," 70; Spanish relations with, 34, 46; tensions among, 40–41; tribal membership of, 119, 132; U.S. government responsibility for, 90, 94. *See also* pan-Indian movements
Neitzel, Robert, 95
Nerisse, Marie, 49, 75–76, 84, 161n62
New Orleans: Acadians near, 39; archaeologists from, 131; Choctaws on trial in, 46; corrupting effects of, xvi, 141; English soldiers hospitalized in, 38; ethnic groups in, xxi; fortification of, 42; founding of, 7, 17, 150n8; French attitude toward tribes near, 25–26; Houma presence in and near, 20, 28, 29, 31, 39, 41–42, 48, 118–19, 139; Houma trade in, 24, 27, 29, 43, 52, 95, 142; hurricanes in, xv, 136; lawyer from, 90; map of, 21; marriages in, 58; Native activist from, 110; population of, 22, 71; schools in, 102; Spanish control of, 32, 33, 35
New Orleans, Bishop of, 58
New Orleans *Daily Picayune*, 73
Ng-A-Fook, Nicholas, xx
"Nicolas," 22

Nonintercourse Act (1970), 125–26
North Carolina, 160n47
Nuyu'n "Marion" (Félicité Billiot's grandmother), 120, 121

Oakley, Christopher Arris, 160n47
O'Brien, Jean M., 160n47
Odin, Archbishop, 63
oil companies: effect on Houma's quality of life, 79, 111; encroachment on Houma land, xvii, 88–90, 92, 93, 106, 144, 162n26; and recognition of Indian tribes, 109, 114, 125–27, 131–33
Okchina Indians, 37
Oklahoma, 143
Okmulgee Indians, 19
O'Reilly, Don Alejandro (Alexander), 33–35, 38, 46, 155n30
Orleans Parish, 71
Orleans Territory. *See* Louisiana
otters, 88

Pacana Indians, 40
Pailmastabee, 47
pan-Indian movements, 109–11, 139
Papeles Procedentes de Cuba, 154n22, 154n26
Parfait (surname), 59
Paris, 120
Pascagoula Indians, 40–41, 151n16, 154n26
Pearl River, 18, 150n1
Pénicaut, André, 148n5, 150n7
Pensacola FL, 43
people of color, 84–85. *See also* blacks; free people of color
Perdue, Theda, xxi
Périer, Governor, 25–26, 29
Pesantubbee, Micheline, 150n5
piastre, 155n39

IN THE INDIANS OF THE SOUTHEAST SERIES

CPSIA information can be obtained
at www.ICGtesting.com
Printed in the USA
LVHW031934120220
646727LV00006B/217